TIGER TANKS

Michael Green

Motorbooks International
Publishers & Wholesalers

To my good friend Charles Lemons
whose help on this book was invaluable.

First published in 1995 by Motorbooks International
Publishers & Wholesalers, PO Box 2, 729 Prospect Avenue,
Osceola, WI 54020 USA

Library of Congress Cataloging-in-Publication Data

Green, Michael.
    Tiger Tank/Michael Green.
        p. cm.
    Includes index.
    ISBN 0-87938-954-0
    1. Tiger (Tank) I. Title.
    UG446.5.G694   1995
    623.7'4752--dc20   94-34376

On the front cover: On the outskirts of the French city of
Vinouteirs, located in the Normandy area of France, sits one
of the surviving handful of World War II Tiger Is still in
existence. *R.J. Fleming-Panzer Prints*

On the title page: The G.I.s who managed to block a main
road with Tiger 204 eventually pushed it off and down the
steep hillside slope to the right of the vehicle. *British Army
Tank Museum*

On the frontispiece: Visible within this Tiger II turret
(Henschel) is the gunner's TZF 9d articulated monocular
(single lens) telescopic sight. This device provided either a
three or six power magnification for the gunner. *Tank
Magazine*

On the back cover: *(top)* The vehicle pictured is the Tiger I
that used to be on display at the US Army Ordnance
Museum and is now on a ten year loan to the German
military museum system. The vehicle is seen here on its
arrival in Germany on a dock were it was unloaded from the
ship that delivered it. *Thomas Anderson*

On the back cover: *(bottom)* A Tiger II almost completely
intact, numbered 332, was found sitting abandoned on the
side of a road. The Americans who recovered the vehicle
believed the tank tracks had become frozen to the ground,
causing the German crew to quit the vehicle. After
pouring gasoline all around the outside of the tank, the
Americans lit a fire which thawed the ice in and around
the tracks. The vehicle was then loaded on a trailer.
Patton Museum

Printed in Hong Kong

CONTENTS

ACKNOWLEDGMENTS

As with any book of this type, the help of many people made it possible. This includes the senior tank buff of them all, Dick Hunnicutt. Others include Jacques Littlefield, Richard Byrd, Dennis Riva, Gregory T. Jones, Bob Wright, Walter Magness, Samual Katz, Dave Jones, Bill Nahmens, Richard Pemberton, Richard Cox, Arnold Roussine, Jeff McKaughan, Roy Hamilton, Dr. Giuseppe Finizio, Dennis Spence, Ron Hare, Jim Mesko, Steven Zaloga, Chris Foss, the late Bob Icks, Andreas Kirchhoff, and Frank Schulz.

The many veterans of World War II that were willing to share their stories and pictures. This includes Bill Hamberg, Erling Foss, Michael Altamura, Frank Kurtz, Don Bourne, Bud Hartman, Ken Hockman, Jimmy Leach, Bud C. B. Pettet, Henry Gardiner, Charles Geissel, Otto Carius, and Will Fey.

Translation support provided by Dr. Wolfgang Sterner and Dave Sampson.

Special thanks are due to Dr. Wolfgang Sterner for arranging permission from the German publishing firm of *VerlagsGesellschaftBerg* (VGB) to reprint extracts from Otto Carius's 1960 book titled "Tiger im Schlamm".

Organizations and their staffs that kindly extended their help with both pictures and information include David Fletcher and George Forty of the British Army Tank Museum, Charles Lemons of the US Army Patton Museum, Bill Atwater and Ken Powers of the US Army Ordnance Museum, Oberstleutnant Kulke and the staff of the Panzermuseun Munster, Fred Pernell and the staffs of the National Archives and National Records Center, Armor Magazine and its managing editor Jon Clemens, Wheels and Tracks magazine and its editor Bart Vanderveen, Tank Magazine and its managing editor Hideya Ando, plus AFV News and its editor George Bradford.

A special note of thanks is due to my wife, Gladys, who allowed me to spend many nights and weekends with my terminal instead of with her.

INTRODUCTION

Like a well-known movie star, the one tank that doesn't really need any type of introduction is the famous German Tiger tank of World War II. With more books and articles written on this one vehicle than any other tank ever built, it was with some trepidation that this book was approached by your author. With a number of excellent German language books dealing with the Tigers recently being reprinted in English, a wealth of new information on both technical and unit histories has become available for tank buffs.

With the years having taken a heavy toll on the few remaining Tiger crewmen, finding such veterans that have both new stories to tell to your author, or supply him with those never before published pictures of Tigers in action becomes harder. Yet, there are many different ways of looking at the Tiger tank story. Rather than trying to rehash the same basic Tiger material as has been done by so many others, I have sought out as much unpublished material as possible, including a number of very interesting technical intelligence reports done on the Tigers by the Allied armies. Numerous extracts from a series of articles by Garrett Underwood that were published in *Armor* magazine shortly after World War II will give the reader and outlook on both German and Russian tank development from a top wartime authority that would be impossible for your author to give a half a century later. Additional extracts from Otto Carius' 1960 book on his wartime experiences as a Tiger tank commander will provide a feel for its use on the actual battlefields of World War II. To complement the text, a large number of less known and unpublished pictures of Tiger tanks currently on display are included. Hopefully these will provide the scale modelers among us the much sought after close-up detail shots.

This book does not attempt in any way to be the definitive work on the Tiger tanks. That would be impossible in the amount of space provided by the publisher. Rather, it is the author's hope that the readers will find his interpretation of the Tiger story adding to their knowledge and understanding of this historical and very interesting vehicle.

TIGER BACKGROUND AND DESCRIPTION

To help explain German tank development leading to the Tiger, the following extracts are reprinted from an article entitled "German Armor" published in the 1949 July-August issue of *Armor Cavalry Journal*. The author was the famous *Life Magazine* military journalist Garrett Underhill, who served on the United States War Department's General Staff (now known as the Joint Chiefs of Staff) for three years during World War II. This vantage point gave him an overall view of German tank development not available to most others outside of American and Allied intelligence agencies during World War II: "To the post-World War I Germans, a 'tank' was a turreted, tracked combat vehicle, armored all over. Tanks were primarily the armament of the armored regiment of the armored division. The German designation was *Panzer-Kampfwagen*, followed by a Roman numeral. The word 'tank,' though commonly used, was 'verboten' because it reminded the Nazis of unpleasant British World War I achievements. The original abbreviation was Pz.Kw. which during the war was changed to Pz.Kpfw. to avoid confusion with the P.Kw.'s *Personenkraftwagen*, which were personnel-carrying vehicles."

[NOTE: The wartime Western Allies used the term Mark or it's abbreviation Mk. to describe various German tank models. As an example; the Panther medium tank in the German military nomenclature system was referred to as the *Panzerkampfwagen V*, which the Allies referred to as the Mark V. This form of nomenclature has continued to be used in most English language books dealing with German World War II tanks. This system of Allied and German nomenclature, as well as the official and unofficial German and Allied nicknames for various German tanks will appear in this book since it draws from many different sources.]

In 1940, there developed the idea that thick armor and a small gun might be the proper basic characteristics for future heavy tanks. Henschel—famous for trucks and locomotives—began work on a project for a VK 4501 (71 US tons) in this class. Interesting—recalling American objections to heavy tanks because of trans-port complications—the Germans planned to have this tank break down into three loads for rail travel. The project was never completed.

Henschel also tried the VK 1801—a heavily armored Mk.II. A similar VK 1601 improvement on the little Mk.I was also attempted before the Germans would give up their early tank models and write off the production investment, or use it for self-propelled mounts exclusively.

As is obvious from production orders and actual early combat experience, the Germans did not consider big tanks essential. They do not seem to have been impressed by late World War I French efforts to build monsters—or similar British efforts in the 1920's—and actual Russian production in the 1930's. The experimental work done above appears to have been in the nature of insurance to acquaint German industry with problems of design, should a pressing need for larger vehicles develop.

In general, German industry tried to get experience on the next larger tank, before there was a call for it. They knew that it had taken Krupp two and a half years to get the Mk. I designed and into production.

Moreover, during the period up to the Russian campaign, tanks seem to have been pretty much the Army's business. And Guderian—as the prime Panzer advocate—has shown throughout his career that he prefers a proven tank in the hand (albeit it may not be the best) to a gaggle of super-doopers in prototype form, which industry is vainly trying to produce in a form that will be reasonably bugless.

But the practical military leaders had reckoned without propaganda-conscious Mr. Hitler. The *Fuhrer* liked his weapons bigger, if not better. Growth of his interest in weapons coincided with his strong interest in the direction of the military campaigns—which may be said to have begun in earnest with the Russian campaign of 1941. With his taking over the job of Army Commander-in-Chief, in addition to his role as Commander-in-Chief of the Armed Forces, the *Heereswaffenamt* (army ordnance) and the tactical experts were at

In an effort to keep the German Mark IV medium tank a viable weapon system able to deal with Soviet tanks like the T-34 medium and KV heavy tanks, the Germans mounted a long-barrel, high-velocity, 75mm gun in the vehicle. While this gun helped to put the Mark IV on a more even par with Allied tanks, the Mark IV neither had the long-range firepower or thick armor protection advantage that the German Panther medium or Tiger heavy tanks possessed. The Mark IV pictured had been captured intact by American soldiers during the fighting around Bastogne, Belgium. Almost 9,000 Mark IV tanks were built by the Germans during World War II. Because of it's box-like shape, it was often mistaken by American soldiers as a Tiger I. *US Army*

the mercy of capricious Hitlerian whim. It was General Buhle who, as Hitler's weapons expert, consulted the troops, and then handed down weapons characteristics to ordnance.

Mr. Hitler naturally took personal interest in the VK 4501 (49 US tons) project, which began four weeks before the attack on Russia. The experienced Henschel firm competed with the eminent automotive engineer Dr. Ferdinand Porsche. The latter, thanks to his famous racing cars, had obtained personal contact and a pull with Hitler. He finally managed to get 90 tanks of his Tiger P version built, but—although he had wonderful ideas, such as diesel-electric drive—the order went to Henschel.

The tacticians had now decided on a powerful big gun in a not-so-well-armored tank. The common or garden 88mm AA gun (Flak 36) was adapted as the 8.8cm Kw.K. 36 (L/56). As the project progressed, the original VK 4501 specification was built up into a tank weighing 60-62 tons, with armor over 4 inches thick. The first Pz.Kw. VI (Sd. Kfz. 181)—as the Tiger was originally called—was delivered to Hitler on 20 April 1942, construction of the prototype having been begun the previous November.

In August of 1942 the first dozen came off the production line, and the first Tigers went into action on the Leningrad front in the fall. They didn't get to Tunisia until 1943—just about making it a dead heat with the propaganda photos reaching the Allies via neutral channels. (Though a propaganda picture of a Tiger on the march through Tunis was picked up and circulated by US press services, concurrent pictures and reports on the first Tiger encountered by the British-American team were circulated as "Secret.") It would seem that, even if Hitler refused to keep the Tiger a secret weapon, the high school fraternity mentality of certain Anglo-American intelligence folk caused automatic correction of his error. In 1944, the *New York Mirror* published photos of the first Royal Tiger specimen well before secret photos of the same vehicle were received in the US.

Despite the Germans drawing up a set of requirements for a new forty-five ton heavy tank mounting the deadly "88" at least one month before the invasion of the Soviet Union, it was the German panic at finding the Russian T-34 tank outclassing their own existing tank fleet which really initiated the quick development of both the Tiger I and Panther tanks.

In August 1941, German Army tanker Otto Carius was serving aboard a Czech-designed light tank known as the *Panzerkampfwagen 35(t)* which was armed with a 37mm main gun. At the time, he belonged to the 20th Panzer Division taking part in the invasion of the Soviet Union. In an extract from his 1960 book titled *Tiger im Schlamm* (reprinted with the publisher's permission), he describes his first impression of the Russian T-34 tank: "The T-34 with its excellent armor, ideal shape and magnificent 76.2mm long-barreled cannon was universally feared and a threat to every German tank up until the end of the war. What were we supposed to do to these monstrosities that were being committed in quantity against us? We could only knock at the door with our cannons; inside, the Russians were able to play an undisturbed hand of cards. At the time, the 37mm antitank gun was still our strongest armor defeating weapon. If lucky, we could hit the T-34 on the turret ring and jam it. With a whole lot of more luck, it became combat ineffective. Certainly not a very positive situation."

A background history of the T-34, the armored vehicle that led to the utilization of the Tiger I, is provided in the March-April 1950 issue of *Armored Cavalry Journal* with an article by Mr. Garret Underhill:

It was the first to make full use of the principle that well-sloped armor adds greatly to its effectiveness. The front plate sloped at 60 degrees up over the driver, but was pierced on the left with the driver's hatch (fitted with periscope) and on the right for a ball-mount DT machine gun. The sides of the superstructure sloped at 41 degrees, the rear at 49 degrees. The armor was 1.8 inches thick—though original models had sides and rear a quarter inch thinner. The turret was shaped with sloping sides. The side plates dovetailed with the front. Cast turrets were fitted to the T-34 at about the same time as to the KVs [Russian heavy tank]. Turret armor was also 1.8 inches. Unfortunately, the turret had a rear overhang, leaving only a slit between the hull top and turret bottom. Into this slit the Germans found it convenient to slip teller mines (standard AT mines) or demolition charges. One such would blow the turret off— and did. About the same time as the KV got a cast turret, the T-34 got one too. The change brought about some slight armor increases, the hull front increasing to 2 inches, and the turret to what must have been a minimum of 2-in on the sides. However, this slight increase may only have been due to different procedures by different factories.

The 76mm M1940 gun fitted was slightly more powerful than the US 75. At first it appeared only in unit commanders' tanks, later wholly replaced the M1939 of 30.5 calibers. The armor on the US tank was about the same in thickness—though vertical on the sides (although there can be no doubt that US plate was always far better in quality).

The T-34 with cast turret compares interestingly with the US M4A3 Medium. The T-34 was designed in [1939-40], and was fielded in [1941]. This tank had remarkable mobility. Its power combined with broad

tracks made easy work of fall and spring muds and the quagmires in the Ukraine after summer rains. The T-34 was designed to negotiate snow 3 feet deep, so it had no trouble in winter. (In Task Force Frigid exercises in February 1947, US heavy (now medium) Pershing tanks were overheating engines even in 30 inches of light snow.)

The T-34's modified V-12 Diesel gave it a 15.6 mph road speed, according to the Russians, and burned 3/4 gallons of fuel a mile going cross country or along bad roads. (Since most Russian roads are bad, this was the typical fuel consumption.)

Its outside dimensions were 19'-4" long and 9.82 feet wide—showing that Morosov, too, had width to play with to gain form and power. He managed to pack 77 rounds of 76mm ammo in the hull, plus 46 drums for the DT's.

With its speed, mobility, gun power, and particularly the form of the hull, the T-34 made a great impression on the Germans. It completely outclassed their tanks, and resulted in the Panther 45-ton medium of 1943—whose form was obviously borrowed from Morosov's conceptions. When the Germans began to be impressed with the Sherman's qualities, they could think of no better compliment than to dub it "the T-34 of the West."

The T-34 was not a perfect tank. It was difficult to drive on hard roads; its Christie fast suspension, inherited from the BT's, gave a rolling and unstable platform when going cross-country. It was of course most uncomfortable, but comfort was never a high priority to the Soviets.

Transmissions do not appear to have been very reliable. There are photos of T-34s with spare transmissions secured by cables atop the rear. The original crew of four was sufficient for the mission of an armored

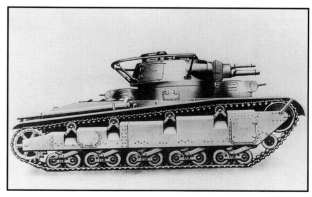

This side view is of a prewar German prototype tank known as the NeubauFahrzeuge (NbFz). In English it meant new construction vehicle. There were two different versions of this vehicle which when first ordered, were designated the PzKpfw V and VI. As these vehicles never went into production, their designations were later passed on to the Panther and Tiger tanks. *US Army*

It is quite surprising to consider that, when the 46-ton heavy KVs and the 30-ton (original weight) T-34s were going into production in 1939, the US was procuring a 10-ton M-3 Light for its only "armored force" (the Mechanized Cavalry), and an 18-ton "medium"—both of which were armed with 37mm guns. Both US tanks had riveted armor and open slits for vision in combat.

When the Germans went into Russia, they attacked with the 21-ton Pz. Kpfw. III (37mm or short 50mm) as their main weapon, supported by 23-ton IV's with short 75's and 11-ton light II's with 20mm automatic cannons. The Germans learned fast, though. The Tiger appeared first on Lake Ladoga in November, 1942. The Tiger, Panther, and Royal Tiger were the direct results of the first meetings with the Russian wonder tanks.

As soon as the Tiger I began reaching the battlefields of the Soviet Union in growing numbers, they began to take a heavy toll of T-34 tanks whenever they met them.

Otto Carius, who was assigned to one of the first Tiger I units deployed to the Eastern Front, was responsible for the destruction of a large number of T-34 tanks during his time on the Eastern Front. One of his wartime encounters with the T-34 tank is recounted and translated by Dr. Wolfgang Sterner, who commanded Mark IVs and Panther tanks during World War II:

The combat engagement took place on November 4, 1943, deep in the Soviet Union in the Witebus-Newel area. The Soviets had achieved an unexpected breakthrough in the swampy area north of Witebus. Carius and his lone Tiger were ordered to stop any further advances by Soviet forces in the Newel area and to keep the main highway in the area open.

After taking a hull-down position near the main highway. Carius observed twelve T-34 tanks with infantry being carried on top of the vehicles, heading towards his position over a hill to his right at about 2,000 meters. Coming towards his position at a fairly high speed, he observed that the enemy tanks had their hatches open. Yet, neither the tank crews or the infantry riding the tanks spotted his Tiger since it was very well camouflaged.

When the Soviet tanks were within sixty meters of his own vehicle, he opened fire with his '88' and within minutes, ten of the enemy tanks were burning with their onboard infantry scattered all over the battlefield. Only two T-34 tanks reached cover from the Tiger's main gun. Carius' Tiger did not receive a single hit during the entire engagement.

Two days later, Carius had just returned to the same position opposite the main highway in the Newel area, after leading a counterattack in the Schelkunicha area, when five more T-34 tanks came from the same direction as their doomed predecessors had done. The only difference was that their was no infantry riding on the tanks and they had all their hatches closed. Again, the Soviet tank crews failed to spot his position and were instead headed in the direction of an 8.8cm antiaircraft gun opposite Carius' position on the main highway.

When the five T-34 tanks tried to drive around the hulks of the ten T-34 tanks destroyed by Carius two days before, he again opened fire with his main gun and within a couple of minutes destroyed three more enemy tanks. The gun crew of the 8.8cm antiaircraft gun finished off the other two enemy tanks. Like the first Soviet tank attack, neither Carius' tank or the 8.8cm antiaircraft gun sustained any hits despite heavy return fire from the Soviet tanks.

With it's deadly long-range 88mm cannon and thick frontal armor, the Tiger I was the world's most powerful tank when used properly. When not used properly, the Tiger I was just as vulnerable as most other tanks to a number of weapons ranging from antitank guns to antitank mines. The Tiger I pictured, was formerly on display at the US Army Ordnance Museum. It is now on a 10 year loan to Germany's military museum system. *Andreas Kirchhoff*

Rushing into action, these low-slung Russian T-34 medium tanks were a nasty surprise to German tankers who were unaware of it's existence until meeting it in combat in mid-1941. With it's well-sloped armor and outstanding cross-country mobility, the T-34 made the entire German inventory of existing tanks and antitank guns obsolete almost overnight. In response to the serious threat the T-34 posed to the German war efforts, the Tiger I and the Panther medium tanks were rushed into production. *British Tank Museum*

Tiger I Description

The British Army always had a keen interest in German weapon systems. Any information the British acquired was normally supplied to the American military. The following extracts are from a British Army technical report on the Tiger I, given to the American military attaché in London on October 19, 1943.

No complete Pz.Kw VI vehicle has as yet been examined in Great Britain. Our information as to its construction is gathered from reports on the examination of captured vehicles in North Africa. Various samples of the armour have, however, been received by D.T.D. and subjected to metallurgical examination and, in two cases, to ballistic trials. Ballistic trials have also been carried out in North Africa.

The following brief particulars of the vehicle may be of interest:

Weight	56 tons
Length (excluding gun)	20ft 6in
(including gun)	27ft 1in
Height	9ft 6in
Width (over cross-country tracks)	11ft 8in
(over road tracks)	10ft 4in
Belly clearance	1ft 6in

It may be noted that the width of 10ft 4in after the removal of the cross-country tracks just brings the vehicle within the continental loading gauge.

The suspension is by front sprocket, rear idler, and large disc type interleaved bogie [road] wheels on eight load carrying axles on each side of the tank. The overlapping of the bogie wheels affords additional protection to the hull side plates. There is independent torsion bar springing.

[Note: The Germans first used interleaved road wheels during the 1930's on their early unarmored half-tracks. While the extra road wheels found on the interleaved type suspension system slightly lowered a vehicle's ground pressure, it also meant repair of any damage to an inner road wheel involved the removal of many outer road wheels.]

The main armament is an 88mm. gun (KwK.36). A 7.92mm. machine gun is mounted co-axially with this in the turret and another is mounted in the front of the hull.

The vehicle is provided with very comprehensive sealing arrangements and an air intake pipe is fitted at the rear so that it is submersible to a depth of at least 13ft.

The Pz.Kw.VI has a crew of five, of whom the driver, hull gunner, and wireless operator are accommodated in the forward compartment, to the near and offside of the gearbox respectively, while in the turret the commander and gunner are on the near side of the gun, with the loader and co-axial M.G. on the offside. The 88mm. gun is slightly offset to starboard and its recoil guard extends backwards until it nearly reaches the turret ring, thus dividing the fighting space into two unequal parts. The gunner's seat is well forward and low down on the port side and the commander's immediately behind it and higher up; they occupy the larger of the two portions of the chamber but both are rather cramped. The loader, with the starboard side to himself, has rather more room, but this is needed on account of the size of the ammunition. The co-axial M.G. is readily accessible.

Tiger I Special Features

An interesting feature of the Tiger I tank captured by the British in North Africa was its ability to cross water obstacles. The following British Army report was supplied to the American military attaché based in London in early 1945:

The clean well-sloped lines of the Russian T-34 medium tank were quite an innovation in their day. Well-sloped armor can almost double the effectiveness of any given thickness of armor. Sloped armor achieves this by deflecting many types of armor-piercing rounds by causing them to slide or bounce off a tank's hull or turret. The Germans quickly saw the benefits of sloped armor and applied them to many of their own later tank designs. As the Tiger I was already in the prototype stage when rushed into production, it was impossible to redesign it with sloped armor. The early-model T-34 pictured is on display at the US Army Ordnance Museum. *Michael Green*

Two systems of ventilation, one for normal running and one for submerged running, are used in the German Pz.Kpfw Tiger Tank Model H. For normal running air is drawn through two mushroom type intakes one of which is located in the engine cover plate and the other in the front top plate between the driver's and co-driver's escape hatches. Circulation of air inside the tank is induced by a centrifugal fan which is bolted to the engine flywheel. Air is drawn by the fan from the bottom of the engine compartment and from within the cowling which surrounds the transmission, and is transferred to the downstream side of the engine cooling radiators through two independent jackets which surround the exhaust manifolds. Air for the combustion process in the tank engine is taken into the vehicle through two flexible metallic hoses mounted on top of the engine cover plate at the rear of the tank. The intake ends of these hoses are covered with gauze protectors. Through these hoses the air is led through two pre-cleaners at the rear of the tank and is then delivered to the main air cleaners in the engine compartment through a manifold bolted on top of the engine cover plate. An electric fan mounted in the turret roof above the loader expels the fumes resulting from the firing of the turret armament.

For submerged running the two mushroom intakes are closed and a four-section, telescopic intake pipe is erected at the rear of the tank. Butterfly valves, which alter the path of the air being circulated, are closed by remote controls mounted on each side of the rear bulkhead of the fighting compartment. Air brought into the crew and engine compartments through the telescopic intake pipe is drawn through the transmission cowling by the centrifugal fan referred to above and is circulated through the jackets surrounding the exhaust manifolds in much the same manner as is done in normal running. Instead of being directed through the radiators (which in the case of submerged running are surrounded by water), the air is now led to the top of the engine compartment where it is available for the combustion process in the tank engine. Engine exhaust is through flutter valves.

Flow charts of the tank ventilation system are included in the report. Previous section of the S.T.T. report on the Pz.Kpfw Tiger Tank Model H were transmitted by M.A. London 65639, 66923, 69586, and 1390-44.

A captured German order forbids submersion of tanks, and recently captured German tanks have not been equipped with the means for running submerged.

This will be of special interest to the Technical Intelligence Branch of Ordnance Research and Development Service, Armored Board, Tank Destroyer Board, G2-Mil, O.C.O.-Detroit, Foreign Material Branch of Aberdeen Proving Ground, and other recipients of the original reports.

Tiger Tactics

When German tanks like the Tiger I were used in large-scale offensive operations, they normally worked in conjunction with the support of artillery, infantry, and aircraft. Their job to was help neutralize enemy antitank guns and create gaps in the enemy lines through which the Tiger tanks could pass. An example of this type of offensive action involving Tiger I tanks occurred during the famous tank battles of Kursk in July 1943. Named "Operation Zitadelle" by the Germans, the entire operation had already been leaked to the Soviets who had plenty of time to prepare their defensive positions. The following extract which describes German tactics during that series of battles is reprinted with permission from the late Robert J. Icks, from his book titled *Famous Tank Battles*:

The attack in the south began in the middle of the afternoon on a hot and sultry July 4. It was preceded by a short artillery and air bombardment. Just before it began, Russian air bombed German airfields as the planes were being fueled. The tanks to be used in the assault had been moved up during the night of July 3 and faced a morass resulting from a brief cloudburst which stopped the XLVIII Panzer Korps until the night of July 4. The formation employed by the tanks was the "wedge." This comprised the placing of a Tiger at the spearhead of the wedge with the base made up of Pz Kpf Wg IVs or Panthers.

After encountering Russian defenses, tank tactics were changed from the "wedge" formation to the "tank

The very thick box-like hull armor of this early-model Tiger I can be seen in this photo of a captured vehicle in Italy. On the front superstructure hull plate can be seen both the hull-mounted 7.62mm machine gun and the driver's vision port which consisted of a double sliding shutter arrangement. This type of vision port was a weak point in terms of ballistic protection for the Tiger I and was done away with on the Tiger II. *US Army*

bell." In this formation, a Pz IV became the lead tank and a Tiger was placed in the center of the formation. Other Pz IVs were located to right and left in a spreading arc. Halftrack engineer vehicles were behind the tanks to clear mines and tape paths when called upon while behind them were infantry halftrack mortar or other mortar vehicles. Pz IIs and IIIs were in the rear in readiness for pursuit in case of break-through. The "bell" commander with a forward artillery observer for the self-propelled assault guns to the rear traveled in a *Panzerbefehlswagen* or command tank behind the leading Pz IV. These command tanks usually were Pz III or other tanks with a dummy cannon to disguise it and equipped with several types of radios, one of them for communication with the Stuka squadron assigned to cooperate with the particular tank bell.

The following extract was originally published in the July 18, 1943 issue of the Soviet Army magazine known as *Red Star*. It describes the official Soviet military view of German Tiger tanks in action during the battles around Kursk:

During the last few days the Germans have been bringing up new tank reserves, resulting in more determined counterattacks. Since our tanks pave the way for our infantry, tank battles have now become the usual thing.

Occasionally a small percentage of the counterattacking tanks are "Tigers" (T-VI's). They prefer to operate on one of the flanks of the attacking echelon or immediately to the side and behind, acting as self-propelled artillery or an armored shield in case of a sudden flank attack by our tanks. The Germans endeavor to use their "Tigers" economically—probably because of a lack of them. They are brought into battle only when it is obvious that the other tanks will be unable to achieve success.

The combat formation of the German tanks is usually the following: ahead of all the rest are the heavy tanks; then come the mediums; followed by light tanks. At the present time, in a single echelon, the Germans use tanks of various makes, striving to create an appearance of a mass attack on a wide front.

By massing our tank forces we have many times put the German machines to flight.

From an article by Lt. Colonel Albin F. Irzyk (US Army) that appeared in the January 1946 issue of *Military Review*, published by the US Army, comes this interesting comparison between American and late war German tank tactics: "One must not forget that the German requirements and our own were totally different. They were fighting a slow war, a defensive war where they picked their spots. They had fewer tanks then we, so their tactics, of necessity, had to be different. We were

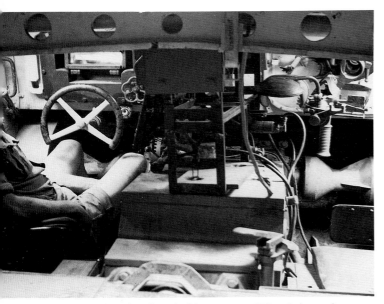

An interior shot from inside a captured Tiger I shows the driver's position on the left and the hull machine gunner's position on the right. The small desk-lamp-looking item located at the machine gunner's position is a shoulder grip. The 7.62mm machine gun is not mounted in this vehicle, however the weapon's mounting bracket is still fitted. Due to the box-like shape of the Tiger's hull the vehicle was very spacious when compared to many other tanks of that era. *British Tank Museum*

fighting an offensive war, we were hurrying to get it over with, we wanted to shake loose, and we had many tanks with which to do it. Virtually never did a scrap take place with fifty German tanks against fifty American or twenty against twenty. The proportion was usually five American to one German, even ten to one, rarely if ever less than two to one."

Lt. Colonel Irzyk went on in his article to discuss why the German heavy tanks, like the Tigers, took such a heavy toll of American tanks in late 1944: "The terrain was admirably suited for him. It was rough, and this enabled him to pick the key terrain features on which to post his men and vehicles. The ground was so muddy that advancing, attacking elements could not maneuver, could not outflank. They had to slug it out toe to toe, face to face. Without a doubt the tank of the Germans was ideally suited for such a fortunate turn in the war for them. The tank could pick dominating ground, and with its huge gun and thick armor proved to be a roving pillbox par excellence. On many occasions it picked off American tanks as they floundered in the mud in an effort to gain valuable ground and dislodge their adversary."

From the personal collection of Otto Carius, German Army Tiger tank ace, comes this extract from a January 1943 *After Action Report*. The report was based on combat experience gained by the 502nd Heavy Tank Battalion, equipped with the Tiger I tank. Within the re-

port are some suggestions on how to best utilize the Tiger tank on an tactical level: "Without exception, it must be ensured through the issuance of strict orders at all levels of command that Tiger units are never employed under company strength [14 tanks] and that Mark IV and Mark III tanks are never separated from the Tigers. The Tigers must be and remain the battering rams in an ongoing attack and the center point of the defense. The field forces hold the general opinion that the Tiger can do everything. [This has to be blamed partly on the German's own propaganda.] They do not understand that a new weapon system has strong points and weaknesses which can only be corrected through experience and further development. For this reason, the danger exists that Tiger units will be assigned missions which the standard tank companies could solve without any problems."

Improved Tiger I

Like most tanks that are rushed into service, the Tiger I was continually upgraded throughout its production run as shortcomings in its design were discovered during field use. Actual Tiger I production ran from August 1942 till August 1944, with 1,350 vehicles being built. Other design features incorporated into the Tiger I tank were the result of production decisions made at the factory because of cost or efficiency.

The Tiger I tank was originally designated the Pz.Kpfw VI Tiger Ausf H, but was later redesignated the Pz.Kpfw Tiger I/Ausf E in 1944. This change in the vehicle designation was merely of nomenclature and does not reflect any particular model type for the Tiger I tank. The many notable differences between production mod-

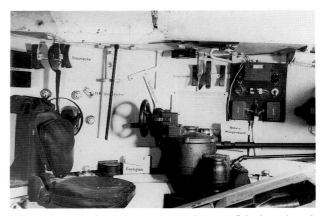

Viewed from the loader's position is the top of the breech end of the 88mm gun as found in the Tiger I. Behind the breech end of the gun is the elevation hand wheel for the tank commander, which is attached to a hydraulic turret power-traverse unit. The seat pictured, belongs to the Tiger tank commander who sits directly behind the gunner. The gunner's seat and controls are hidden from view in this picture. In German tanks the vehicle commander and gunner are located on the left of the main gun, the loader on the right. This is just the opposite of American and British tanks. *British Tank Museum*

els of the Tiger I have more to do with when it came off the assembly line than anything else. As many early model Tigers were returned to the factory or depots for rebuilding, they came away with different component parts from various production periods.

Some of the most noticeable visual features that distinguished early production from later models were: (1) The replacement of the original rubber-rimmed road wheels with stronger steel-rimmed road wheels; (2) The fitting of a Panther tank type commander's cupola instead of the older more vulnerable drum-type cupola; (3) Preproduction and early model vehicles did not have the escape/loading hatch located on the right-hand side of the vehicle's turret that appeared on mid-production vehicles and beyond; (4) The earliest production vehicles had mudguards which were made from one piece of diamond plate, angling slightly downward, end to end from midpoint. Most later production Tiger Is had larger flat mudguards with folding extensions hinged at the side. These mudguards could be folded during rail transport.

British Museum Tiger

The world's best known Tiger I tank (vehicle number 131) resides at the British Army Tank Museum, located in the beautiful rolling countryside of Southern England. Much of the information and many of the pictures in this book and others are based on wartime research done on this single vehicle. George Forty, director of the British Army Tank Museum discusses the history and future plans for their vehicle:

This famous example of the Tiger tank, production number 250112, was completed by the Henschel plant at Kassel in February 1943. It was issued to 504 Heavy Tank Battalion which it served in Third Platoon of number 1 Company.

It was captured, in Tunisia, on 21 April 1943 following an action with 48th Royal Tank Regiment. It would seem that the Churchill tanks of 4 Troop, A Squadron 48RTR were not aware of a Tiger in the vicinity during this action at Medjez-el-Bab and the shots that put the German tank out of action were entirely fortuitous. One round from a Churchill's six pounder gun struck the underside of the Tiger's 88mm gun. Deflected downwards, it chipped a groove in the bottom of the mantlet and buried itself in the turret ring, causing the turret to be jammed in the forward position. Incidentally, the blow seems also to have wrecked the tank's radio. A second round fired by this Churchill struck the boss of the mantlet pivot on the left side of the turret. It carved a big chunk out of it and then ricocheted upward, taking off the top smoke discharger pot and whistling past the commander's hatch. There is no reason to suspect any more damage to the tank, which was still in running order, yet the crew immediately abandoned their tank and made off. At the same time, the crews from some German tanks in the vicinity also made their escape.

For a while the tank remained where it had been abandoned, acting as the focal point for a collection of captured equipment, but in due course it was removed to Tunis, tidied up in First Army workshops and even painted with the appropriate British markings. Here it was inspected by the Prime Minister, Winston Churchill and King George VI during their visits to the area following the Allied victory. Later the tank was brought back

On display in the main hall of the British Army Tank Museum in Southern England is the museum's most popular exhibit, Tiger I number 131. *British Army Tank Museum*

to Britain on the merchant ship SS Ocean Strength. It was exhibited to the public on Horse Guards Parade in London and then despatched to the School of Tank Technology at Chertsey where it was subjected to Armored Corps Gunnery School at Lulworth, presumably undergoing firing trials, which resulted in the famous, and oft quoted report. Unfortunately this activity caused damage and loss to many components, while the engine itself was cut open for instructional purposes.

After the war the School of Tank Technology was transferred to the RAC Centre at Bovington Camp and its collection of enemy tanks, including the Tiger, was incorporated into the Tank Museum collection then being re-established after its wartime suppression. As an exhibit the Tiger has always been most popular. More visitors come to look at it than any other single exhibit and there were even stories of it being haunted by the spectre of Herman the German.

Naturally there has always been a lot of interest in the possibility of returning the Tiger to running order, but it was considered to be a difficult and expensive task. Now the project is under way. The hull has been entirely dismantled, a suitable engine obtained from another exhibit and considerable research done in Germany, France, and Russia for missing items to complete the restoration. One day, it is hoped, Tiger 131 will roll again.

Pictured after the war in Europe was over, a captured Tiger I has been fitted with a four-section telescopic air-intake pipe by British troops prior to being test run through a 20ft deep wading pit. While some early model Tiger Is had been fitted with a system allowing them to cross water obstacles, it did not prove to be a success in field use and was soon discontinued. However, the Germans did continue trying to improve the system up until the end of the war. The same basic system of running tanks underwater was later copied by the Allies and saw widespread use in both NATO and Soviet-designed tanks up until current times. *British Tank Museum*

Tiger II Description

As early as May 1941, one month after the first prototypes of the Tiger I were shown to Hitler, decisions had already been made by German tank producers and their military counterparts to start the ball rolling on the design of another heavy tank that would eventually become known as the Tiger II. (It was also called the Tiger Ausf. B or Kingtiger by the Germans.) It would mount an improved version of the basic 8.8cm. gun as found on the Tiger I. Because of a very confusing development history, the first three production models of the Tiger II didn't come off the assembly line until January 1944.

Extracts from three US Army technical intelligence reports give a fairly comprehensive description of the Tiger II tank. The first report is dated August 21, 1944:

A preliminary report as yet unchecked has been received on a 67-ton redesigned Tiger tank mounting an 8.8cm. Kw.K 43 gun. The general appearance of this equipment is that of a scaled up Panther and it conforms to normal German tank practice in so far as the design, layout, the interlocking of the main plates, and the welding are concerned. The engine is in the rear and the gear box and the steering and driving units are in front.

Suspension

This consists of front driving sprockets, rear idler, and independent torsion bar springing with two steel rimmed rubber cushioned disc bogie wheels on each of the nine axles on each side. The bogie wheels are interleaved and there are no return rollers. The driving sprocket centres are at about 29in above the ground and the bogie wheel centres at about 21in. The contact length of the track on the ground is about 160in. Every alternate track link has two ground contact bars cast in one piece. These bars have half inch raised strips in a fine chevroned pattern for better grip. The track pitch in the main links is 150-mm and for the alternate connectors about 100-mm. On the left hand side (the only side capable of being examined) it was found that there were five external twin bogie wheels and four internal twin bogie wheels. These were genuine "twin" and not spaced wheels.

Turret

The turret has 360 degrees traverse and is long for its width. It has bent plates and on the left hand side the plate is bulged to the vertical to accommodate the cupola. [Note: This indicates the tank was fitted with one of the fifty original Porsche turrets rather than the series turrets built for the Henschel version of the Tiger II. On the Henschel design, the commander's cupola no longer protruded from the left-hand side of the turret.] The turret sides are interlocked with the turret floor. The upper turret ring is 70 3/8 inches in diameter and the lower ring 73 inches; there is a total of 298 teeth. The turret front is rounded and has an opening for a monocular telescopic gun sight on the left hand side and for the coaxially mounted MG 34 on the right hand side. The gun mantlet is of the same width as the turret front and moves about it. There is a long rectangular hatch in the turret rear plate and a series of plugged pistol ports.

The cupola is of the latest Panther type and has seven vision openings. It also has a rail for mounting an AA MG. The ventilator is central in the turret top and the rectangular hatch is on the right hand side. The turret is mounted slightly to the left of the center line of the tank with the circular hatch centrally in the turret top.

Engine

It was not possible to examine the engine but the external structure and layout of the engine cover was similar to that of the Panther and it is thought therefore, that the engine may be the HL 230. The gear box has eight forward speeds.

Miscellaneous

There is a ball-mounted MG 34 on the right hand side of the front glacis plate as in the latest Panther, and no other openings. The opening for the driver's

On display at the Swiss Army Technical Museum in Thurn, Switzerland, is a Tiger II fitted with an Henschel production turret. This particular vehicle is missing it's muzzle brake. Protected by thick well-sloped frontal armor and armed with a powerful long-range 88mm gun, the Tiger II was a dangerous opponent despite it's numerous mechanical shortcomings. *Wheels and Tracks Magazine*

periscope is on the left hand side of the front super-structure roof. The chassis number of this vehicle is P 280637.

The second US Army report dated September 13, 1944 describes additional features of the Tiger II in more detail:

A badly damaged specimen of the new redesigned Tiger tank, mounting the 8.8cm. Kw.K 43 L/71 gun, Sd.Kfz.182, has been examined in the British Sector in Normandy.

This tank bears little resemblance to the previous Tiger tank, first encountered in North Africa, but has many features in common with the Panther, particularly as regards the sloping of the main armour plates. However, it would be a mistake to compare it with any previous German tank, as it mounts a gun with a much superior performance to the gun in either the previous Tiger or Panther tanks and its armour affords a much greater degree of protection. Thickest armour is 150mm. (5.9 in.) on the glacis plate, which is sloped at 40 degrees from the vertical.

Semi-official names which have been used for this tank are Tiger II and *Konigstiger* (Royal Tiger). [Note: *Konigstiger* really translates to Kingtiger, but the Allies often used the term "Royal."]

Armour

The armour appears to consist of rolled plate, except for the cupola and exhaust pipe sockets, which appear to be castings, and the gun mantlet and turret ring protection strips, which appear to be forgings.

In the construction of the turret, extensive use has been made of plate bending.

As in the case of the Panther tank, all the main joints in the hull and turret are interlocked in addition to being welded. The turret front plate is actually dovetailed into the turret sides.

Owing to the fact that the vehicle examined had been completely burnt out, it has not been possible to ascertain the quality of the armour used.

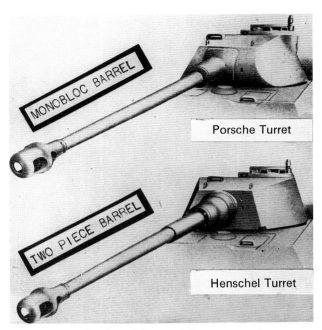

MONOBLOC BARREL

Porsche Turret

TWO PIECE BARREL

Henschel Turret

A comparison drawing of the two different types of turrets found on the Tiger II. The Porsche turret, of which only fifty were built, features a curved front and side plates. This design was not well thought out as it was both expensive and difficult to built. Combat experience also showed that the curved front plate proved to be a shot trap, as it deflected enemy rounds into the upper hull where the armor was the thinnest. In contrast, the Henschel turret was both easier to build and offered superior ballistic protection over the Porsche turret. *British Tank Museum*

All the main armour plates are coated with "Zimmerit" plaster to prevent magnetic grenades and demolition charges from adhering to the metal beneath. [Note: Zimmerit was a thick anti-magnetic plastic coating, made mostly out of sawdust, which was applied to many German tanks. It had been designed to prevent Soviet tank-hunting infantry teams from attaching magnetic mines to German tanks in combat.]

Armament
(a) Main
(i) *General:* This consists of a high velocity 8.8 Kw.K 43, of the normal German tank gun design, mounted in a turret having 360° traverse. The gun has a sleeve mantlet which is centered by a screwed collar at the front, and, towards the turret terminates in a square bell-shaped skirt with rounded corners. The cylindrical portion of the mantlet is 28in long while the overall length is 42in.
Apart from a somewhat longer muzzle brake and slightly different breech mechanism, the gun appears to be similar to the 8.8cm Pak 43 on Panther chassis described in Summary 142. Ballistic details were given in Summary 137 Appendix A.
An official German document states that the gun has an elevation of 15° and a depression of 8°. The length of

the ordnance from rear of the breech ring to end of barrel is 20ft 8in. The length of the rifling is 16 feet 11 7/8 inches and the length of the chamber is 2 feet 9 7/8 inches. The rifling has a RH [right hand] uniform twist of 6°.
(ii) *The piece:* This appears to be of monobloc construction and is secured to the closed jaw breech ring by a securing collar. The muzzle brake is approximately the same size as those fitted to the 8.8 Pak guns.
(iii) *Breech Mechanism:* This is generally similar to previous German tank guns. The breech block is of the vertically sliding wedge type and may be operated by hand or at SA. It differs from the 8.8 Pak 43 on the Panther chassis mainly in that the breech is closed by a coil spring contained in a housing around the actuating shaft. The housing is extended to form an LBM, similar to the 8.8cm Flak 18 guns. And air blast gear is fitted, consisting of nozzles arranged each side of the breech ring to direct jets of air into the chamber and prevent flame or gases passing back into the turret while the breech is open.
(iv) *Firing Mechanism:* This is electric and from the charred remains it appears that the normal safety devices are incorporated.
(v) *Muzzle brake:* This is of the double-baffle type and has an overall length, with securing collar, of 23 inches and without, 20 3/4 inches.
(vi) *Recoil Mechanism:* Buffer and recuperator cylinders are mounted side by side above the piece on two plates, suitably curved, which are welded to the ring type cradle. The liquid buffer is on the right while the eccentric cylinder hydropneumatic recuperator is on the left. The piston rods are nutted to lugs at the top of the breech ring. Maximum recoil is 22 inches.
(vii) *Elevating Mechanism:* This is carried out by a nut and screw, the screw being attached to the right rear of the recoil mechanism bracket, while the nut is carried in a housing bolted to the floor of the turret. The nut is rotated by a bevel pinion meshing with teeth formed on its edge, probably through a universally jointed shaft.
(viii) *Gun Supporting Arrangements:* The gun is supported on two trunnion supporting arms, bolted to prepared surfaces in the forward floor of the turret. The trunnions are bolted to brackets which are welded to each side of the ring type cradle through which the piece recoils.
(ix) *Sighting arrangements:* The monocular sight, TZF 9 d, is graduated up to 5000 metres for HE and 3000 metres for APCBC and Hollow Charge.
(b) Subsidiary
One 7.92mm MG 34 is mounted co-axially on the offside of the 8.8cm gun in the turret and there is another 7.92mm MG 34 in a ball mounting on the offside of the glacis plate.

Smoke
There is a small circular opening in the horizontal portion of the turret roof on the offside through which projects a tube, fitted with a detachable metal cover. The tube, which may be traversed, leads to a small cylindrical

container, to which some kind of firing mechanism appears to have been attached.

It is believed that the whole apparatus is designed to enable smoke generators to be projected in the required direction from within the fighting compartment."

Ammunition

A total of 80 rounds of ammunition for the 8.8cm gun is carried consisting of 50% HE and 50% APCBC. Most of it appears to be stowed horizontally in panniers in the sides of the hull.

Construction and layout

The hull is somewhat larger than that of the original Tiger tank and has been completely redesigned to incorporate the principle of sloping armour plates, successfully achieved in the Panther tank. The superstructure sides are sloped from the vertical and taper slightly outward toward the rear of the vehicle.

The engine is at the rear and the gearbox, steering and final drive units at the front.

The crew appears to consist of five, namely; commander, gunner, loader, driver, and wireless operator.

Turret

The turret [Note: one of the fifty original Porsche turrets], which is of exceptional length, is mounted centrally, and the side and rear plates are sloped at an angle of 25 degrees to the vertical. The side plates are bent inwards both at the front and at the rear and the top centre of the near side turret wall bulges to the vertical to receive the cupola. There are no pistol ports or hatches in the side plates.

The front of the turret consists of a single plate which bends round the turret front from the front end of the turret roof to a point on the turret base about 3 feet 6 inches from the front of the turret. This plate is 80mm thick from where it joins the forward edge of the turret front to a point immediately below this junction at the bottom of the turret front. It is then stepped down to 60mm and from here to its end it tapers down to 50mm. The plate is dovetailed, interlocked, and welded to the turret side plates. At the point where the plate is stepped down from 80mm to 60mm, there is a large weld, incorporating a filling piece.

There is a single hole in the rounded turret front plate on the near side of the 8.8cm gun to receive a monocular gun sight and an opening on the offside to receive the coaxial MG.

The turret roof consists of three separate plates. The front portion slopes down towards the gun mantlet, the centre portion is horizontal, and the rear portion slopes down towards the engine compartment.

The cupola, which is 15 inches high, is of the type found in recent models of the Panther and original Tiger tanks, and is offset to the near side of the centre portion of the turret roof. It has seven vision openings and is fitted with a rail extending from 10 o'clock to 5

o'clock to receive a mounting (Fliegerbeschussgerät) for an AA machine gun.

Protection for the turret ring is provided by a circular strip of armour, divided into 12 arc-shaped segments, 3 3/4 inches wide at the base, 1 inch wide and 4 inches high.

Engine

This is a water-cooled V-12 petrol engine and is understood to be the 23 litre H.L. 230 as fitted in Panther and in the original Tiger tank.

Gearbox

The gearbox is situated centrally at the front of the vehicle with the gear levers on the right of the driver's position. There appears to be 8 forward gear ratios, and a separate gear lever for reverse travel. The clutch is fitted immediately behind the gearbox.

Suspension and Tracks

The suspension arrangement consists of large disc type, interleaved bogie wheels, sprung independently on torsion bars, with nine load carrying axles each side of the tank. There is a front driving sprocket and rear idler, but no return rollers.

Altogether there are 36 bogie wheels, which have steel rims and embody some form of internal rubber cushioning. There is one pair of bogie wheels on each of

This photo—taken at the British Army Tank Museum, located in Southern England—shows the three best known German tanks of World War II. On the far left is the Tiger I with it's box-like hull which first came off the production line in Sept. 1941. Next to the Tiger I is a Panther medium tank which came out in May 1942. The Panther was the first German tank to feature sloped armor in it's design. The Tiger II prototype on the right of the Panther is fitted with the Porsche turret and clearly shows the influence of the Panther design. In combat, many Allied soldiers had a very hard time telling the difference between the two vehicles. The Tiger II reached the field in November 1944. *British Tank Museum*

The sole remaining Tiger II presently still in running condition is located at the French Army Tank Museum at Saumur. The tank is a Tiger II with an Henschel turret. The vehicle has been restored to near-perfect condition with only the inability to find a number of interior components preventing them from finishing the job. At least once a year, the Tiger II is brought out on display under it's own power. This photo shows the French Tank Museum's Tiger II entering the display area to be put through it's paces before the assembled crowd. *Tank Magazine*

the nine axles on each side of the tank. On the first, third, fifth, seventh, and ninth axles, the pairs of bogie wheels lie outside the bogie wheels on the remaining axles.

There are two torsion bars for each side, coupled together in series, the arrangement being similar to that on the Panther tank. Shock absorbers are provided for the front axles. The diameter of the torsion bars is about 60mm.

The jointed metallic tracks are of a new pattern not hitherto found on German tanks and consist of main and connecting links. Altogether there are 90 links and each of the main links has two spuds on which there are five chevron patterned half-inch raised strips, designed to afford better grip.

The pitch of both the main and connecting links is 5.9 inches. Approximate track pressure is 14.7 pounds per square inch.

Vision arrangements

Seven horizontal openings round the cupola give the commander all round vision.

There is a small rectangular opening suitable for receiving an episcope in the offside of the sloping front portion of the turret roof. It is protected by a large flat armour plate.

For the gunner there is a monocular gun sight on the left of the gun.

For the driver there is an opening at the front edge of the superstructure roof plate above the driver's position for receiving a periscope. It is protected by a U-shaped guard. Part of the top of the glacis plate is cut away to provide a clear view from the periscope.

At the forward edge of the top of the superstructure roof plate on the offside, there is an opening for an episcope set at about 1:30 o'clock.

Hatches and pistol ports

There is a rectangular hatch in the offside of the horizontal centre portion of the turret roof measuring 19 inches by 14 inches. It is closed by a single cover plate hinged to open upwards and forward. In the sloping rear portion of the turret roof there is a circular hatch 9 inches in diameter closed by a cover plate on a single hinge.

In the turret rear plate there is a rectangular hatch, 20 inches by 14 inches closed by a cover-plate opening outwards and downwards. In the centre of this cover-plate there is a wedge shaped pistol port closed by a plug attached to a chain.

In the hull, there are two large irregularly shaped hatches, one each above the driver and hull MG operator. They appear to be operated in the same way as the equivalent hatches on the Panther tank and are provided with a spring balancing mechanism.

Ventilation

There is an electric extractor fan, similar to the one in the Panther tank, in the centre rear of the horizontal portion of the turret roof.

An air intake opening in the front of the superstructure roof between the driver's and hull MG operator's position, is protected by a large circular plate.

Communication

No details of the wireless equipment are obtainable. An aerial is mounted on the offside of the superstructure roof at the rear.

Dimensions

Lengths

Overall including 8.8cm gun	32'- 8"
Overall excluding 8.8cm gun	23'- 10"
Superstructure roof	19'- 2"
Rear of turret race to rear of superstructure roof	7'- 11"
Front of turret race to front of superstructure roof	4'- 9"
Glacis plate	4'- 3"
Sloping front of turret roof	2'- 11"
Horizontal centre of turret roof	3'- 3"
Sloping rear of turret roof	3'- 4"
Muzzle brake overall	1'- 11"
Track on ground (by measurement)	13'- 4"
Front to rear bogie wheel centres	13'- 6"

Widths

Overall	11'- 11"
Hull	6'- 4"
Front bottom of superstructure	9'- 9"
Front Top of superstructure	8'- 6"
Rear bottom of superstructure	10'- 5"
Rear Top of superstructure	9'- 5"
Overall turret base	8'- 3"
Turret roof at rear	3'- 5"
Turret roof at centre	5'- 6"
Turret roof at front	3'- 5"
Track	2'- 8"

Heights

Overall	10'- 2"
Top of superstructure above ground	5'- 10"
Turret including cupola	4'- 4"
Turret at rear	2'- 3"
Turret at centre	2'- 10"
Cupola	1'- 3"
Driving sprocket centres above ground	2'- 5"
Bogie wheels centres above ground	1'- 9"
Rear idler centres above ground	1'- 11"
Track guide horn	3/4"

Diameters

Turret upper race	6'- 6 3/4"
Turret race ball bearings	1 3/4"
Cupola (external)	2'- 11"
Cupola (internal)	1'- 6"
Hatch in rear of turret roof	0'- 9"
Bogie wheels (external)	2'- 7"
Driving sprocket (external)	2'- 7"

While the thick well-sloped armor protection of the Tiger II gave it a decided advantage in head-on combat with Allied tanks, the weight penalty imposed by the heavy steel armor did cause mobility problems. Even with it's very wide tracks the Tiger II pictured—with a Porsche turret—had become completely bogged down somewhere in France in 1944. Because of it's weight (almost seventy tons) the Germans often had problems in recovering Tigers that had become immobilized due to man-made or natural obstacles. *Private collection*

Rear idler (external)	2'- 3"
Torsion bar (60mm. approx.)	2"

An October 16, 1944 US Army report includes observations by 1st Lt. George B. Drury, Ordnance Technical Intelligence Unit "E" attached to First US. Army:

Examination of two Tiger II tanks revealed the ammunition stowage locations and also several design changes. Principal changes are as follows:

a) New type gun mantlet—The mantlet on these tanks was of a type similar to that found on the 5cm. Kw.K. 39 as mounted on the 8-wheeled armored car.

b) Turret front—Instead of the rounded front turret as found on the first Tiger II examined, a flat plate 185mm. in thickness and sloped at an angle of approximately 10° has been substituted. [Note: This was the series or standard production turret as built for the Henschel Tiger II design.]

c) Turret rear—A different arrangement of the escape hatch has been made. Instead of the old type hatch which was mounted on a plate bolted to the turret rear plate, a hatch mounting directly on the rear plate has been substituted. This hatch hinges at the bottom similarly to the old type. Dimensions of the hole in the turret rear were 18 3/4" high by 20 1/4" wide. The hatch door measured 25 1/2" high by 25" wide.

A manual found in one of the tanks gives the designation of the tank as TIGER Model B. It is not known, however, whether this or TIGER II is the accepted nomenclature.

Chassis numbers as taken from the two vehicles were 280101 and 280105.

Stowage space for 70 rounds of ammunition was found in the tanks. 69 rounds in one tank were accounted for and these consisted of 39 rounds of A.P. and 30 rounds of H.E. Stowage of the ammunition was all in the sponson sides and turret rear.

A US Army technical intelligence report dated October 17, 1944 describes the items attached to the outside of the Tiger II:

At rear of tank
1 Steel winch with lifting housing and folding crank for weight up to
20 tons
1 Wooden block for 20 ton winch
1 C Hook

At Left side wall
1 Cable steel 8.2m long, 32mm diameter
1 Wrecking bar 1800mm long
1 Hand crank for starter
1 Spade
3 Cleaning rods

At right side wall
1 Cable steel 8.2m long, 32mm diameter
1 Cable steel 15m long 14mm diameter with two hoops for installation of tracks
3 Cleaning rods

On deck
1 Tetra fire extinguisher (2 liters for Pz.Kpfw.) with handle
1 Axe
1 Sledgehammer
1 Wire cutter

Tiger Ergonomics
As late as 1947, the British Army was still conducting tests on both models of the Tiger tanks as well as the Panther medium tank. These tests were conducted by the Motion Study Wing of the Military Operational Research Unit. Using experienced British tank crewmen, their aim was to determine both the operational efficiency and comfort of the various German tanks compared to British tanks of the same period.

The modern term for this type of testing is referred to as ergonomics. Ergonomics is a biotechnology term indicating engineering that considers human factors and anatomy in the design of and use of both machinery and clothing. While the study of ergonomics, as related to military equipment, began before World War II, most World War II tanks were designed with little thought for the crew's comfort or operational efficiency. In other words, the tanks were not very user-friendly. In studying the German wartime tanks, like the Tiger II, the British were surprised at how little thought was given to the crew's positions and controls within the vehicle. The following extracts are from a 1947 British military report concerning their motion studies of the Tiger II tank:

1. Description of the Vehicle
The Pz Kpfw VI (B) is commonly known as the Royal Tiger. It weighs approximately 70 tons in battle order. It mounts an 8.8cm. Kw.K 43 gun and a 7.92mm MG in the turret, and a hull MG 34 is mounted in the glacis plate.

2. The Commander
(a) Seat and Positions. The commander's station is in the left rear quarter of the turret. He has three alternative positions: first, seated in the seat, secondly, standing on the footrests, and thirdly, standing on the turret floor.

The seat is saddle-shaped and the top is 11" long and 1' 2&1/2" wide and covered with imitation leather. It is mounted on a hinged arm on the turret wall and can be stowed against it when not required. No other adjustment is provided.

The backrest is also covered with imitation leather and is 11" wide and 4" high. It is hinged, and can, like the seat, be stowed against the turret wall when not required. It is badly positioned in relation to the seat,

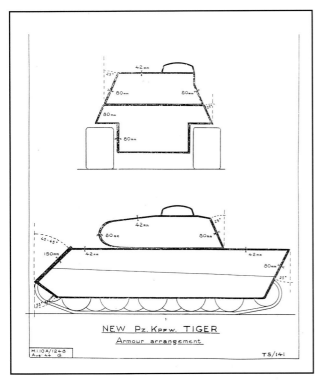

From an August 1944 American Army technical report comes these rough line drawings of the approximate thickness of the steel armor fitted to the Tiger II. Also shown are the angles at which the Tiger's armor is inclined at. By sloping armor plate, it's ballistic protection can be greatly improved. The vehicle as drawn, was based on a captured Tiger II fitted with a Porsche turret. The armor thickness of modern tanks using non-steel types of protection can be as thick as 600mm (2ft) on just the front of their turrets.

since it is mounted so far forward that it tends to push the commander off the seat. This tendency would become more pronounced when the vehicle is on the move.

The commander's left footrest is hinged and can be folded against the turret wall when not required. His right footrest is fixed to the right side of the gunner's backrest. When the commander uses the footrests, he can stand in relative comfort.

(b) <u>Vision.</u> The commander's vision facilities are reasonable. When seated, he can see with comfort through any one of the set of seven episcopes mounted in his fixed cupola. When standing on the footrests, his head and shoulders are outside the turret and his vision range is reasonable. However, when standing on the turret floor, a commander of average size cannot see either out of the turret or through the episcopes. He would therefore use his seat or footrests when the vehicle was in action.

(c) <u>Conclusion.</u> The commander's position is spacious and comfortable, although the backrest to his seat is mounted too far forward. His vision facilities are reasonable.

3. The Gunner

(a) <u>Seat and Position.</u> The gunner sits on the left of the main armament and in front of the commander. His seat is saddle-shaped, padded, and covered with imitation leather. It is 11" long, 1' & 1/2" wide, and 1' 6 & 1/2" high, mounted on the turntable, and is not adjustable.

The backrest is curved and padded. It is 11" wide and 5" high and can be lifted on a hinge on its right side to allow the gunner greater access to his seat.

American soldiers were always impressed with the German Tiger tanks. Compared to the Sherman tank the Tiger II was huge. This wartime photo, by Charles Geissel of the 5th Armored Division, shows a destroyed Tiger II fitted with an Henschel turret. Notice the lack of anti-magnetic plastic coating on the hull and turret of this vehicle. This vehicle took two close-range 3in hits from an M10 to its front hull plate without any interior damage to the vehicle. It was only when another 3in round managed to penetrate a welded armor joint on the turret (opposite to the camera) that the vehicle finally started to burn and the crew abandoned it.

The Tiger I's "88", firing it's standard armor-piercing round, could punch a hole through 4in of steel armor at 1,000yds. Modern tank guns can penetrate double that amount of tank armor at 3,500yds. At the end of the Tiger's barrel was a large muzzle brake that was designed to cut down on both recoil and dust when the main gun was fired. This feature was later copied by Allied tank designers as they to began to mount bigger guns on their own tanks. The Tiger I pictured took a high-velocity round into its thinner side-hull armor. The penetration hole can be see about halfway down the hull of this vehicle. *British Tank Museum*

Both the seat and backrest are satisfactory, but the position is cramped and uncomfortable. This is due to the bad layout and design of the gun controls, which are described below.

(b) <u>Gun Controls.</u> The traverse handwheel is very badly positioned. When the gunner is seated, the linkage between the wheel and the gearing is between his knees, which must be kept apart. In such a cramped station, the gunner would soon become very uncomfortable and probably fatigued.

The handwheel is 10 & 1/4" in diameter and the handle is 3 & 3/4" long. A lever on the forward end of the gunner's seat operates a cam, which allows adjustment of the handwheel forwards and backwards through an arc. The wheel can be locked in the required position. We found that the best position was in an almost horizontal plane, with the front rim of the wheel lower than the rear. Even in this position, the rear rim chafes the gunner's wrist when he turns the wheel. In general, the control is very unsatisfactory, since in any position it is uncomfortable to use.

Fortunately for the gunner, the turret can also be traversed by power. There are two controls which can be used either independently or, as is more likely, together. The first control is a tilting floorplate which is set into the floor in front of the gunner's seat. The plate is 1' & 1" from front to back and 1' wide and is pivoted along its length. It can be locked in the neutral position when not required.

The axis of the plate is mounted approx. 6" to the right of the centre of the gunner's seat, and traversing is

This picture of a Tiger I in action shows to good effect the long overhang of the vehicle's main gun, the famous "88". Because the gun was mounted so far forward on the vehicle's hull, it was considered muzzle-heavy. To overcome this problem, the German tank designers attached a large compression spring within the turret to help balance the gun in it's mount. British military personnel who had a chance to test captured Tiger I's felt that both the main gun and the turret to be out-of-balance. *Private collection*

difficult in either director. On left traverse, the gunner's left foot depresses the left half of the plate; this is awkward because the gunner's left leg jams against the traverse handwheel spindle. On right traverse, the side of the gunner's right boot scrapes against the side of the hole cut into the turret floor and his boot tends to slip off the plate. The plate inspected was stiff to operate independently, though when used in conjunction with the hand lever, it proved more satisfactory. The hand lever is a plain steel bar mounted on the left side of the seat. The bar is operated by moving it either forwards (left traverse) or backwards (right traverse), and it is mounted on the same linkage as the footplate. When the bar is pulled backwards, the gunner's left elbow tends to strike the commander's left footrest.

Although more satisfactory then just a footpedal, the combination of footpedal and hand lever is still, in our opinion, not as efficient as the spade-grip type of control.

The elevating handwheel is 9 & 1/2" in diameter and mounted in a vertical plane to the right of the gunner's seat. The 3" long handle is too short to be gripped by the whole hand. When the handle is at the bottom of its arc of movement, the gunner's right hand tends to jam on a lever on the power traverse gearbox, as there is only 1" clearance between the two.

The gun is fired electrically. The trigger comprises a steel bar hinged to the shaft cover of the elevating wheel. The bar is curved and lies parallel to the rim of the wheel. It is operated (satisfactorily) by the gunner's right hand.

No emergency firing gear was evident in the vehicle inspected.

(c) <u>Sighting and Vision.</u> The sight, type TZF 9d, is articulated at the front end and the eyepiece is clamped to the turret roof. The sight is mounted about 4" to the right of the seat centre line and the gunner must therefore lean to the right when sighting. The browpad inspected was very hard, and the gunner would be liable to injure his nose on the eyepiece when sighting on the move.

(d) <u>Conclusion.</u> The gunner's position is very unsatisfactory. It is cramped and uncomfortable and some of the controls are badly positioned. The hand and power traverse controls are badly designed, and the gunner is given inadequate vision control.

4. The Loader

(a) <u>Seat and Position.</u> The loader's station is on the right of the main armament. A mounting in the front part of his station indicates that he is provided with a seat, but no such seat was available in the vehicle inspected. Its probable position is in the centre of the right half of the turret.

As it appears from the mounting that the seat is removable, the designer's intention would seem to have been that the seat would be removed during an action to allow the loader greater access when loading. It would be replaced only when immediate loading was not anticipated.

The loader has ample space for handling ammunition on his side of the turret. In addition, if his hatch is open, a loader whose height is 5' 7" or less can stand erect with his head not touching the turret roof. However, when the hatch is closed, the fitting on the inside of the door projects about 3" below the level of the roof. Since the loader would probably strike his head against it when loading he would probably keep the hatch door open when loading.

(b) <u>Controls.</u> An auxiliary traverse handwheel is provided for the loader so that he can assist the gunner to traverse the turret when the power traverse mechanism is not being used. A latch on the gunner's wheel prevents the loader from operating his wheel independently.

(c) <u>Vision.</u> The sole vision device provided for the loader is a 5" wide episcope in the turret roof above the coaxial MG 34. This seems satisfactory, and moreover it does not project into the loader's station.

(d) <u>Conclusion.</u> The loader's position is very spacious and allows adequate room for loading the large ammunition. The auxiliary handwheel is badly positioned and awkward to operate. The loader has adequate vision facilities.

5. The Driver

(a) <u>Seat and Positions.</u> The driver's position is in the front left quarter of the hull. The seat is padded and 1'2" square, and the height can be adjusted so that he can drive "closed-down" (lower position) or "opened-

Somewhere in North Africa, American soldiers are examining the destroyed remains of a Tiger I. Tiger crews were under strict orders to blow up any vehicle that might fall into Allied hands. In this picture, the force of an internal explosion has completely blown the vehicle's turret off of the hull. The turret itself, landed upside down on what was left of the vehicle's hull. The picture also shows the large cast steel armored mantle that protected the front of the Tiger I's turret. On the Tiger I, the mantle armor was up to 8in thick. *National Archives*

up" with his head and shoulders outside the hatch (upper position).

The padded backrest is 1'0" square and its angle can be adjusted by a cam, which is locked by a lever on the right side of the seat.

(b) Controls. Since the seat is adjustable for upper and lower positions, the controls have been designed to be accessible when the driver is in either position.

Power-assisted steering is controlled by a semi-circular wheel 1'3" in diameter. The wheel column is jointed and the wheel can be raised or lowered to suit the driver's position. The wheel column is also telescopic and can be extended through 11" as required.

In general, the wheel is very satisfactory, and more comfortable to use than the orthodox steering levers fitted in most A.F.V.s.

A disadvantage, however, is that the wheel is effective only for power-assisted steering. If the power system is not running (e.g. when the vehicle is being towed), the usual manual steering is used. This is controlled by two standard steering levers, each 1' 9 1/2" long, mounted on the hull floor, one on each side of the driver's legs. The levers are accessible only when the driver is in his lower position, and valuable space is required for two sets of steering controls. The driver's hand is liable to catch on the gearbox direction lever as he pulls back the right steering lever.

The preselective gearbox gives 8 forward and 4 reverse ratios. The control lever is a short rod with a knob at the top end, and is mounted in a semi-circular "gate" on top of the gearbox on the right of the driver, who does not have to use the clutch pedal when changing gear, and who has no need to "rev-up" when changing down. Both of these operations are performed automatically by the gearbox, the clutch pedal being used only for engaging a gear before the tank moves off.

The handbrake is a heavy-duty ratchet type and is operated by pulling towards the rear. Though the brake lever is mounted on the left of the driver, two hands would probably be needed to pull the brake "hard-on," since the return spring is very powerful.

The foot controls are arranged in the order clutch, footbrake, and accelerator from left to right. The clutch and footbrake pedals are identical, being 3 1/4" long and 2" wide. Both are quite satisfactory to use and can

By early 1943, the first few Tiger I's to see tank-versus-tank combat in the Soviet Union quickly began to prove their technical superiority over anything in the Soviet inventory. Tiger Is on the Eastern front were used both in offensive and defensive actions. Because of the vehicle's short operational range and poor automotive performance they did best in defensive actions that required little movement. The early model Tiger Is pictured are waiting for the orders to move forward. Notice the spare track links attached to the front hull of the vehicle in the center of the photo. *Private collection*

be quickly adjusted (by means of jointed pedal arms) to either the upper or lower position.

Two separate accelerator pedals are provided. The lower control is a plate 3 1/2" wide and 10 3/4" long, which is pivoted to the floor. The pedal is almost vertical and consequently difficult to operate. The upper control is a roller 4" long and 1 1/2" wide mounted on a common linkage with the lower pedal. A hinged plate 4 1/2" wide which can be folded when not in use, is fitted as a footrest. The pedal is rather difficult to find with the foot but is otherwise satisfactory.

(c) Vision. When driving "opened-up" the driver has an adequate vision range, since his head and shoulders are outside the hull of the tank. When the vehicle is being driven "closed-down" his sole vision device is a 5" wide episcope. A handle on each side of its mounting is used to control the episcope's angle of tilt and rotation. Although the driver can see the ground from 6 yds. onwards in front of the vehicle, the fitting of only one episcope for the driver of so large a tank is bad.

The vision range with the episcope is so restricted that, probably, even an experienced driver would have to rely on his commander's instructions when driving "closed-down" along a narrow or devious route. This is undesirable, as the commander should at all times be free to look for targets, instead of concentrating on whether or not the driver is keeping the correct course.

Unlike modern main battle tanks which can fire on-the-move. The Tiger I and Tiger IIs lacked any type of stabilization system for either azimuth or elevation. As a result, they were unable to fire accurately while moving. The only way for a Tiger crew to successfully engage and destroy an enemy target was to bring their vehicle to a complete halt. Unfortunately, when stopped, they themselves became an easier target to hit. The only country to provide their tanks with a stabilized-turret gun system was the United States which fitted both their M3 and M4 medium tanks with such a system in elevation only. The Tiger I pictured had been knocked out in combat somewhere in Europe. *British Tank Museum*

(d) Conclusion. The driver's seat and positions are comfortable and his controls are mostly satisfactory. His vision range when driving "opened-up" is excellent, but inadequate when he is in the lower position.

6. The Bow Gunner

The seat was missing and the bow-gun could not be fitted in the vehicle inspected. Therefore, there is little which we can say about the bow-gunner's position. The seat is presumably similar to the driver's except that it is probably not adjustable for height.

The spacious position would probably be comfortable, but the long drop from the hatch to the seat would make "bailing-out" rather difficult.

7. Lighting

Festoon lamps are fitted:
(i) Above the gunner's position
(ii) Above the coaxial MG 34
(iii) On the roof in front of the commander's cupola
(iv) On the driver's dashboard
(v) On the wireless set

Thus a lamp is fitted in each crew member's station. The arrangement is reasonable, although the fitting of a lamp in the turret bulge would have facilitated loading when the tank interior was dark though still light enough outside.

8. Crew Access

(a) Hatches. The commander's fixed "cupola" is circular, 1'7" in diameter, and is situated in the left-rear quarter of the turret roof. In this cupola are fitted the seven episcopes the commander looks through when seated. Although fairly deep, the cupola allows quick access to and from the turret. The cupola door is pivoted, and lifts and swings sideways to open. When the door is open, it does not increase the overall height of the tank. The door can be closed from inside or outside the tank, but can be locked only from inside.

The other turret roof hatch is on the right side and is for the loader. The hatch is rectangular, 1'2" long and 1'8" wide and opens with spring assistance. It is locked by a set of levers operated by a handwheel on the inside of the door. This seems a cumbersome arrangement and moreover probably a dangerous one since the levers project below roof level when the door is closed. They obstruct the loader, who is liable to injure his head on the projections when loading.

A turret escape hatch is fitted into the rear wall of the turret and is 1'8" wide and 1'2" high. When the turret bulge ammunition bins are full, the rounds project around and beneath the hatch, making evacuation almost impossible, even for a slim crew member. When the bins are emptied (a situation which would be operationally dangerous) the hatch is more accessible, but can still be used only by a very thin man. In emergency, the crew members would probably prefer to risk getting out

Because the Germans could never build enough Tiger tanks to fulfill all their military needs, they sometimes turned to decoys to fool Allied air and ground forces. This picture—taken from a World War II US Army report—shows a crude wooden replica of a Tiger I hidden under a tree. It is unknown if the German military used many such decoys to make the most productive use of their limited number of Tiger tanks. The Germans formed most of them into special heavy tank battalions that were controlled at Corps level, from which they were assigned to various divisions based on the mission. Only a few divisions ever had Tigers as part of their normal compliment of tanks. *US Army*

A most unwelcome sight for any Allied tanker of World War II had to be the front of a Tiger I. With it's thick armor and very accurate long-range main gun, the Tiger I possessed a big advantage over most Allied tanks. Adolf Hitler considered a battalion of Tiger Is (47 at full strength) equal to a division of standard German medium and light tanks (150 at full strength). In the fighting for Italy, New Zealand troops typically found Tiger Is in hull-down positions that were both well-sited and well-camouflaged. They also observed that the Tigers were almost invariably supported by at least one other tank or a self-propelled gun. *Private collection*

"with the smoke" through the roof hatches rather than chance being caught in the escape hatch or one of the many projections surrounding it.

A circular empty-case ejection hatch 9" in diameter is fitted in the turret roof towards the rear. The hatch can be closed and locked when not required.

The driver's hatch is mounted in the hull roof on the left side of the vehicle front. It is 1' 2 1/2" long and 1' 6 1/2" wide and, like the commander's hatch, opens on a pivot by swinging sideways. When open, the door does <u>not</u> foul the turret traverse. The door can be opened and closed from inside the vehicle, and is very satisfactory from a user standpoint.

The bow-gunner's hatch is identical to the driver's but is mounted on the right side of the hull roof and opens in the opposite direction from the driver's.

(b) <u>"Bailing-Out"</u>. The men taking part in the loading trials took the following times (in seconds) to leave their stations and get outside the vehicle:

	Comdr.	Gunner	Loader	Driver
Hatch open	5	10.3	6.7	3.4
Hatch closed but locked	10.2	14.1	9.8	6.9

Since no bow-gunner's seat was fitted, no trial could be made from that position.

Three men were timed leaving the turret via the escape hatch. The biggest became entangled in the bin arms and could not move either way until he was released from inside the turret. The other two men took

13.4 and 15 secs., respectively, the faster man tearing his clothing "en route." These trials took place with the men standing in the loader's station, with no ammunition in the bulge bins, i.e., under the best possible conditions.

(c) <u>Conclusion</u>. The commander's, driver's, and bow-gunner's hatches are all well-designed and satisfactory; the loader's hatch door fittings project inside the turret when the door is closed; and the escape hatch is almost useless for "bailing-out" and its principal use would be for stowing the turret bulge from outside the turret.

9. Main Armament Loading Trials

(a) <u>Loading Arrangement</u>. Although the documents stated that a total of eighty 8.8cm rounds were carried in this vehicle, we found a stowage for only sixty-four rounds in the earlier vehicle and seventy rounds in the later vehicle. In both vehicles, forty-eight rounds are carried in the panniers and the remainder in two racks in the turret bulge. All the rounds are stowed horizontally with bases rear.

When the gun fires, the empty case is ejected but does not stop clear of the deflector guard. Instead, it lies

Because German tanks of World War II were powered by gasoline engines, they were very prone to burn if their armor was penetrated by an enemy round. This was also a serious problem in American tanks as they were also fitted with gasoline engines. The Soviet military on the other hand, went to diesel engines in their tanks. Diesel fuel is much less flammable then gasoline. This early-model Tiger I, suffered an internal fire whose heat was so intense, the paint peeled off the vehicle's turret. *British Army Tank Museum*

with the base on the deflector guard and the neck on the breach ring. It must therefore be removed before another round can be loaded. In the trials, the cases were thrown through the ejection hatch in the turret roof. This took an average time of 2.4 seconds per case.

Although the loader would probably wear gloves when handling the hot case, none were available for the trial. The loading times would not be materially increased by wearing gloves, since the rounds are more or less "man-handled" into the gun and no special finger dexterity is required.

Loading is simplified by the use of a collapsible roller. The roller is hinged on the bulge floor between the two bins and is in line with the gun.

When the gun is elevated, the loader can insert the round into the breech comparatively easily since the deflector guard is low down and allows him a straight push. However, when the gun is depressed, the deflector guard is well above the level of both the loading roller and the breech, making loading very awkward and difficult. The easiest and fastest drill for loading the gun in depression was to remove the empty case, drop the hinged deflector guard, load the round, replace the deflector guard and operate the safety switch. If this drill is not used, the loader is liable to lose control of the round (weighing fifty-one lbs.) and jam his fingers on the deflector guard.

The four loaders used in the trials were:
Loader A - Tpr. Egan, height 5'4",
Loader B - Cpl. Francis, height 5'10",
Loader C - Cfn. Weaver, height 6'4", and
Loader D - Dvr. Liddiatt, height 6'1".

(b) Turret Bulge Racks. The two "ready" racks in the vehicle are Racks A and B which are situated in the turret bulge. Rack A is in the right side of the bulge (nearer the loader) and Rack B is in the left side. Each rack in the earlier vehicles holds eight rounds, and in the more recent vehicles eleven rounds. The rounds are stowed in three layers, each layer resting on two fixed arms. Each round is individually held in position by two straps fastened by toggle clips. Although this arrangement keeps the rounds securely in place, the rearmost clips are not easily accessible and time is lost both in fastening and unfastening each round.

The drill for loading from either rack is to remove the empty case from the gun and throw it through the ejection hatch, move to the rack, undo the toggle clips holding the round, roll the round along the rack arms, and then lift (or drop) the round onto the roller. Holding the round by the right hand, pull the round forward on the roller, and guide the projectile into the breech. Still holding the round by the right hand, push the back of the round with the left hand, lifting it clear of the roller and the deflector guard, and ram the round home. Operate the safety switch with the right hand.

The average loading times per round (in seconds) are as follows:

RACK	GUN LEVEL	MAX. ELEV.	MAX. DEPTH.
A	9.6	8.2	10.1
B	8.0	8.0	9.3

Although Rack A is nearer to the loader than Rack B, rounds can be loaded faster from Rack B because the rack is directly opposite the loader. Consequently, the clips are more accessible and the rounds are easier to remove. However, Loader A, who is 5'4" tall, could not reach two of the rounds in Rack B.

Since the racks hold a total of either sixteen rounds (earlier model) or twenty-two rounds (later model), they would provide adequate "ready" ammunition for any normal engagement. They would be replenished from one of the pannier racks.

(c) Pannier Racks. There are three pairs of pannier racks, C and F, D, and E, and G and H. In these racks, the rounds are stowed horizontally in layers, carried hinged wooden blocks, which wedge against the underside of the rounds and keep them in position. The hinges on these blocks get rusty and dirty and then require considerable force to operate. This is undesirable, since it leads to increased round-handling times.

This type of stowage would have been greatly improved if the layer arms had been hinged and sprung so that they lifted upwards when the rounds were removed. This would have allowed greater access to the layer below.

Racks C and F. Each rack is designed to hold eleven rounds in three layers, but in the vehicle inspected, only eight rounds could be stowed. A curved rail has been fitted on the hull roof to carry 7.92mm ammunition belt bags for the coaxial MG 34. Each end of the rail projects into one of the racks and prevents the top layer of three rounds from being stowed. In addition, when the rail is loaded with belt bags, the centre layer of the bin is partly obscured.

The rail appears to be an afterthought, and its designers presumably considered that it would be better to have a large stock of MG 34 ammunition, and lose stowage space for six 8.8cm rounds.

The two racks A and B contain an adequate number of rounds (16 to 22) for any normal engagement. Eight rounds were loaded from Rack G with the turret at 12 o'clock, in an average loading time per round of 17.8 seconds.

Racks D and E. Racks D and E are situated in

front of Racks C and F respectively. The racks each hold 7 rounds in two layers. The rounds are even less accessible than those in Racks C and F.

Racks G and H. These racks are situated on each side of the extreme front of the hull. Each rack holds 6 rounds in two layers of three rounds each. Replenishing Racks A and B from these racks would be very awkward and fatiguing.

10. Conclusion

The Royal Tiger allows a very reasonable degree of comfort to all the crew members except the gunner. His seat is badly positioned in relation to his controls, his position is cramped and not easily accessible, and the gun traverse controls are badly designed.

The loading arrangement is good; the loader has a spacious position, and the ready rounds need not be lifted appreciably when loading. The arrangement should be compared with the UK tank arrangement having no rounds stowed above the level of the turret ring. This latter is probably safer, but it makes the loading of large and heavy rounds very slow and fatiguing to the loader.

Despite the good loading arrangement, the loading times are high in this vehicle, because:

(a) The empty case must be disposed of before another round can be loaded.
(b) The design of the rack fittings is unsatisfactory.
(c) The extreme size and weight of the rounds makes them awkward to maneuver.

The following are the outstandingly good and bad features of the vehicle as revealed by this Motion Study:

Good Features
(i)   Very few projecting fittings in fighting compartment.
(ii)   Driver's seat and two positions. Steering wheel.
(iii) Driver's and bow-gunner's hatch doors.
(iv) Driver's open-up vision.
(v)   Loading roller in bulge.
(vi) Number of 8.8cm rounds stowed.

Bad Features
(vii)   Commander's backrest.
(viii) Position of gunner's seat.
(ix)   Gunner's cramped station.
(x)   Gun traverse controls.
(xi)   Position of loader's handwheel.
(xii) Loader's hatch door.
(xiii) Driver's closed-down vision.
(xiv) Design of ammunition rack fittings.
(xv) Empty case must be removed before next round can be loaded.
(xvi) Rail for stowing MG 34 belt bags fouls

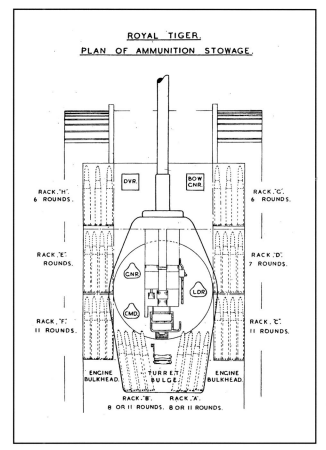

From a 1947 British Army report done by the Motion Study Wing of the Military Operational Research Unit, comes this overhead drawing of the placement of main gun rounds in the Tiger II. In looking over captured Tiger IIs and documents, the Allies found different ammunition stowage arrangements in various vehicles. The crews of Tiger IIs sometimes preferred to keep all main gun rounds within the thicker armor protection of the vehicle's hull. The Tiger II crews found that keeping main gun rounds stored in the vehicle's turret could result in complete destruction of the tank and crew if hit in the wrong place by an antitank shell.

CHAPTER 2

FIREPOWER

When the Germans invaded the Soviet Union in 1941, they found to their surprise that the armor protection on the Russian T-34 medium tank and the KV heavy tank had almost rendered their entire inventory of tank and antitank weapons obsolete. In desperation, the German Army was forced to use an existing weapon originally designed as an antiaircraft gun. This weapon was best known to Allied soldiers of World War II as the "88." Although the name "88" was often erroneously applied to any high velocity German gun, the name actually belonged to the family of antiaircraft, antitank, and tank guns of 88 millimeter caliber. (Caliber is the diameter of the bore, not including the depth of the rifling of a gun tube.)

On display at the US Army Ordnance Museum is an example of an early model of the well-known multipurpose "88". This particular gun was fitted with an thin armored shield to provide it's crew at least a basic level of protection from small arms fire and artillery fragments. Primarily designed as an antiaircraft gun, the "88" proved to be the best antitank gun of World War II. Coming in many models, the German fitted the "88" to a wide variety of different platforms ranging from non-turreted tank destroyers to turret equipped tanks like the Tiger I and Tiger II. The basic gun itself was constantly improved by the Germans throughout the war to retain it's advantage over Allied tanks and planes. *Michael Green*

The widespread use of these highly effective weapons led to an almost legendary reputation and like most legends, it was often exaggerated. However, in the case of the 88 there was a solid basis in fact. The Germans themselves did not use the term 88 but referred to these weapons as 8.8 centimeter guns in their military paperwork. The typical German soldier called the gun *"acht/acht,"* the English translation being "eight/eight."

The 8.8cm guns that proved so effective in World War II originated during World War I when 88mm caliber guns were widely used for naval guns. These weapons were fitted with pedestal mounts on trailers for mobility to combat the rapidly increasing effectiveness of military aircraft. 88s were used from 1917 onward to protect vital rear-area German military installations.

With the end of the First World War in 1918, the Treaty of Versailles drastically limited the activities of the two major artillery producers in Germany. Two famous competing companies, Rheinmetall and Krupp, were prohibited from designing weapons in the same caliber. Rheinmetall was restricted to guns above seventeen centimeters in bore. Krupp was restricted to guns smaller than that caliber, and was thus eliminated from antiaircraft gun competition.

To circumvent these restrictions, Krupp entered into an agreement with Bofors of Sweden, whereby Bofors received the right to manufacture guns for foreign sale using Krupp technology and designs. In return, Krupp received details of Bofors development work and was permitted to send three of their engineers to Sweden to work with Bofors. It was during this period that the weapon that was to become the first production model 8.8cm antiaircraft gun was developed. In 1931, the Krupp design engineers returned to Essen, Germany, and completed the prototype at the Krupp plant in early 1932. The long years of careful development paid off and the gun was an instant success.

The new German rearmament program was now underway and the weapon was put into production and introduced into service in 1933 as the 8.8cm Flak 18, L/56. (Flak was a German abbreviation for antiaircraft gun.) The L/56 referred to the length of the gun that measured fifty-six calibers from the muzzle to the rear face of the breech ring. The Flak 18 had a barrel life of only 900 rounds. With the introduction of a new type of propellant, this increased to about 3,000 rounds. Even this number was not considered satisfactory by the Germans, so a large research program was started in 1935 to increase barrel life. The solution came from Krupp's rival, Rheinmetall, with their barrel design known as the Rohr Aufbau Nine.

Standardized as the 8.8cm Flak 36, the Rheinmetall barrel design and new trailer mount (the *Sonderanhaenger 201*) constituted a substantial improvement over the Flak 18 with its simple cruciform (cross-shaped) mount. The Flak 18 mount was designed primarily for antiaircraft fire and required the weapon to be emplaced by lowering the cruciform mount to the ground and removing the wheels before commencing fire.

Experiences in Spain (1936-39) with German volunteers during the Spanish Civil War had shown that under many combat conditions it was highly desirable to be able to open fire immediately, without any delay caused by emplacing the gun. With the Rheinmetall carriage, the gun could be brought into action to engage targets simply by lowering the side outriggers and locking the hand brakes on the rear wheels. For planned targets, the cruciform mount was lowered to the ground by winches on the wheels assemblies. The wheels tilted as the platform was lowered.

The wheels were then removed and the sidearms lowered. Jacks were fitted to each arm of the cruciform to permit leveling the mount which was then spiked to the ground. Cross-leveling handwheels permitted leveling of the top carriage. If a rammer (a device used to force a round into the firing chamber of a gun) was present, the rammer guard was unfolded to the operating

The ability of the "88" to punch through Allied tank armor can be clearly seen in this picture of an early cast-hull Sherman tank that took a hit from an "88" into the lower front hull. The round itself has passed completely through the armor into the vehicle's front-mounted transmission housing. What happened to the vehicle's crew is unknown. This ability to punch holes so easily in Allied tanks did much to lower the morale of tankers who had to go up against the "88" in combat. In many cases the antitank rounds fired from an "88" would pass through one side of an Allied tank and out the other. *6th Armored Division Association*

Because the ground-mounted "88" was so widely used by the Germans throughout World War II, the total number of losses of these types of weapons and their crews were quite heavy. Once the position of a ground-mounted "88" was identified in combat, Allied forces would bring as much firepower to bear as they could on the gun, or guns, to wipe out the deadly threat that this weapon posed to their soldiers and vehicles. The ground-mounted "88" pictured, was caught by Allied aircraft in it's traveling position and destroyed somewhere in Western Europe. *US Army*

position, the gun was cocked and the weapon was ready to fire. Later in the war, an improved trailer designated the *Sonderanhaenger 202* was placed in production by the Germans. It is readily identified by the twin wheels front and rear compared with the single front and twin rear wheels of the *Sonderanhaenger 201*.

Antitank Role

Beginning in 1940, the 8.8cm Flak weapons were frequently used in ground combat. They were fitted with thin armored shields to provide limited protection for the gun crew from small arms fire and artillery fragments. There are also many examples of shields being added as field modifications and in many cases these precluded the use of the weapon in the antiaircraft role. A standard shield fitted on the Sonderanhaenger 201, however, permitted the use of the weapon at all levels of elevation. Because of the large size of the deployed gun (roughly 6.9 feet tall, 9.5 feet wide, and 19 feet long), it was vulnerable to high explosive artillery fire. Hence, German gun crews did their best to camouflage their positions from enemy observation.

British tankers first experienced the full might of the German ground-mounted 88s on May 20, 1940, during The Battle for France when an English tank attack on German units was stopped dead in its tracks by both artillery and a number of 8.8cm antiaircraft guns

pressed into the antitank role. The British lost thirty-six tanks that day, eight of them to the 88s. The success of the antiaircraft guns in this battle was well-noted by the German military as a whole and in particular by the German officer in charge that day, Major General Erwin Rommel. Rommel later made excellent use of his 88s in North Africa against Allied tanks. Typical German tactics involved luring the enemy tanks within the killing zone of the ground-mounted 88s. German gun crews would then use the superior range of the 88 to destroy their opponents before they could defend themselves with their shorter-range weapons.

Major Allerton Cushman (US Army), attached to the British Army in North Africa as an observer, commented in a wartime report dated March 29, 1943: "Any attempt by tanks or (tank destroyers) to attack German mechanized elements, even those that appeared to be isolated and vulnerable, was likely to bring down a murderous converging fire from concealed antitank guns. Any Allied attack that did not provide for the neutralization of this antitank defense risked defeat and disaster."

American tankers first met the 88 during the 1942 invasion of North Africa. Lt. Col. Henry Gardiner (US Army), commander of a tank battalion, wrote in his diary about his first encounter with ground-mounted 88s in North Africa:

Our tanks [M3 mediums] which had charged across a little flat between two hills with the infantry still riding on the tanks had suddenly been engaged by enemy antitank guns and four knocked out and set on fire. I went up to take a look and could see our tanks burning with a dense black column of smoke pouring out of the turrets of each of them. Much confusion. There were men lying all around the tanks, most of them dead. We could observe a few crawling and could hear some cries for help. Lt. Jehlik, one of our best officers and finest men, had his head shot off. We laid him back over the hill and I put a shell case upright at both ends of his body to keep him from being run over and so we could find him in the dark.

Later during a night movement, Gardiner had another encounter with a deadly ground-mounted 88 that he describes in his diary: "Just at dusk, we started to move back to an area about two miles towards Tebourba. The Germans had slipped an 88 in just across the river from us and it opened fire on the column and hit the lead tank. It continued to fire apparently at the exhaust flashes and with its screaming sound and flaming tracer it was a scary affair. The rest of the tanks kept swinging wide of the one that was hit. I was in a tank and waited until they had all gone and the firing had stopped before I made a run for it, and wasn't fired on."

A few weeks later Gardiner's luck ran out and his M3 medium tank was hit by a ground-mounted 88: "Just then we were hit! There was a blinding flash in the tank, a scream, and I realized I had been hurt. I jumped out of the tank and ran back a short distance and

This picture of a captured "88" in an antiaircraft position shows American soldiers preparing to load and fire a round in the general direction of the German Army. As an antiaircraft weapon the "88" required a host of supporting systems, including a gun direction device, height finder, range finders, and possibly a radar unit to effectively engage Allied aircraft. The typical "88" configured as an antiaircraft gun could throw a twenty-one pound shell up to 50,000ft. Massed in large numbers to defend important targets, the "88" took a heavy toll of attacking Allied aircraft throughout the war. *US Army*

What does actually happen when an armored vehicle is hit by a high velocity antitank round from a gun like the 88? The actual ability of a projectile to damage a target depends on a variety of conditions relating to the projectile and the target. The principal damage to a tank is caused by penetration of its armor by a projectile and the subsequent ricochet of the round within the target vehicle.

In addition to the round entering the vehicle, the armor is usually damaged by spalling. Spalling is a condition wherein a tank's armor shatters due to the impact of the round, and scatters pieces of armor into the vehicle at high velocity.

Sgt. Michael V. Altamura, who saw action with the 750th Tank Battalion in Europe during World War II, was his unit's weapons expert. He was often called upon to check out the destroyed and normally burned-out hulks of his unit's tanks for booby-traps set by the Germans. He describes the sight of looking into an American tank hit by an 88: "It wasn't pretty—an 88 round that had bounced around the inside of a Sherman tank pretty much tore to shreds any crewman that was unfortunate enough to get in its way. If a tank had been hit by an 88 and had burned, the smell of burnt flesh could be overwhelming. In the intense heat of a burning tank, the blackened bodies would shrink to half their normal size."

So horrible were the wounds caused by high-velocity German antitank rounds (fired from weapons like the 88) striking and penetrating American tanks that the US

As an early stop-gap measure to provide the German Army some form of mobile antitank defense from Soviet vehicles like the T-34 medium and KV heavy tanks, the Germans quickly developed a number of tracked self-propelled (SP) tank destroyer vehicles to mount the deadly "88". Early models were open-topped and thinly armored. These vehicles were not as versatile as a tank with a 360 degree fully-traversable turret. A self-propelled tank destroyer's gun was usually mounted in a fixed position which only allowed for a very limited amount of traverse. But they were both cheaper and quicker to build in large numbers than the much more complex tank designs. As time went on these vehicles later evolved into a family of well-armored and low-slung tank destroyers. The vehicle pictured is a Nashorn which was based on the chassis of a Mark 4. Almost 500 of these vehicles were built by the Germans. *Michael Green*

crouched. There had been seven of us in the tank and I saw four get out."

What is it like inside an American tank being shot at by high-velocity German antitank rounds? In the March-April 1943 issue of *The Armored Cavalry Journal* comes this very colorful description by Lt. Colonel Louis V. Hightower.

We could actually see the shells coming along close to the ground like a ricocheting stone on water.

One shell fragment came right down the tube of our gun but caused no serious injury among our crew. Another shell went through the bogey wheels under the tank and tore out the other side like a rabbit. Another hit our turret but didn't penetrate. Then a shell stuck our suspension system.

Each shell that hit sounded like a giant anvil or tremendous bell. It made your ears ring. As soon as our gun was unjammed we began firing again, but another shell smashed the bottom of our left rear gas tank, and flaming gasoline spurted over the back of the tank, its tracks, and on the ground about us.

I shouted to my boys, "Now is the time to git!" We bailed out of there like peas from a hot pod before the tank had stopped running.

Army's 4th Armored Division had a standing policy that if one of their tanks was hit and had to be abandoned, the crew was only allowed to assist their wounded comrades out of the tank. If any member of the tank crew was killed, it was forbidden for the remaining crew members to remove the body or bodies. Ordnance vehicles would be used to tow the destroyed tank and dead crewmen to a rear area where non-combat soldiers would be used to remove any remains. Colonel Jimmy Leach, a battalion commander of the 4th Armored Division in World War II, remembers the reason for this policy: "If the tank crews had a chance to really see what happened to their fellow crewmen and the terrible ways in which they died within our tanks when struck by high-velocity German antitank rounds, they might become disinclined to be more aggressive during their next combat encounter with German forces. We couldn't risk our tank crews' morale from suffering this fate."

German gun crews of ground-mounted 88s didn't always have it their own way. Captain Charles L. Davis (US Army) describes the actions of a single Sherman tank in a wartime report from the 1st Armored Division in Tunisia (North Africa) in early 1943: "An 88mm gun came into the platoon leader's vision, about eight hundred yards to the right front, with the gun pointed to his right. He gave 800 to the gunner, and the round was high. He gave 700, and the round was still over. 600 was again high. The German crew began traversing to lay on the tank. About then the platoon leader became a bit frantic and began screaming 'FOUR!, FOUR!' The next round was close enough to stop the gun, which got off one round that was barely wide of the tank. The gunner polished off the 88 with several more rounds."

Taken inside the turret of a Tiger I, this picture shows a German tanker carefully loading an 88mm round into the breech end of the main gun. The Tiger-tank loader was also responsible for loading the coaxial MG34 machine gun located on his side of the turret. It was the gunner however, that controlled the firing of this weapon with a foot switch. The loader in a Tiger I had the most space in the vehicle since he needed the room to load the fairly large 88mm rounds into the main gun. The loader was also provided with a padded seat and backrest that could be lifted and swung out of the way when not in use. *Private collection*

In the Tiger I all ninety-two main gun rounds were stored horizontally in ten unarmored sheet metal bins on either side of the vehicle's hull. There were no main gun rounds stored in the Tiger I turret. This picture shows two of the ten onboard ammunition bins in the Tiger I hull. The bins were normally covered by thin-hinged doors which folded down when opened. Each bin held up to sixteen rounds, stowed in four layers of four rounds each. Postwar British tests showed that after the front rounds were taken out the loader would have a much harder time removing the remaining rounds. *British Army Tank Museum*

Ground-mounted 88s could also be destroyed by individual soldiers. Described in the files of the US Army Center for Military History is this account of an American infantryman during the invasion of Salerno (Italy): "T. Sgt. Manuel S. Gonzales of Company F discovered an 88-mm gun firing from the dunes towards our landing craft. Machine gun tracers set fire to his pack, but he wriggled out of it and crawled on past exploding grenades towards the gun. Then he threw his own grenades, killing the crew, and blew up their ammunition."

Unlike a howitzer that normally has a medium muzzle velocity and a curved trajectory which allows it to fire at indirect targets hidden from view, the 8.8cm Flak gun (befitting its original role as an antiaircraft gun) had very high muzzle velocity and a very flat trajectory. This meant that the 8.8cm gun was not particularly effective against targets hidden from its view. Ken Hockman, who served as a driver of a US Army M5A1 light tank in Europe during World War II recounts: "On a number of occasions dug-in German 88s were unable to score a hit on our tank because they couldn't depress their barrels low enough to fire at us!"

This tactical limitation often allowed Allied soldiers the opportunity to turn the tables on 8.8cm guns being used in ground defense roles. The American-built Sherman tank had the ability to use its 75mm gun in an artillery indirect-fire mode. By remaining behind cover, the Sherman could on occasion destroy German 8.8cm gun positions with high-explosive (HE) rounds without exposing its thin armor to the deadly 8.8cm rounds. Bud Hartman, a US Army infantryman in Europe during World War II, remembers: "Our unit would often use its 4.2 mortars from under terrain cover to lob high-explosive rounds on top of dug-in German 88 gun positions. When they called in their own artillery support, we just packed up the mortars and moved to another position."

Anti-Aircraft Role

In an antitank role, the 8.8cm gun required only its excellent direct-fire sights to effectively engage enemy vehicles. On the other hand, to aim an antiaircraft gun requires specially designed sighting systems and fire control equipment to keep the gun continuously aimed on a plane that may be simultaneously changing in azimuth, range, and altitude. The high speed of aircraft also necessitates the rapid mechanical or electronic calculation and transmission of firing data to the gun. Sighting and fire control instruments are therefore provided to automatically keep one gun (or many) aimed at a flying target and automatically set the mechanical time fuse on each shell so it will explode at the correct altitude. The typical 8.8cm Flak gun could be elevated 90 degrees straight up and throw a twenty-one pound shell to altitudes of 50,000 feet.

A data transmission system known as the *Uebertragung 30* was originally fitted to both the Flak 18 and Flak 36. This device connected the gun to its fire-control instruments (which normally consisted of a gun director device, height finder, stereoscopic range finder, and possibly a sound detector or radar unit) by a 108-strand remote-control cable. A new data transmission system designated the *Uebertragung 37* was introduced into service in 1939. When the weapons were modified to use this new equipment, they were redesignated the 8.8cm Flak 37. The Flak models 18, 36, and 37 weighed approximately five tons.

Vehicle Mounted

The success of ground-mounted 8.8cm Flak guns as antitank weapons in Russia and North Africa led to their quick consideration by the German Army for mounting on a variety of self-propelled (SP) mounts. By simply mounting 8.8cm Flak guns on obsolete or surplus tank hulls, the Germans fielded a weapon system that effectively repelled Allied tank fleets until newer more powerful tanks could be designed and built.

The German industrial base, always short of raw materials and under constant air bombardment after 1943, was never able to build enough tanks to even keep up with combat losses. The Allies consistently out-produced the Germans in numbers of tanks built during the war.

The distinction between a World War II tank and self-propelled (SP) gun is derived from the way the main gun was mounted. The Germans defined a tank as a fully-tracked armored vehicle fitted with a gun in a crew-operated 360 degree traversable turret. In contrast, a German SP gun of World War II was fitted in a fixed armored superstructure which constrained it to a very limited traverse arc of fire.

The requirements of a gun on a SP mount were somewhat different from the standard Flak weapon, so a redesign was carried out to optimize the gun for this application. A one-piece barrel enclosed in a light jacket was designed and fitted with a muzzle brake to reduce the recoil. Originally, this gun was intended for installation in three prototype vehicles designated the 8.8cm Kanone (Pz. Sfl.) auf *Sonderfahrgestell*. In the meantime, however, development of the L/71 8.8cm guns had proceeded to the point where they were available for SP mounts. The superior performance of these weapons resulted in displacement of the smaller L/56 gun used previously on SP gun mounts.

During this same period, a weapon similar to that for the SP mount was developed for installation in the new Tiger tank prototype built by Porsche. The points of

The Tiger II was armed with the final and most powerful version of the "88" family of guns, known as the KwK 43. This gun was 20ft 7in long. Like the KwK 36 version of the "88" mounted on the Tiger I, the KwK 43 as found on the Tiger II had a large double-baffle muzzle brake fitted. Some later production models of the Tiger II featured a slightly smaller version of the standard Tiger muzzle brake. The Tiger II pictured is currently on display at the German Army Tank Museum in Munster. *German Army*

Because the "88" was originally envisioned as only an antiaircraft weapon, the size, weight, and height of the gun was not a real concern for the designers. However, field use of the "88" in an ground emplaced antitank role quickly showed the Germans how vulnerable the very large and stationary "88" was to any enemy vehicle that could get close enough to use it's own weapons. In an effort to make the "88" an easier weapon to hide on the battlefield, the Germans built a number of "88s" on strictly antitank ground mounts. In this picture a captured "88" (known as the Pak 43) on an antitank mount is being used by an American crew to fire back at it's former owners. Clearly visible is the cruciform mount for this weapon. This mount lowered the silhouette of the "88" to only 5ft 8in tall. This was in sharp contrast to earlier antiaircraft versions of the "88" that were almost 7ft tall when emplaced in position. *US Army*

difference were primarily those required to mount the weapon in the tank's turret. Both of the guns designed for vehicle mounting were equipped with vertical sliding breech blocks contrasting with the horizontal breech blocks of the Flak guns.

Ballistically, the SP weapons were identical to the Flak 18, 36, and 37. With the production of the standard Henschel-built Tiger I tank version, the gun was adopted and produced in quantity as the Kw.K 36 (Kw.K was a German abbreviation for tank gun). A total of 1,355 Tiger I tanks were produced during the war equipped with the 8.8cm Kw.K 36 L/56. The Kw.K 36 L/56 gun was itself seventeen feet long and had thirty-two grooves with a right-hand twist.

Barrel length plays an important part both in tank gun accuracy and the transfer of energy from the propellant charge to a kinetic energy round. The more energy a round has when leaving a barrel, the faster and harder it will hit an opponent's armor. This force is called muzzle velocity.

Because Allied tanks, like the Sherman, were originally armed with only a short barreled 75mm gun (seven feet long), its accuracy and muzzle velocity were poor compared to that of the Tiger.

In a World War II report, Sgt. William Braden of the 2nd Armored Division stated: "I believe the German anti-tank gun is a better weapon than the guns the United States uses because they have a longer barrel and they use a 'souped-up' ammo."

Unlike the Flak gun, the Kw.K 36 L/56, when mounted on a Tiger tank, was equipped with an electric primer. (A primer is the component used to ignite the propelling charge.) Flak versions of the 8.8cm gun fired percussion-primed ammunition. In contrast to a percussion primer, which fires a round of ammunition by a blow from a firing pin, an electric primer fires a round of ammunition by the heat generated when an electric current passes through a resistance wire embedded in heat-sensitive composition explosive. All German tanks of World War II used an electric primer firing system for their main armament. In the Tiger I, the gun was fired electrically from a trigger bar control placed behind the gunner's elevating hand wheel.

Kw.K 36s in Tiger I turrets were also fitted with a large double-baffle muzzle brake. A muzzle brake is a short cylindrical extension for the muzzle of a cannon which redirects and partially dissipates the high-pressure gasses expelled by the projectile. When redirected, the force of the gases reduces recoil energy by partially counteracting the rearward force of recoil. The muzzle brake also cuts down on the amount of dust and dirt thrown up by the firing of a large caliber gun. This is a very important factor for tank crews, since they need to clearly see the fall of their shot to decide if another round is necessary.

Recoil is the backward movement of a gun tube after being fired, caused by the reaction to the forward motion of a projectile. Counter-recoil is the forward movement of a gun tube and connecting parts returning to their original position. A recoil system, as found on all large caliber tank guns, is a mechanism designed to gradually absorb the energy of recoil to prevent violent movement of the vehicle. Because of the Tiger's great weight and bulk, they were well suited to absorb the recoil from the very powerful 8.8cm gun. The Tiger I's recoil gear was of the standard German tank pattern, with a counterrecoil hydraulic buffer on the right of the main gun and a hydro-pneumatic recuperator on the left. A recuperator is that part of a tank's recoil mechanism that adds energy to return the barrel to its original firing position within a tank's turret. When a Tiger I's 8.8cm gun was fired, the recoil would push the gun's breech rearward almost two feet. Hydro-pneumatic meant the Tiger's recuperation used the action of hydraulic dampers (shock absorbers) and air springs to control the motion of the main gun's recoil. Other types of counterrecoil mechanisms use powerful mechanical springs to return a gun to its original firing position.

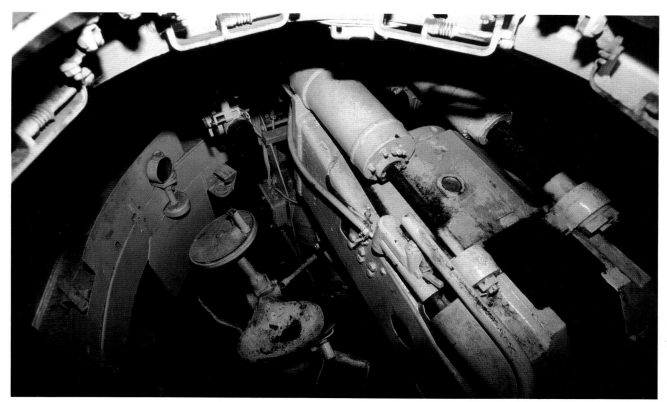

Looking down the commander's hatch of the Tiger II on display at the French Tank Museum, both the massive breech mechanism of the KwK 43 gun and the recoil cylinders located on top of the gun itself can be seen. On the left of the main gun can be seen the gunner's seat. In front of the gunner's seat is the manual turret traverse hand wheel. The manually operated elevation hand wheel for the gunner is hidden from view in this picture under the main gun. Both the Tiger I and Tiger II also had a hydraulic power traverse system controlled by the gunner from a foot operated pedal located on the bottom of the turret floor. *Tank Magazine*

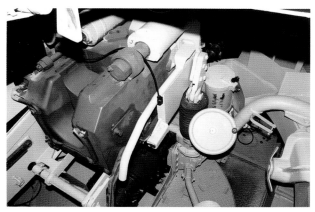

This turret-interior photo of the Tiger II belonging to the Patton Museum shows both the breech end of the KwK 43 gun and the loader's position. A breech mechanism is a mechanical opening and closing device located on the end of the barrel which provides for the entry and sealing of the ammunition in the weapon. On the other side of the breech is the folded-up seat and backrest of the tank commander. The gunner seat and controls would be located in front of the tank commander's position. Directly behind the main gun breech would be the ammunition racks for the main gun. *Jacques Littlefield*

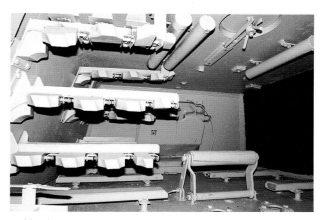

Unlike the Tiger I which had no main gun rounds stored in it's turret, the Tiger II with it's larger turret had space for up to twenty-two rounds when fitted with a Henschel turret and sixteen rounds when fitted with one of the fifty Porsche turrets. This interior photo of the Tiger II on display at the Patton Museum, shows the brackets for storing the main gun rounds in the rear of the turret. Located at the very rear of this Henschel turret can be seen the rear escape hatch. Seen at the bottom of the picture between the two sets of ammo racks is a wooden roller used to help the loader with placing the rounds into the gun's breech. *Jacques Littlefield*

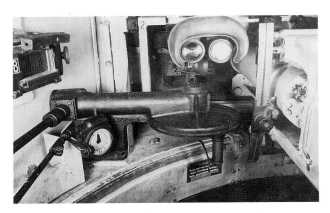

This photo shows the gunner' TZF 9b articulated binocular (two lens) telescopic sight as found on the Tiger I. Located above the sight is a brow pad for the gunner to steady his head when looking through his sights. Directly below the sight is the gunner's manually operated traversing hand wheel. This device is connected to an secondary hand control that can be operated by the tank commander if needed. To the left of the picture can be seen a direct vision port. Under the turret traversing control on the left of the picture is a turret indicator device. *British Army Tank Museum*

Since German tactical doctrine made wide use of the 8.8cm guns as antitank weapons, a number of antitank rounds were developed. The most widely used was a projectile with an armor piercing cap and a streamlined ballistic cap (APCBC), known to the German soldiers as the *Panzergranate 39* (Pzgr.39). Like almost all World War II German tank gun rounds, the Pzgr.39 contained a small high explosive bursting charge with a fuse designed to detonate it after the round had pierced the armor of an enemy tank. According to a wartime German Army handbook on the Tiger I, the Pzgr.39 could destroy enemy tanks at up to 2,000 meters.

Another round, the Pzgr.40, was dubbed APCR (for Armor Piercing Composite Rigid projectile). The APCR was a super-hard sub-caliber core within a larger light alloy body. Because the tank cannon imparted more kinetic energy to the sub-caliber core when fired, the core's armor penetration was better than the Pzgr.39. However, the lighter weight of the Pzgr.40 meant that its velocity and armor penetration abilities dropped off at ranges over 1,500 meters. Because the sub-caliber core was made out of tungsten, the Pzgr.40 was fairly rare, owing to a wartime tungsten shortage.

Visible within this Tiger II turret (Henschel) is the gunner's TZF 9d articulated monocular (single lens) telescopic sight. This device provided either a three or six power magnification for the gunner. Some of the original fifty Porsche Tiger II turrets were fitted with a binocular (two lens) TZF 9b1 sight similar to that found on the Tiger I . Vehicles so equipped could be identified by the two small openings on the front of the turrets. Later models of the Porsche turret were fitted with the same single lens sight found on the Henschel turrets and one of the two openings was then plugged. *Tank Magazine*

The Germans also developed a shaped charge high explosive antitank (HEAT) round known as the HL-Granate (hollow core). Shaped charge rounds concentrate energy over a small area to better penetrate thick armor. Because of a very sensitive warhead, camouflage nets and tree branches would often detonate it prematurely. In the Tiger handbook, the *Hohlladung 39* round is described as, "a high explosive shell, without a delayed action fuse, that produces shrapnel 20 meters to each side and 10 meters in the forward direction. It is effective against antitank guns, artillery, massed targets, and machine gun nests. It perforates gun shields, rips apart tires, tracks, loopholes, tips over vehicles, and sets everything on fire. Fitted with a delayed action fuse, it functions as a weapon against vertical targets, slamming through and exploding bunkers, houses, foxholes, forest, and early model enemy tanks. It will ricochet off of flat surfaces and then fly another 50 meters before exploding 4 to 8 meters above locations which cannot be seen and could otherwise not be fired on."

The Tiger handbook also describes the duties of the vehicle's commander: "Your quick thinking, your certain commands, brings the tank to life. Your rapid directions in selecting the warhead (armor piercing, high explosive, etc.) has a decisive effect. YOU hold all the trump cards in your hands. Now learn to play the game!"

Both the Pzgr. 39 and the HL-Granate had tracer elements. Like most World War II armies, the Germans color-coded their ammunition. The Pzgr.39 had a black nose with a white tip, the Pzgr.40 had an all black nose, and the HL-Granate round had a gray nose. Shells that had a yellow nose meant that they had an explosive element. So powerful were the various armor-piercing (AP) rounds fired from the different types of 8.8cm guns, that on many occasions these projectiles would pass completely through one side of an Allied tank and out the other. This type of combat encounter with the German 8.8cm gun did much to give the weapon its legendary reputation. A psychological survey conducted by the US Army during World War II concluded that American soldiers who had to go up against the German 88s in combat, feared it more than any other German weapon. In the American 1st Armored Division the saying; "Find German 88 Guns or Die" was often repeated to green tankers seeing action for the first time.

Although the original 8.8 was very effective against the aircraft in service when it was first introduced, by 1938 aircraft performance had vastly improved. Neither the Flak 36, 37, nor the heavier 10.5cm (105mm) Flak proved capable of effectively dealing with faster and more agile aircraft. The 12.8cm (128mm) Flak 40 provided the answer as far as heavy fixed mounts were concerned, but it did not possess sufficient mobility for rapid deployment in the field. (It was later mounted in a modified Tiger II chassis and referred to as the *Jagdtiger*, but only forty-eight were built during World War II).

Clearly, a new weapon was required with a higher muzzle velocity, giving a greater effective ceiling and a

From a German wartime magazine comes this picture of a small scissors-type periscope being used by a member of General Rommel's famous Afrika Korps. This same device was also adapted to fit on the tank commander's cupola of the Tiger I. Used for observation, spotting, and for general conduct of fire, the binocular (two lens) construction increases the observer's stereoscopic (depth) perception. The periscope allowed a Tiger tank commander to keep his head under cover and still observe the fall of his main gun rounds.

shorter time of flight to the target. Such a weapon was intended as a replacement for the 8.8 Flak 18 and 36 then in service. The new weapon would be highly mobile and use ammunition light enough to be handled without the use of power equipment. For these reasons, the decision was made to concentrate on an improved model of the 88 rather than a new higher caliber weapon. In the fall of 1939, Rheinmetall received a contract for the 8.8cm *Gerät 37* to meet these requirements. The specifications called for a higher muzzle velocity with a rate of fire of approximately twenty-five rounds per minute. The new designation caused some confusion with the Flak 37 then in service, so it was changed to the 8.8cm Flak 41 during the summer of 1941. These guns weighed approximately nine tons and were issued to field units in early 1943. Like its predecessors, it was carried on the *Sonderanhaenger 202* and was effectively employed as both an antiaircraft and antitank gun.

The production Flak 41 had a muzzle velocity of 3,280 ft/sec with high explosive ammunition and 3,214

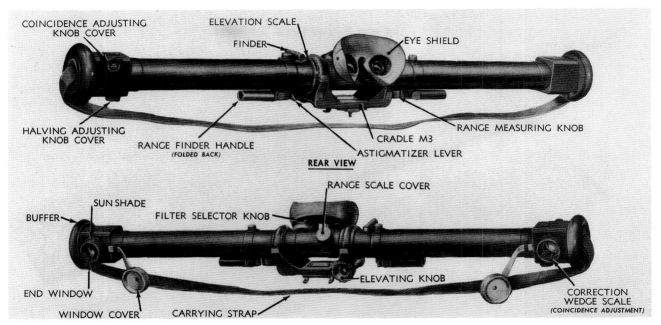

COINCIDENCE ADJUSTING KNOB COVER

ELEVATION SCALE

FINDER

EYE SHIELD

HALVING ADJUSTING KNOB COVER

RANGE FINDER HANDLE (FOLDED BACK)

CRADLE M3

ASTIGMATIZER LEVER

RANGE MEASURING KNOB

REAR VIEW

RANGE SCALE COVER

SUN SHADE

BUFFER

FILTER SELECTOR KNOB

ELEVATING KNOB

END WINDOW

WINDOW COVER

CARRYING STRAP

CORRECTION WEDGE SCALE (COINCIDENCE ADJUSTMENT)

From a destroyed Tiger I in North Africa, the British Army found a badly burnt example of a hand-held optical range finder known as the E.M. 17. Wartime pictures also showed it's use in other areas of operation by Tiger I crews. It was a coincidence type range finder, which meant the distance to the target is measured by sighting on the target, and bringing the erect image into coincidence with the inverted image in the field of view. The hand-held range finder pictured is from a US Army manual and is almost identical to the models used by the Germans.

ft/sec with armor piercing rounds. The Flak 41 barrel could be mounted on the Flak 36/37 carriage without overloading the equilibrators. (Equilibrators are springs that are used to balance a gun on its mount so it can be raised or lowered with relatively little effort by the gun crew.)

The Flak 41 design followed normal German practice for this period with a horizontal sliding breech block similar to that found in the Flak 18. The weapon was equipped for electrically primed ammunition similar to that introduced with the 10.5cm (105mm) Flak 38. The height of the weapon was reduced by using a turntable mount instead of the earlier pedestal mounting, thus simplifying the loading of the heavier ammunition.

By the spring of 1942, it was apparent to the Germans that despite full production of the Flak 41, the main burden of antiaircraft defense for the next two years would have to be borne by the earlier 8.8cm Flak 18, 36, 37 and the 10.5cm Flak 38/39. It was therefore desirable to increase the performance of these weapons to the highest degree possible. This required an increase in muzzle velocity to enable the weapons to engage bombers operating at higher speeds and altitudes. With the 10.5cm Flak 38 and 39, the improvement was obtained by fitting a Flak 41 barrel onto the earlier mount. These were designated the 8.8cm Flak 38/41 or Flak 39/41.

Improvements to the 8.8cm Flak 18, 36 ,and 37 proved to be more difficult, so development contracts were issued to both Krupp and Rheinmetall in May of 1942. The Germans' antiaircraft gun improvement program was closely related to the parallel designs for the new 8.8cm tank and antitank guns, which at that time were still designated the Kw.K 42 and the Pak 42. (Pak is a German abbreviation for antitank gun). As late as the winter of 1942, the Krupp antiaircraft gun design was still quite attractive because of its higher muzzle energy and trouble-free cartridge case extraction. At this time it was considered desirable to introduce it as the Flak 42, thereby having uniform ammunition with the new tank and antitank guns when they came into production. It was expected that the prototype would be finished by the spring of 1943 if no other alterations were required. However, suggestions were being made that the gun be lengthened to eighty calibers and the muzzle velocity increased. By February 1943, the pressure of other design work resulted in the cancellation of the entire Krupp antiaircraft gun project.

After work on the Flak gun was stopped, the development of an antitank gun continued with the introduction of the Pak 43 mounted on various ground mounts and vehicles. In parallel with the Pak 43 design, a tank version (Kw.K 43) was developed for the new Tiger II. This used the same ammunition and was ballistically identical with the Pak models. Early versions of the Tiger II with the Porsche turret had the monobloc weapon, but later production vehicles were equipped with the divided monobloc gun. Except for the Pak 43/41, all these weapons were equipped with vertical

Both the Tiger I and II were fitted woth at least two MG34 7.92mm vehicle-mounted machine guns. One of the machine guns was mounted alongside the Tiger's main gun and was fired from the gunner's position. The other machine gun was mounted in the front hull and operated by the vehicle's radioman. later models of the Tiger I and Tiger II tank were provided with an attachment rail on the tank commander's cupola for the mounting of a third 7.92 machine gun. This posed wartime picture shows two American G.I.s with a captured German M34 machine gun. *US Army*

sliding breech blocks and all late production guns used uniform right-hand twist rifling. A breech block is the principal moving part of a gun's breech mechanism. It consists of a large, heavy block at the back end of a barrel which contains the high propelling force of the round.

In order to obtain the maximum number of anti-tank guns as rapidly as possible, an interim model was introduced until the Pak 43 reached full production. This weapon was designated the Pak 43/41. It fired the same ammunition and its ballistic characteristics were identical to the Pak 43. The gun was fitted with a horizontal sliding breech block and the thirty-two groove rifling was of the increasing twist type. The carriage was of the conventional two-wheel type normally found on artillery pieces. This weapon was also fitted on an open-topped Mark IV chassis as a self-propelled antitank gun known as the *Hornisse* (Hornet) and later the *Nashorn* (Rhino). Almost 500 of these vehicles were built. The effectiveness of these SP guns against the American Army's M26 heavy tank is described in Richard Hunnicutt's book on the Pershing tank (reprinted with permission): "This was Pershing number 25 belonging to company H of the 33rd Armored Regiment and it had been knocked out by a self-propelled 8.8cm gun (*Nashorn*) at under 300 yards range. The projectile penetrated the lower front armor, passed between the driver's legs, and set the turret on fire. The crew successfully abandoned the vehicle before the ammunition blew up gutting the turret."

Other experimental developments with the Pak 43 and the 43/41 continued on different SP mounts, including at least one half-track version. The version designated the Pak 43/2 was fitted on the canceled Porsche Tiger chassis and designated the *Jagdpanzer* Tiger (P) Sd. Kfz 184. It's official German Army nickname was the *Elefant/Ferdinand*. Used as a tank destroyer, ninety of these vehicles were built. The Pak 43/3 was also mounted in the most effective tank destroyer of the war, the 8.8cm *Panzerjäger* Panther Sd. Kfz 173, better known to most as the *Jagdpanther*. References indicate that some weapons fitted to this vehicle were designated the Pak 43/4. Based on the chassis of a heavily modified Panther tank, 382 *Jagdpanthers* were built by the war's end.

Widely considered as the best antitank gun developed during World War II, the Kw.K 43 and Pak 43 guns showed a dramatic increase in performance over the earlier 8.8cm guns. The Kw.K 43 gun barrel mounted on the Tiger II was 20ft 7in long. Like the Tiger I, the Kw.K 43 gun on the Tiger II was fitted with a large double-baffle muzzle brake. With armor piercing capped ballistic capped (APCBC) ammunition known as Pzgr. 39/43, a muzzle velocity of 3,282 ft/sec. was obtained resulting in exceptional armor penetration performance. With this

Taken inside of a Tiger I, this picture shows the hull-mounted 7.92mm machine gun as operated by the vehicle's bow gunner/radioman who was located in the front right corner of the hull. The machine gun itself is housed in a ball-mounting and controlled by a pistol grip which is visible in the center of this photo. The weapon is sighted by an episcope telescope fitted with a forehead pad that can be seen on the far left of the picture. On the right of the picture are belt bags which contain 150 rounds each of 7.92mm machine gun ammunition. *British Army Tank Museum*

type of ammunition the 8.8cm Kw.K 43 and the Pak 43 could penetrate over five inches of steel armor at 30° obliquity at a range of 2,000 yards. Even higher penetrations were obtained with an armor piercing tungsten-cored round known the as Pzgr. 40/43. With a muzzle velocity of 3,707 ft/sec it could penetrate seven inches of steel armor! Because this type of round was in very short supply, the Germans tended to save them for use against late-war Soviet heavy tanks. (The Germans began using uranium as a substitute for tungsten when that element became scarce at the end of the war.) Most American and British tanks were under-armored and could be easily destroyed with the standard armor piercing round. Normally both Tiger I and Tiger II would carry an ammunition load split almost evenly between armor piercing and high explosive rounds.

Several variations of the Pak 43 8.8cm weapon were constructed. Some of the original weapons were fitted with monobloc barrels, but later production standardized on the divided monobloc construction. The basic Pak 43 was fitted to a cruciform mount carried on the Sonderanhaenger 204. This was a double wheel arrangement, similar in appearance to the carriers for the Flak guns. Although the weapon could be fired on its wheels, the wheels were normally removed and the cruciform mount lowered to the ground for emplacement yielding a very low silhouette in firing position. The top of the shield was only 5ft 8in above the ground. The Pak 43 was equipped with a vertical sliding breech block and the rifling had uniform right-hand twist with thirty-two grooves.

Gun Optics

One of the major contributing factors leading to the successful use of the 88 as an antitank weapon during World War II was the gun's outstanding optics (sights). The effective use of any gun in the direct-fire mode depends on the weapon's crew being able to spot a target, engage it, and then destroy it in the shortest amount of time possible. Because the German optics industry was the best in the world prior to World War II, German weapons had the ability to see and engage opponents at ranges far in excess of what their Allied counterparts were capable of. Herr Franz Kurtz, a veteran of the Eastern Front, trained for two months on the 8.8cm Flak. He vividly recalls looking through the 88's sight's and in his own words: "You could clearly see a blade of grass over a mile away with the sights on this weapon."

Almost always outnumbered, German tankers exploited the advantage of the Tiger's long-range firepower to reduce the number of enemy tanks getting too close. A good example of this approach is described in a wartime report by Captain Charles L. Davis where he recounts details of an attack on German positions in North Africa by units of the 1st AD in late April 1943:

As the platoon moved back up the ridge to cover the left flank, the Germans responded with high explosives and armor piercing shells. A look through the glasses showed at least one Mark VI tank firing at approximately 3,000 yards (maximum range for the American tank direct fire because of inadequate sights). One round landed about three quarters of the distance to the enemy target. The Platoon Leader put his trust in mobility. He kept moving, issuing similar instructions to his platoon.

The Company Commander urged the Platoon Leader, via radio, to move higher on the hill. The Platoon Leader asked who was going to take care of the Mark VI on the right flank. "What Mark VI?" asked the CO. A moment later the Platoon Leader and his crew were hitchhiking. A near miss had struck near the right rear of the tank, breaking the track and immobilizing the vehicle. Recognizing the futility of using the 75mm gun to compete with high velocity weapons equipped with superior fire control instruments in that situation, the Platoon Leader ordered the crew to abandon the tank.

The crew of another Sherman tank in the same engagement against the Tiger tanks was not so lucky:

That fifth tank had been the one entering the attack with a four-man crew. When the limited supply of ammunition that could be carried in the tank [turret] had been exhausted, it had been necessary to stop the tank for the driver to pass ammo from the racks under the turret and behind the assistant driver. That task is normally handled by the assistant driver while the tank is in motion. On this occasion, when the tank sacrificed its mobility to accomplish the transfer of ammo, the guns of the enemy on the right flank of the battalion laid on the tank and broke a track. Not realizing the futility of engaging in a firefight under those circumstances (he was outranged by the German guns), the tank commander continued to fire. The Germans concentrated on the vehicle and literally pulverized it with high explosive. [Note: High Explosive rounds from an 88 are more accurate at longer ranges than Armor Piercing rounds]. First, the radio and inter-phone were knocked out, then the turret periscopes, and finally the turret traversing mechanism, although not until the last

round of ammunition had been fired.

The crew was trapped in a disabled tank, out of ammunition and without communications, while the enemy laid on the high explosives. Concussion and shock wrecked the instrument panel and all interior control mechanisms. The tank commander alerted the crew to evacuate through the top hatches rather than through the bottom escape hatch because of the many low rounds striking under the tank. As the crew began the evacuation several more hits by German guns killed the tank commander, broke the driver's leg, and wounded the loader. The corporal gunner took charge and moved the wounded from the vicinity. He managed to stop one of the rear tanks of another platoon and place the driver on the vehicle to be transported to the reorganization area. He then took the other wounded man with him to the line of departure, during which trip, with one pistol between them, they took four prisoners.

In Roberts J. Icks' book, titled *Famous Tank Battles* there is a description of Tiger I tanks in Russia, using their long-range firepower advantage to slow down advancing Soviet armored forces:

Most of the Russian tank losses occurred as a result of following too closely the elements of the German rearguards. Often these rearguard units consisted only of a few infantry or combat engineers riding on a Tiger tank. Defilade positions or locations just inside an orchard or woods would be prepared and when Russian tanks exposed themselves the Tigers with their longer range 88mm guns would pick them off, usually concentrating on tanks behind the leading Russian tanks, throwing the leading tanks into confusion and quick re-

Visible in this photo taken inside a Tiger I, is the breech end of the KwK 36 version of the "88" and the rear of the coaxial 7.92mm machine gun mounted to fire along side the main gun. While the loader was responsible for the feeding of ammo into the machine gun and it's maintenance, it was the Tiger gunner who both sighted and fired the weapon. Beneath the rear of the machine gun is the loader's seat. The large black metal tube behind the loader's seat is a compressed-spring, counterweight cylinder used to balance the main gun in the Tiger turret. *British Army Tank Museum*

This picture was taken inside the Tiger II located at the French Army Tank Museum and shows the view of the vehicle's loader looking towards the front of the turret. In the center of the picture is the auxiliary turret traverse hand wheel for the loader. The coaxial 7.92mm machine gun is not mounted in this vehicle, although the small opening in the front of the turret through which the muzzle of the gun is fired is visible. *Tank Magazine*

tirement. The Tigers then would move off to the west a few miles to repeat the action.

Despite Tiger crews doing their utmost to use their long-range firepower advantage to offset superior number of Allied tanks. There were numerous occasions throughout World War II when the Tigers were forced into dealing with enemy tanks at very close ranges. Just how close is related in a story from Tiger tank ace Otto Carius' 1960 book titled *Tiger im Schlamm* (reprinted with the publisher's permission). The combat action occurred during a nighttime encounter with Soviet T-34s in December 1943:

I saw muzzle fire in the woodline. It moved farther to the right from flash to flash. Those had to be tanks moving along the woodline. They wanted to reach the road at the opposite end of the village. Sergeant Zwetti

was in position there.

Behind him was Von Schiller's tank. I radioed to Zwetti. With the help of a flare, I could see that a T34 was moving no more than 50 meters away from Zwetti. Due to the firing, we couldn't hear any engine noises. Because of that, the enemy had already entered the village. Zwetti shot his neighbor into flames. But, to our astonishment a second T34 was in the middle of the village street, right next to Von Schiller's tank.

It often proved deadly to the Russians that they kept their tanks completely buttoned up. Because of that, they could barely see anything, especially at night. They also had infantrymen riding on the tank, but even they didn't recognize the situation until it was to late.

Von Schiller wanted to turn his turret, but in the process hit the Russian tank with his cannon. He had to back up first in order to be able to knock it out. I didn't feel confident enough to shoot. One of the craziest situations I ever experienced.

Tiger Fire-Control Systems

Early tank designs had been fitted with straight-through telescope sights that were attached directly to a tank's main gun. While simple in design, this type of arrangement was very awkward for tank gunners to use. Whenever the main gun moved up or down, the gunner was forced to follow the sight.

The gunner on the Tiger I was provided with an articulated binocular (two lens) telescopic sight known as the TZF 9b. Telescopic sights that are articulated (joined to the main gun) have an eyepiece that remains in a fixed position for ease of the gunner's sighting. The TZF 9b sight had a magnification of 2.5 power. Some later models of the Tiger I had the TZF 9c sight fitted.

All Tiger II tanks with the standard production Henschel turret (and some late production models of the Tiger I) were fitted with a monocular (single lens) telescopic sight, known as the TZF 9d. This sighting system gave the Tiger II gunner a choice between two magnifications, either three or six power. The six power magnification was used at longer ranges while the three power magnification was for closer range. The first fifty

Mounted in the front hull plates of both the Tiger I and Tiger IIs was a single 7.92mm machine gun fitted in a ball mount. It was employed by the gunner who controlled it with a pistol grip and fired it with a hand trigger. The gun was aimed from a K.Z.F. 2 telescope as shown from this World War II US Army picture. The telescope was mounted alongside the machine gun in it's ball mount. This same ball mount and telescope was also used in a number of other German tanks.

Taken from the left side of the Tiger II on display at the French Army Tank Museum, this picture shows a close up view of the vehicle's main gun mantle. A mantle is an armored housing that protects the gun mount in the front of a tank's turret. On the left of the mantle is the small opening for the coaxial MG34 machine gun. Below the mantle can be seen both the driver's hatch on the right and the bow gunner's hatch in the foreground. In between the hatches can be seen an armored cover for the hull-mounted ventilating fan. The cord located below the mantle, on the front hull plate leads to a single headlight. *Tank Magazine*

Tiger II tanks built with the Porsche turret were fitted with the binocular TZF 9b1 sight. Some were later re-built with the monocular TZF 9d telescopic sight.

All versions of the TZF 9 sights fitted on the Tiger I and Tiger II were limited to a field of view of roughly twenty-three degrees. This somewhat limited field of view is fairly common for most tanks. Because of the better overall view from the top of a tank, target acquisition and initial range determination is normally the responsibility of the vehicle commander, although he can be assisted by other crew members. *The Tiger I Handbook* states: "The distance can only be properly estimated by the driver and the commander, because they can see the target unhindered with the naked eye. It is worse through the telescopic sight, first because the telescope sight magnifies everything by a factor of 2.5 and second because you cannot estimate that well with a single eye."

This same manual also describes the typical process to find the correct distance to a target: "If you have the time, do it like this: The tank commander measures or estimates the distance. The driver, he takes a little longer, reports his distance [estimate]. The tank com-

mander then calculates the middle [e.g. the average]. The gunner [who in the meanwhile has estimated or measured] reports his distance. The tank commander recalculates the middle and gives the right range. The gunner then sets the range."

The tank commander usually sees a target before other crew members. Upon spotting a target, a typical Tiger commander would give directions to his gunner over the intercom regarding the location and approximate range of the target. The gunner would then turn the turret and gun to the general direction of the target. Hopefully, the target would appear in the gunner's sight.

The sight contained two illuminated transparent discs. The first had a range scale inscribed around its circumference. This disc was turned by the gunner until the appropriate range to a target was set against a small pointer. This action would simultaneously raise the other transparent disc which incorporated the gunner's graticules (graticules are the aiming marks in any type of sighting device). The gunner would then overlay the aiming marks on the target using his hand operated elevation and traverse controls. As long as the gunner knew the correct width of the target, he could make a fairly accurate range determination. This range estimate is known as a stadiametric range determining system (most World War II tank commanders' binoculars also had a stadiametric range scale incorporated in them).

From the *Tiger I Handbook* comes this simple hint for gunners: "When a painter wants to measure exactly 'a stretch' [i.e. something], he compares the size of the model with a pencil. You should compare the size of the graticule mark with the target! Then you will know how large your target is; you can measure with the graticule marks its distance."

Both the Tiger I and Tiger II sometimes suffered a disadvantage in tank combat since the great weight of their turrets meant it took longer to turn the main gun in the direction of an enemy target. Extracts from a March 15, 1945, US Army report discuss the speed of the Tiger II turret:

General: Tests were made with a German Pz. Kpfw. Tiger Model B [Tiger II] tank to determine the speed of traverse of the turret in relation to the engine speed.

Turret Traverse Mechanism: Since the turret is driven by the engine through a transfer case, the speed of the turret traverse is dependent upon the engine speed. A gearbox provides two ratios for controlling the speeds of traverse. Selection of the ratio to be used is made with a shift lever located on the left of the turret drive housing.

The traverse is controlled by two foot pedals located on the turret floor ahead of the gunner. The left pedal is used for left traverse and the right pedal for right traverse. The traverse can also be controlled by a hand lever connected to the foot pedal linkage. The lever is pushed down for right traverse and pulled up for left traverse.

A hand traverse wheel is also provided. 700 revolutions of the handwheel traverse the turret through 360°.

Method of Testing: Before starting the time tests, the engine and gearing were warmed for 30 minutes. Engine temperature during the tests was 60°C (150°F). The time required for the turret to traverse 360° was measured for engine speeds of 500, 1000, 1500, and 2000rpm for both the high and low ratio of the gearbox and for right and left traverse. In all cases the turret was traversed from a standstill. Engine speeds in excess of 2000 rpm were not used because of the possibility of damage to the engine.

Results: It was found that, with the engine turning over at 2000rpm and with the high ratio engaged, the turret traversed 360° in 19 seconds. With low ratio, the time required was 40 seconds.

In contrast, the American Sherman tank turret could turn 360° in about 10 seconds. This sometimes allowed the Sherman the advantage of the first shot in duels with Tiger tanks.

Optical Rangefinders

Tiger tank commanders were provided with a small optical coincidence-type rangefinder to assist in the observation and ranging of targets. (In a coincidence rangefinder, the distance to the target is measured by sighting on the target, and bringing the erect image into coincidence with the inverted image in the field of view. The range is then read on a range scale.) Used together with the auxiliary hand traverse, the commander could fairly accurately align the main gun onto a target which his gunner couldn't see.

Coincidence-type rangefinders work very well under conditions of clear visibility or when used on sharply defined objects. It is also relatively easy to train competent operators. Only a couple hours of instruction are usually required. On the minus side, they are ineffective at longer ranges or on targets having indistinct outlines.

In wartime US Army documents, the German optical rangefinder device used by Tiger tank commanders is referred to as the TZR1. It was listed as having an overall length of fifty-five inches and a field of view of six degrees according to tests conducted by the First US Army and others in the United States. The TZR1 was typically used for observation by a German tank commander to see over the flash or muzzle obscuration (dust) from the firing of his tank's main gun. In many cases this would temporarily hide a tank gunner's view of a target. According to a US Army report: "When in use, the periscope is mounted on a bracket attached beneath the base of the cupola, so that it enables the tank commander, with his head below the top of the cupola, to see from a point approximately 39 in. above the cupola machine gun mounting ring. When not in use, it is stowed on the near side of the turret. The mounting bracket is adjustable and allows the periscope to be tilted approximately 5 degrees to either side of the vertical. Two clamping handles are provided for locking the periscope in position after adjustment."

Early production Tiger I tanks with the drum pattern cupola did not have the bracket for mounting the TZR1. Instead, the crew used a hand-held optical rangefinder similar to those used by the crews of Flak guns.

Lt. Col. Wilson M. Hawkins (US Army), commanding the 3rd Batallion, 67th Armored Regiment wrote in a wartime report about his opinion of German tank sights: "The matter of tank gun sights has caused us much concern. I have looked through and worked with sights in German Mark V (Panther) and Mark VI (Tiger) tanks as well as our own. I find that the German sight has more magnifying power and clearness than our own, which is a big advantage to a gunner."

Sgt. Lewis A. Taylor (US Army), of the 2nd Armored Division, stated in a wartime report: "The German telescopic sights mounted in their tanks are far superior to ours, in particular it is more powerful. In fact all their optical equipment is superior to ours."

Sgt. George A. Barden (US Army), also of the 2nd

This beautiful cut-away color illustration of a Tiger I was done by a World War II British military technical team that had examined a number of captured vehicles. Almost all the vehicle's major components and sub-systems are both clearly visible and marked. Today, there are five Tiger Is on display in in various military museums. Currently, none of them are in operational condition. Fortunately, both the British Army Tank Museum and the German Auto & Technik Museum have plans to restore their respective Tiger Is to operational condition. *British Army Tank Museum*

Armored Division,, confirms this fact in a wartime report: "I took from a German officer a pair of field glasses 10x50, the best glasses that I've ever seen. On two occasions, I was able to pick up an antitank position and a mortar position at a range of about one mile, when these same two targets could not be seen using a pair of G.I. glasses, 7x50."

From a World War II US Army report dated March 1943 and titled *Training Notes from Recent Fighting in Tunisia* comes this description of German tank tactics from an American tank officer: "When the German tanks come out, they stay out of range and sit and watch. Then they move a little, stop, and watch some more. They have excellent glasses [binoculars] and they use them carefully."

Backup Fire Control Systems

The Tiger gunner's firing accuracy was improved by an illuminated clinometer on his right side. (A clinometer is a device used to measure slopes.) In artillery pieces and tank guns the clinometer is used to form a base for applying certain corrections in elevation in order that the gun may be aimed or pointed in exactly the right direction and elevation. In American military parlance the device is known as a quadrant.

A traverse or turret-indicator device driven by a pinion from the turret was mounted to the left of the Tiger I gunner. It was marked with a counter-rotating clock-like device graded from 1 o'clock to 12 o'clock. The arm for the 12 o'clock position remained in the same spot to indicate the forward direction of the vehicle's hull. When the gunner moved the vehicle's turret (when tracking a moving target for example), the second hand of the turret-indicator device would follow the direction of the turret and its main gun. This allowed the tank commander who had a matching counter-rotating clock (fitted around the interior of this cupola on a toothed annular ring) to follow the gunner's actions and give commands to the gunner if he decided to switch to a more-dangerous target that the gunner may not be aware of due to his narrow field of vision. If a Tiger gunner was taking aim at an enemy target slightly to the left of his tank at the 2 o'clock position and the tank commander suddenly spotted an enemy tank directly to the rear of his vehicle. The tank commander would tell his gunner over the intercom that the tank's main gun and turret should be turned to the 6 o'clock position.

As a very basic and crude aiming device, the Tiger I had a simple blade foresight mounted in front of the tank commander position. The Tiger II commander had access to a different system which incorporated a small blade foresight fitted in front of his cupola. By dropping his head within the confines of his cupola, he could look out through a rear sight attached to the forward cupola

This picture is from the Tiger I located at the British Army Tank Museum, who's turret has been removed prior to rebuilding. The vehicle's empty engine compartment is located at the rear of the picture. The vehicle's drive train linkage has also been disconnected and removed. Seen on the bottom of the hull floor are the traversing torsion bars. *Jacques Littlefield*

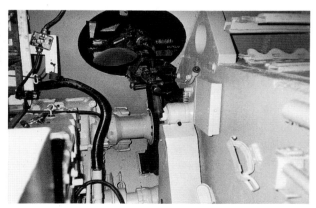

This interior close-up picture of the bow gunner's position on the Tiger II currently on display at the Patton Museum of Cavalry and Armor, shows the ball-mounting for a MG34 7.92mm machine gun. The machine gun and it's mount are shown in this photo. *Jacques Littlefield*

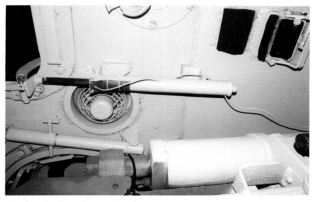

The loader hatches on both the Tiger I and Tiger IIs were spring assisted. This interior view of a Tiger II taken from the loader's position shows the spring piston and arm mounted on the inside of the turret roof. Located behind the spring piston and arm is the turret ventilating fan. On the far right of the picture is the loader periscope mount, with an overhead pad so the loader won't bump his head on the turret roof when looking through the periscope. *Jacques Littlefield*

periscope and quickly determine what his gunner was looking at (or should be looking at). According to gunnery test results conducted by the British on captured Tiger I's and later supplied to the American Army, the accuracy of the Kw.K 36 8.8cm gun on the Tiger I was excellent. The test results stated: "A five round grouping of 16"x18" was obtained at a range of 1,200 yards. Five rounds were fired at targets moving at 15mph and, although smoke obscured observation by the gunner, three hits were scored after directions were given by the commander. Normal rate of fire was estimated to be from five to eight rounds per minute."

Tiger Tank Commanders

One of the most important elements of any tank in battle is the man in charge. An interesting look at Michael Wittmann, the best known German Tiger tank commander of World War II, is provided in an article in the August 3, 1944, issue of the *Das Schwarzkorps* (The Black Corps). This was the official newspaper of the "SS." The article begins:

He has a sixth sense in assessing a situation, which gives a unique gift to his method of fighting. But he also knows what his success has cost him in terms of spiritual strength and the totality of the situation, which places him under the shadow of death and in the midst of great efforts. All this changes people, creates different standards. Too much hinges on this performance for one to act like a hero out of a storybook. The mood which encloses the combat sphere of the Tiger tank with a commander like Wittmann aboard included cold-bloodedness and presence of mind, complete mastery of all means of war. His marvelous victories are not the victory of the "heroic," but of the "human."

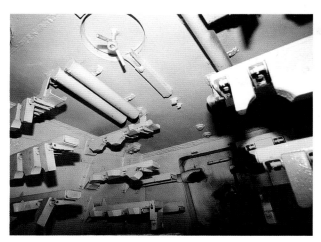

This interior picture of a Tiger II fitted with a Henschel turret, was taken from the gunner's position. Visible at the top of the picture is a small hatch. Other than being used as an opening for firing a flare gun or showing signal flags, it could also be used by the loader to get rid of empty shell cases from the main gun. In the lower rear of the picture can be seen the turret escape hatch. It was also used to either mount or remove the tank's main gun. On either side of the rear turret bustle are the racks for the storage of twenty-two main gun rounds, eleven on either side. The rounds themselves were held in place by the painted wooden clamps seen attached to the metal rails. *Tank Magazine*

Looking directly up from the bottom of a Tiger II's turret floor can be seen the interior components that made up the commander's cupola. The cupola contained several episcopes which are missing from this vehicle. Seen in this picture are the mounted points for the episcopes. On the far left of the picture can be seen the commander's lever for opening or closing the hatch. The big advantage this cupola had over the early drum type found on the Tiger I was the commander's head and upper chest was now kept within the protection of the turret armor. *Tank Magazine*

He, and all others on whom the battles hinges, were not made by nature without nerves or feelings. They are not Supermen. They are human beings, with wishes, longings, hopes, and thoroughly bourgeois love for their wives and children.

Otto Carius, a highly decorated Tiger ace who saw heavy combat on the Eastern Front, describes his feelings on what makes a successful Tiger tank commander in his 1960 book titled *Tiger im Schlamm* (reprinted with the publisher's permission):

The personal aggressiveness of the commander while observing was decisive for success against numerically vastly superior enemy formations. The lack of good observation by the Russians often resulted in the defeat of large units. Tank commanders who slam their hatches shut at the beginning of an attack and don't open them again until the objective has been reached are useless, or at least second rate.

No one can deny that the many casualties among the officers and other tank commanders were due to exposing their heads. But these men did not die in vain. If they had moved with closed hatches, then many more men would have found their death or been severely wounded inside the tanks. The large Russian tank losses are proof of the correctness of this assertion. Fortunately, for us, they almost always drove cross-country buttoned up. Of course, every tank commander had to be careful while peering out during positional warfare. Especially since the turret hatches of tanks in the front

On the outskirts of the French city of Vinouteirs, located in the Normandy area of France, sits one of the surviving handful of World War II Tiger Is still in existence. Abandoned by it's crew during the war without being destroyed, this Tiger I managed to avoid all the postwar scrap dealers who cut up almost all of the derelict armored vehicles which littered so much of Europe after the war ended. Fortuitously, the nearby city finally realized the Tiger's historical value and in 1983 went about preserving the vehicle for display. The Tiger I's camouflage paint scheme as pictured, is not based on any actual wartime vehicle. *R.J. Fleming-Panzer Prints*

A large number of Tiger tanks were lost during World War II because of mechanical breakdowns or lack of fuel. Colonel Bill Hamburg, who commanded a battalion of Sherman tanks during the war in Europe, remembers that his general impression was that many of the Tiger tanks engaged by American tankers were already deserted by their crews for one reason or another. In combat however, it pays not to take any chances. The Tiger I pictured was abandoned by it's crew in a small French town, who's inhabitants along with some American soldiers are examining it with great interest. *Patton Museum*

lines were continuously watched by enemy snipers. Even a short exposure could be fatal for the tank commander. I had commandeered a folding artillery scope for just such cases. Actually, such a scope shouldn't be missing in any fighting vehicle.

While very few German soldiers would question the personal bravery of the typical Soviet tanker in battle. There were a number of serious command and control problems that hindered Soviet tank commanders and their combat formations from being as effective as their German counterparts. From an November-December 1976 article in *Armor* magazine by Capt. Ronald J. Brown, titled "Manstein's Winter Miracle", comes this extract:

> There were three glaring weaknesses in the Soviet system: a rigid, inflexible command system; the lack of an effective, rapid communications system; and a poor logistical process.
>
> These three factors resulted in the heavy handed, unresponsive tactics that gave the *Wehrmacht* [German

Army] the upper hand. The Soviet command system allowed for no deviation from the prepared script. Doomed attacks were carried out even though their futility was apparent to all on the scene. Subordinate commanders were mere automatons, only echoing their orders from above. Individual initiative was stifled, and only complete compliance was tolerated. This sterile atmosphere was compounded by the fact the Russians were never able to implement an effective, rapid communications system that could operate on a tactical level. Even in the elite Guards units, individual vehicles (other than command types) never had radios installed. Lacking such a system, they often had to commit entire units to accomplish simple tasks.

Captain Brown went on to describe why the German command and control system was so superior to that of the Soviet Army during World War II: "The German command system neatly meshed strong central control with individual initiative at the tactical levels.

This seeming contradiction was achieved by a single proviso. The *Wehrmacht's* chain of command went from the front to the rear. The staff at headquarters was expected to anticipate problems and have solutions ready when requested. The staff handled the everyday affairs at headquarters. The leader's position was at the front. Commanders went to the action and made their decisions based on personal observation, not at a rear headquarters as did the Soviets."

An interesting view of combat from the tank commander's position of a Tiger I, comes from a personal letter sent to Gregory T. Jones by World War II *Waffen SS* Tiger tank ace Willi Fey. In his letter, Fey describes a battle action in France. The date is August 7, 1944, the place is Chinedolle, France. A large force of British Sherman tanks are attacking:

> We had already moved our Tiger into firing position and the gunner had had his first target in sight for some time; it was the tank at the point, exactly in the center of the attacking pack. The second and third targets were also determined, first its neighbor to the left and then the one on the right. Then we search the extreme left and extreme right. If those tanks were to outflank us, even our Tiger's could be vulnerable inside 400 M [meters] range.
>
> Then came the order to open fire. "Antitank-shell,

The Western Allies first encountered Tiger IIs in France in July 1944. Most of the Tiger IIs that fell into Allied hands during those initial encounters were fitted with the Porsche turrets, as is the vehicle pictured. The Tiger II's highly-sloped frontal armor was so similar in layout to that of the earlier Panther medium tank that in combat action, most Allied soldiers had a hard time telling them apart. This often led to the belief that the Germans were employing many more Tiger II's in France then there actually were. In actual numbers, German wartime reports show that there were never more than fifty Tiger IIs in France at one time. The Tiger II with a Porsche turret pictured is on display at the British Army Tank Museum. *Bill Nahmens*

600, FIRE!" But the first shot was wide! We momentarily froze. "Gun sight, 400, FIRE!" That was a hit. A second shell into the breech. Another hit. Then the next target: "Tank on the left! FIRE!" That one took two shells.

Then the surviving Shermans opened fire.

> Now we took hit after hit, on the turret, on the front, to the tracks. Nuts, bolts, rivets whistled through the interior of our tank. In between finding plenty of work for the bow machine gun, our radio operator reported constantly on the battle developments. Message from the commander: "Withdraw to our own lines!" By then we counted six burning and smoking tanks. There must have been chaos on the other side. Their infantry dismounted and dodged for cover, vehicles ran into each other as they tried to reverse course. Then we knocked out our seventh, then our eighth tank. Our 88 had brought a quick end to the tangled traffic jam. They burned out, so close to each other.

Thus the Tiger's 8.8cm gun could be deadly in the hands of a well-led and well-trained crew. However, Lt. Col. Bill Hamberg (US Army) commander of a tank battalion from the 5th Armored Divsion during World War II remembers: "As the war was nearing its end, I noticed that the accuracy of German tank firing steadily de-

Beginning in July 1944, the French city of Caen and the surrounding terrain were the scene of a number of fierce battles as Allied forces attempted to wrestle control of the area from German military units. One victim of these encounters was this Tiger II, fitted with a Porsche turret. *British Army Tank Museum*

The Tiger's Last Battles

By March 1945, the once all-mighty German military and it's elite tank divisions no longer existed. Allied air power was everywhere. Almost nothing could move during daylight hours. Running short of everything from ammunition to fuel, the last few remaining Tiger tanks left in the German wartime arsenal were thrown together in ad-hoc units in a useless attempt to stem the onrushing Allied armies that were then overunning what was left of the Third Reich.

An example of how the famous Tiger tanks were employed during the last few weeks of the war can be found in an extract from an article titled *The Little Known History Of Kampgruppe Schulze,* by the military historian Dr. Giuseppe Finizio: "In late March 1945, the 9th US Army and 2nd British Army moved to break through to the Elbe. During the night of April 4-5, near Hameln, the 119th US Infantry Regiment managed to bridge the Weser River. It is at this point that our story begins.

On April 1,1945, the commander of the Aufstellungstab Lehrtruppe, [tank training school] Major Paul Schulze, reported only six Tiger Is from the school, and five Panthers, probably from the Panzer Jager und Versuchskompanie, available from a special unit entrusted with the job to test infra-red equipment for AFVs. (The first German AFV fitted with infra-red periscopes was a Marder II in late 1942.)

Major Schulze decided to form a Kampfgruppe [Battle group] with these tanks and move towards the Weser River to strengthen the depleted German forces in that sector. Major Schulze personally commanded the five Panthers, and Oberleutnant (Lieutenant) Fehrmann the six Tigers (F01, F11, F12, F13, F14, F15, however, only F01 and F13 are identified with certainty), as indicated by the large "F" on the turret sides. On April 6 the Kampfgruppe moved from Fallingbostel and reached Rethem, where one Tiger was abandoned due to gear-box problems. On April 7 the column passed through Nienburg, and near Stolzenau was joined by a motorized infantry company. On April 8 they grouped in an area near the Forestal Militia Post of Landwehr at the northern edge of the Schaumburg Woods, near Wiedensahl. Until then, due to the constant threat of Allied fighter bombers, they had moved only at night and made no contact with the enemy. That evening, Major Schulze decided to launch an attack against the British bridgehead on the Weser near Wietershiem, south of Petershagen. [The] next morning, he lead his Panthers in an attack, but with little success. Towards midday only his tank was left. Fehrmann's Tigers immediately repeated the attack. About three kms from Wietersheim, on the western outskirts of Frille, they were attacked by elements of the 6th British Airborne Division entrenched on the road sides. A PIAT (Projector Infantry Anti-tank) shell hit Fehrmann's Tiger F01 on the right side of the turret, damaging the rotating mechanism. The following two Tigers advanced and flanked F01, enabling it to reach a nearby hill. After this brief encounter the five Tigers returned to Frille with thirty prisoners. At Frille, Oberleutnant Fehrmann ordered Unteroffizier (Corporal)

Pictured is the staff of 1st Battalion Panzer Lehrregiment 130 at Fallingbostel in early 1945. *Oberleutnant* Fehrmann is first from the left, Major Schulze the fourth from the left and wears the Knight's Cross around his neck; the ribbon of the Iron Cross 2nd Class is in lapel buttonhole; the Iron Cross 1st Class and the Silver Tank Battle Badge on his left chest. On his right chest below the silver eagle is the War Order of the German Cross in Gold. The Individual Tank Destruction Badge is on his right sleeve. *Photo from the Giuseppa Finizie collection*

Pictured is the second of two Tiger I tanks that were abandoned by *Kampfgruppe* Schulze on April 1,1945, near the small German town of Bruckeburg after an encounter with elements of the US Army's 5th Armored Division.
Photo from the Giuseppa Finizie collection

Franzen to take the prisoners to the Kampfgruppe command post at Landwehr and drive Tiger FO1 back to Fallingbostel for repairs. On April 11 the surviving tanks (Schulze's Panther and four Tigers) moved towards Buckeburg. That same day, three kms northeast of Buckeburg, the Kampftruppen clashed with forward elements of the 5th US Armored Division and lost two Tigers, Schulze's Panther, and two half-tracks. Schulze managed to escape unharmed and slid into a Tiger, but Fehrmann was captured. One of the two surviving Tigers, Feldwebel (Sergeant) Bellof's tank, was hit later and caught fire. None of the crew survived. Major Schulze's Tiger, thanks to its skillful driver Unteroffizier Frieling, reached Achum and hid behind a burning farmhouse. Meanwhile the armored spearhead of the 5th US Armored Division was advancing on the road in front of the farm. Suddenly the wind shifted and the smoke cleared away, leaving the Tiger wide open. The US column stopped and the leading Sherman steered towards the Tiger. The Tiger's gun traversed onto them and fired four shots. Three US tanks and an armored car were knocked out. The German tank then reversed behind the farm, turned around and zig-zagged through an open field at full speed. More Shermans fired, and two rounds hit the Tiger on the turret, another on the hull. The gunlayer was slightly injured, but the tank managed to escape. That same day, near Wendthagen, Schulze stopped a US petrol tank truck. Although it was almost empty, he found a very useful set of maps in the cab. Finally a new plan was established to regain the German lines. During the night the Tiger crossed the bridge over the highway at Lauenau, while below an endless American column proceeded at full speed. Schulze decided to take the road to the Nienstedt Pass. The Americans, he figured, would have avoided this narrow and steep road with several bad curves in it. Major Schulze did not know that the British spearhead had already crossed the Aller River, and the US Army was on the Elbe. At dawn on April 12 the Tiger ran a military-police roadblock. Meanwhile one Sherman

with an armored car and two trucks with white stars were coming up the road. The German gun-layer adjusted his sight to the base of the olive green silhouette and fired. The Sherman and the armored car were hit and caught fire immediately. The US soldiers in the trucks surrendered, and then released close to 200 German prisoners from a nearby barn. Some of them joined Schulze's Tiger and followed it in an American truck. During its march this improvised Kampfgruppe encountered some US ambulances which were permitted to go on, and captured a jeep fitted with a heavy machine-gun. By early morning they reached the Southern outskirts of Egestorf. Here a young villager informed them that Egestorf had been occupied since April 8 and that three kms from there there was a US Command Post. As the Tiger's petrol tanks were almost empty Schulze decided to capture the US Command Post with the hope of refueling. The young villager from Egestorf led the Tiger and accompanying infantry to the north-east edge of the Deister Forest. But it was impossible to approach the US position without alerting the guard posts all around it. Consequently, Schulze decided to move towards Bad-Nenndorf, but eventually ran out of fuel. This incredible adventure was fast coming to an end. Schulze shook hands with the soldiers and suggested they head for home. Unteroffizier Frieling placed a charge inside the tank and blew it up.

As the F01 arrived in Fallingbostel a repair unit did its best to fix it up, so that by dawn on April 12 the Tiger was finally back in fighting order. The tank was immediately assigned to the Kampfrugge Grosan, which was ordered to hold a line south of Ostenholz. The British were superior in infantry and armor (the 3rd RTR), but fighter bombers were not widely used. The headquarters of Kampfgruppe Grosan was near Unteroffizier Frieling's home, where the F01's crew settled in (Frieling's daughter Gisela married Franzen after the war). On the morning of April 12 the F01 was ordered to support the 7th Company of the 12th SS Battalion at the northern edge of the Essel Forest. Franzen's Tiger crossed the Drebber stream and eased its way around a righthand bend in the road. Here he saw three British Comets on the roadside. They belonged to 1st Troop, Squadron A of the 3rd RTR (under Lieutenant Colonel Edward Mitford MC) attached to the 29 Armoured Brigade (11th Armoured Division). The 1st Troop was commanded by Lieutenant John Langdon, who later wrote an interesting report on this action.

According to this report and Langdon's letter to the author, the F01 was at a distance of 300 to 400 meters. Franzen judged the British tanks to be 600 to 800 meters away, and this was confirmed by Brigadier Mitford to the author. However, in the confusion of seeing three enemy tanks on rounding the bend Franzen's wrong appreciation can certainly be excused. Anyway, the hatches of the Tiger
continued on next page

were slammed closed and Franzen shouted to his gunlayer: "Feuer!" (Fire). On the British side, Lieutenant Langdon described what it was like at his end. "As I looked through my glasses directing trooper Rice, my gunner, onto the target, I saw its 88mm gun slowly traversing onto us. We fired. I gave trooper Charlton, my driver, the order to reverse. The tank we had encountered was a Tiger. The Tiger continued to fire down the road, and a scout car which had been left at the side of the road was blazing. Another vehicle was brewing up further down the road. I glanced across the road and saw corporal Brindle was also attempting to reverse into the woods. An AP (armor-piercing round) ricocheted into his offside track, smashing it completely. He ordered his crew to bale out. Immediately afterward a second shot went through the front of the tank, and a third tore into the turret. An infantry patrol was dispatched, but the enemy withdrew." In actual fact, Franzen had moved back to his previous position. The British tanks did not advance further and spent the night in leaguer near the Aller. The following morning, Friday April, 13, Lieutenant Langdon recalls that: "Just as we were about to move off the Tiger reappeared at the top of the road and fired a few rounds of AP! A troop carrying vehicle belonging to the infantry was brewed up. A heavy artillery concentration was put down in the vicinity of the Tiger, which produced the desired effect of making the enemy retire a little way, enabling us to niggle slowly up the road. Sergeant Harding, who was commanding the lead tank of C Squadron managed to get within 100 yards (about 90 meters) of the road. He was concealed by trees and bushes when the Tiger which was still on the road, suddenly appeared broadside on to him." The F01 had reached the point where the Ostenholz road entered the woods and stopped. It was now 12.00 hours. Franzen, seated on the turret cupola hatch, decided to go forward around that bend again. When he realized that Sergeant Harding's tank was waiting for him among the trees, he shouted to the gunlayer: "Take aim, enemy tank at ten o'clock." Too late! One of

A picture of *Unteroffizier* Eberhard Frieling, the very skillful driver of Major Schulze's Tiger I tank which managed to take such a heavy toll of American equipment before finally running out of fuel in the closing days of World War II. *Photo from the Giuseppa Finizie collection*

This side view of Tiger tank F01 shows the large blackened hole in the hull were Sgt. Harding's Comet tank with it's 77mm main gun had surprised *Unteroffizier* Franzen vehicle and destroyed it. *Photo from the Giuseppa Finizie collection*

the two 77mm AP shots fired by Sergeant Harding had perforated the Tiger's hull side. Flames spread through the vehicle and the crew jumped out of the tank. What impressed Franzen was the fact that the Comet allowed his crew to escape without firing on them. A real noble action, in spite of total war. The five crewmen, all of whom had slight burns, returned to Fallingbostel on foot, and two days later managed to get a lift on a halftrack. Unfortunately, on April 17 it was blown up by a German mine. The gunlayer Karl Specht and the driver Otto George scrambled clear, but the loader and radio operator were killed. Franzen was seriously wounded and lost an eye. Only on May 6 did he awake from his coma. Sergeant Harding was subsequently awarded the Military Medal for his action.

The May 9, 1945 the German military and government formally surrendered to the Allies. The war in Europe was over. The surviving Tiger tanks were gathered together in huge vehicle dumps. Most of these vehicles were eventually cut-up for scrap during the following years.

Fire Control Improvements

The German Army High Command ordered in late 1942 that a second type of optical rangefinder be developed for both the upcoming Tiger II tank and a future Panther tank, which was to be armed with an 8.8cm gun. The rangefinder prototype developed for the Tiger II was stereoscopic in design. (A stereoscopic rangefinder differs from a coincidence type rangefinder in that the two target images are brought together "in depth." A tank gunner would therefore see a 3D image of his target.) The rangefinder was fitted on an anti-vibrational mount to withstand the heavy vibrations of a moving tank. The Germans based their new tank rangefinder on a number of Flak rangefinders already in widespread use.

An extract from a US Army report dated September 12, 1945, describes the device known as the Em.1.6m. R (Panzer):

> This instrument is a large 1.6 meter (5ft 3in) base stereoscopic rangefinder of wandermark type, designed for mounting in the turrets of Tiger I and Royal Tiger tanks. The instrument is suspended from the turret roof, stretches right across the turret, and the end windows are placed behind small parts at the front of the upper turret wall. An interesting feature is the periscopic arrangement by means of which an inclined tube carrying the eyepieces allows these to be positioned slightly to the left of, and at approximately the same level as, the eyepiece of the gun sighting telescope with only a small movement of the gunner's head.
>
> The instrument embodies several features illustrative of the latest German technique found in larger stereoscopic range-finders of recent manufacture, such as a collimating system for projecting the reticule images into the main optical system of the range-finder and a sliding lens deflecting system.
>
> The optical and stereoscopic properties of the instrument are good, the design of the wandermarks giving a good sense of depth and making setting easy. The main tube and outer parts have obviously been made to speed up manufacture. It is doubtful if this built-up construction will permit the adjustment to remain under ordinary conditions of use. This can only be settled by trial. The workmanship of the optical and internal mechanical parts is of high standard.

By mid-1944 the Germans already had the rangefinder for the Tiger II in production. However, none were ever mounted on a Tiger II tank before World War II ended.

The American Army first began using tank-mounted stereoscopic rangefinders in the early 1950s. While stereoscopic type rangefinders are superior to coincidence type rangefinders, the Army quickly discovered that all gunners could not adapt to them. It was found that only seventy percent of tankers had acute enough stereoscopic vision even to use this type of device, and that it took over ten hours of intensive training for those who had the required stereo vision to acquire the necessary proficiency. In the field, the Army found to its dismay that many of its tankers would unplug the on-board stereoscopic rangefinder because of an inability to use it properly.

Secondary Armament

Some early and mid-production Tiger I tanks had been fitted with hull-mounted single-shot antipersonnel mine dischargers. However, the first Tigers captured by the Allies in North Africa did not have these devices. The Allied technical teams found the mounting provisions covered by plates. The belief was that they had been designed to help repel Soviet infantry tank-hunting teams. There are a few wartime pictures showing Tiger I tanks on the Eastern Front so equipped. However, they must have been fairly rare in field use since few wartime Tiger I photos show them. The American Army had also tested a number of similar tank-mounted self-protection systems during World War II. Because of the danger of accidental activation with friendly troops around, they were never placed into production.

In addition to their 8.8cm main guns, the Tiger I and Tiger II were fitted with a number of 7.92mm machine guns. Both models of the Tiger had a machine gun mounted alongside the main gun. In military terms this is known as a coaxial gun (or coax). Because of the large amount of coax ammunition that can be stowed in a tank (the Tiger I carried 5,250 rounds of 7.92mm ammo) and the effectiveness of area fire up to 1,000 yards, the coax machine gun is used against infantry and unarmored vehicles when they appear within effective range. This helps conserve main gun ammunition for tougher targets. The gunner on the Tiger tank controlled both the aiming and firing of the tank's coax. The gun was fired mechanically by a foot pedal. The loader was responsible for both the loading and maintenance of the coax.

As with most World War II tanks, both the Tiger I and Tiger II had a front hull-mounted machine gun operated by the bow gunner. It was aimed by a simple telescope (the KZF 2) and fired by a hand trigger. The telescope gave the bow gunner a field of view of eighteen degrees. The machine gun itself was breech-heavy and was balanced by an equilibrator spring. In its ball mounting, this weapon could be elevated to twenty degrees, depressed to ten degrees, and had a traverse of fifteen degrees both left and right. The Tiger handbook describes the effectiveness of these weapons: "Hull machine gun up to 200 meters against men, horses, and vehicles. Turret machine gun up to 400 meters against men, horses, and vehicles. If there's a lot of them, then at greater ranges. Also for occupied houses and for enemy soldiers lying prone on the ground."

Both the Tiger I, with the late-model cupola, and the Tiger II were provided with an attachment rail on the tank commander's cupola for the mounting of an additional 7.92mm machine gun. Because this weapon could be used independently of the Tiger's main gun

and coax, the tank commander could engage a second target at the same time his gunner was firing at the first. Like the coax gun, it was also useful for firing at infantry or unarmored vehicles. However, against armored protected Allied ground attack aircraft, it was almost useless.

The 7.92mm machine guns mounted in the Tiger tanks were the vehicle-mounted versions of the well-known German *Maschinegewehr 34* (MG34). First accepted for German Army service in 1934, it didn't reach production until 1936. A first-class weapon, the MG34 was best known among Allied soldiers for its very high rate of fire. Both the coaxial and hull-mounted MG34 machine guns on the Tiger were each provided with a spare parts box that contained a bipod and stock in case of dismounted use. Also within these boxes were two spare barrels. The tank commander's machine gun on Tigers would most often be an MG34, or an improved wartime model known as the MG42.

In addition to the crew's individual pistols, there was normally a single MP38 or MP40 model submachine gun (incorrectly known to most Allied soldiers as the "Schmeisser") in both the Tiger I and Tiger II turrets. It was also nicknamed the "Burp gun" by many Allied soldiers. It could be used for guard duty by the crew if there was no infantry support or as a close-in defense weapon of last resort. The Tiger I handbook stated: "Use pistols from the pistol port against guests on the hull. Submachine gun can also be used out of the pistol port against emplacements and machine gun nests in the dead zone. Eggs [grenades] out of the pistol port against foxholes and concealed targets."

Destroyed or abandoned Tiger IIs were always of great interest to American soldiers since there were so few of them ever fielded by the Germans on the Western Front. The large size of the vehicle compared to American tanks of that era left an lasting impression on any soldier that ever had a chance to see or explore one close-up. The vehicle pictured is being checked-out by some American soldiers, two of whom are posing in front of the vehicle with an empty 88mm round. *Private collection*

Sgt. Harold Smith, a tank commander from the 2nd Armored Division, commented on the German submachine guns in a wartime report: "The German Burp gun has a very good demoralizing effect with its rapid rate of fire (as all their small arms do), but is not a very accurate weapon after the first few rounds of the burst have been fired. As my crew and I dismounted from the tank recently, two burp gunners fired at us from the rear and two opened up on the front, and none of us collected any Purple Hearts. But they sure scared us plenty with that 'burp.'"

There were two small pistol ports in early versions of the Tiger I turret, reduced to one in later models. Porsche-designed Tiger II turrets were fitted with a single small gun port on the left side that was later welded over. The standard production turret for the Tiger II had no provisions for the firing of small arms from within the vehicle. Instead, a small armored hatch on top of the turret was designed to mount a multi-purpose 360 degree rotatable launcher called the *Nahrerteidigurswaffe* [anti-personnel weapon] that could fire both smoke and signal grenades from within the turret. In case of a threat from close-in infantry attack, this device could also fire an antipersonnel grenade. This bomb thrower was not mounted in all Tiger II tanks, however.

While Hitler's original plans for the December 1944 Ardennes offensive envisioned a large role for the Tiger II, Allied bombing raids on the factories building the Tiger II limited the number that did take part in the campaign. Most of the 100 or so Tiger IIs that were fielded during the campaign were transferred from the Eastern front prior to the start of the German attack on the American lines. One vehicle remains today in Belgium near the small town of La Gleize as a tourist attraction. The vehicle as shown, was fitted with the standard production or Henschel turret. *Andreas Kirchhoff*

CHAPTER 3

PROTECTION

Having an effective mobile gun that outperforms and outranges your opponent's weapons is a big plus for any military force. This is what the various self-propelled vehicles carrying 88s provided the German Army. However, there usually comes a time in every battle when the enemy will probably get close enough to your long-range weapons to use his shorter-ranged guns. To survive such encounters and to give a vehicle the ability to move freely around the battlefield requires a certain amount of armor protection. The biggest problem with armor protection is its weight.

During World War II, steel was the only armor material available. The protection of armor improved with the thickness of the steel armor, but with a great penalty of weight. Because automotive technology in the World War II era was unable to provide tanks of the day with both a high level of mobility and armor protection simultaneously, tank designers were forced to decide which characteristics to emphasize.

The Germans chose protection over mobility in designing the Tigers. However, no one tank can ever carry enough armor to completely protect itself from all threats from all directions, so a tank's armor is heaviest on areas which are most likely to be hit. While World War II tank designers used common sense in deciding were to place the thickest armor, postwar studies confirmed that the heaviest armor should be placed on a sixty-degree frontal arc (the centerline of this sixty-degree arc is located at the rear of the turret). This frontal arc encompasses the front of both the hull and turret of a tank.

For ease of construction and to allow the use of the thickest armor possible, the Tiger I's hull was fabricated of flat armor plates joined together by interlocking stepped welded joints. Weighing some fifty six tons, most of the weight of the Tiger I was in its thick armor plating. The front hull and turret featured homogeneous steel armor over 4 inches thick. This made the tank almost completely immune to Allied tank and anti-tank guns firing at it straight-on. The rest of the Tiger's turret was protected by armor 3in thick, with the hull sides having armor plate a little over 3.2in thick above the roadwheels. Behind the roadwheels the armor was 2.4in thick.

The top of the turret, the bottom of the hull, and the rear engine hull plate were about an inch thick. In general, the Germans designed their tanks to have enough frontal armor to be immune to the fire from its own gun. The sides and rear were designed to defeat only long-range fire.

Armor Plate

Homogeneous steel armor is armor plate which has the same physical characteristics through its thickness. Compared to face-hardened or cast-steel armor, homogeneous steel armor could be rapidly produced at low cost because it was readily machined and welded. Unfortunately, high hardness steel armor has a tendency to shatter or crack under repeated impacts because it is so brittle. The very hard frontal armor on the Tiger I sometime developed cracks.

A British Army test report (on firing tests with early-production model Tiger I's) dated October 1943 and supplied to the American military attaché in London describes the problem:

None of the trials carried out so far has demonstrated the use of other than machinable quality armour for the PzKwVI, nor has the examination of battle damage. Much of the armour fired at appeared to be of variable quality and was probably experimental. Though machinable, it was frequently much harder than corresponding British armour, and in many cases caused shot to shatter, while the plates were liable to crack and flake. The side plates from turret, hull and superstructure, have all been found to flake in various cases. The cast mantlet appears to be of good quality, not breaking up or cracking under heavy attack, and no case of a penetration was met. The mantlet covers the entire front of the turret and it was considered that it gives extremely good protection.

Like so many other aspects of building complex machinery. There is always a learning curve involved. As the German factories and workers gained more experience in building the various components that made up the Tiger I tank. Improvements took place, including the overall quality of the armor plates fitted to the Tiger. This is reflected in the comments of German Army Tiger ace, Otto Carius, who stated his opinion of the quality of the steel armor on later production models the Tiger I tank in his 1960 book, titled *Tiger im Schlamm* (reprinted with the publisher's permission):

Again and again, we admired the quality of the steel on our tanks. I was hard without being brittle. Despite it's hardness, it was also very elastic. If an antitank round didn't hit the tank's armor plate dead on, it would slide off on its side and leave behind a gouge as if you had run your finger over a soft piece of butter.

Unfortunately, as World War II went on and German industry suffered under the Allied bomber offense and severe shortages of key minerals used in the manufacture of armor plate. The overall quality of German armor plate went down.

The Tiger Primer, a small instructional handbook first published in August 1943 was issued to all Tiger I crewmen. The Primer describes the effectiveness of the vehicle's armor by telling the story of a Tiger I that fought in a battle on the Russian front: "This Tiger received 227 hits from anti-tank rifles, 14 hits with a 5.2cm gun and 11 hits with a 7.6cm gun in 6 hours of fighting. No shot went inside and the tank made it home on its own power."

From a US War Department Intelligence Bulletin (dated January 1945) comes the following description of a combat encounter by a New Zealand Division with a Tiger I in Italy:

On display at the British Army Tank Museum is this early model Tiger I captured in North Africa. The thick box-like steel armor construction of the hull is clearly evident when compared to the well-sloped frontal hull armor of the Panther tank parked next to it. The front hull and turret armor of the Tiger I averaged in at about 4in thick. The type of armor fitted on the Tiger I was known as homogeneous steel armor. This meant that the steel armor was of the same strength or hardness throughout it's depth. *British Army Tank Museum*

Armor protection on the hull sides of the Tiger I was about 2in thick. The rear engine hull plate and the bottom of the hull was roughly an inch thick. The horseshoe shaped turret of the Tiger I was 4in thick on the front and 3in thick on the sides and rear. The vehicle pictured is the Tiger I that used to be on display at the US Army Ordnance Museum and is now on a ten year loan to the German military museum system. The vehicle is seen here on its arrival in Germany on a dock were it was unloaded from the ship that delivered it.
Thomas Anderson

A tank [Tiger I] hidden in the garage of a two-story house ventured out for about 20 yards, fired a few harassing rounds, and returned to its shelter. Many hits were scored on the building by 4.2 inch mortars firing cap-on, but little damage was visible. Each night the tank was withdrawn from the area, even though it was an excellent concealed position and was protected by infantry. Later the house was examined. Although it had suffered appreciable damage, and there were several dead Germans about, there was no evidence that damage was done to the tank itself.

Sgt. Harold E. Fulton (US Army) describes an engagement with a number of Tiger I tanks in a 1945 wartime report:

We were ordered to engage a column of six Mark VI's of the early model and two Mark IV's. As gunner, I fired 30 rounds from the 75mm gun of our tank. Some were HE [High Explosive], some smoke, and the rest AP [Armor Piercing]. Each time one of the AP's hit the tank you could see them ricocheting two and three hundred feet into the air. Along with my gun firing, there were four more tanks of my platoon, two or three M4 [Sherman] tanks from another company and two M7's [self-propelled 105mm howitzers] firing at the same column. The range from my tank to the targets was five to eight hundred yards.

Two days later, having a chance to inspect these vehicles, we found the Mark IV's with large holes in the front, but of all the Mark VI's there was one penetration in one tank on the back of the turret. The numerous places where the other projectiles hit there was just grooves or penetrations part way through the armor.

In military terms their are a number of ways to describe the effects of high-velocity rounds on the armor protection of tanks. This World War II US Army photo of a Sherman tank used as a test target shows in dramatic detail the results of numerous hits by a variety of antitank rounds. Complete penetration of the Sherman's thin armor is very evident in at least four spots. On the rear portion of the vehicle's turret is an example of partial penetration were a round gouged out the armor and then bounced off. *US Army*

This close-up view of the front armor plate on the German Tiger II on display in the Belgium town of La Gleize clearly shows how the vehicle's thick steel armor deflected or stopped three high-velocity antitank rounds. Modern tanks no longer depend on thick steel armor for protection. Instead, they use composite/multilayered non-metallic products ranging from ceramics like a Kevlar matrix to aluminum and plastics.
Andreas Kirchhoff

The following US Army report, issued shortly after the end of World War II, explains some of the many aspects of this field of study in relatively simple terms:

The damage that may be done to armor plate varies considerably, in both type and degree. Variations occur for numerous reasons: the ratio of projectile caliber to the thickness of the plate, the composition of the projectile and of the plate, the striking velocity, and the angle of impact.

(1) Penetration: The principal damage to armor plate is penetration. There are two degrees of penetration—partial and complete. Penetration is deemed complete by some observers when any portion of the projectile protrudes through the plate; when, by impact, a hole has been made that is sufficient to permit any passage of light; or when spalls, buttons, or slivers are thrown from the rear of the plate. Partial penetration is any penetration which is not complete.

(2) Spalling: Spalling is a condition of the plate caused by plate fractures and lamination which allow pieces to fly off the plate at the time of impact. Spalling may occur on either the front (impact) face or the back face of the plate. Back spall occurring in plates on armored vehicles (tanks, etc.) is particularly hazardous to personnel inside because each of the fragments or splinters is a potential casualty producer. The velocity of the fragments is very high.

(3) Petalling: When a projectile penetrates armor plate, a condition called "petalling" may be produced. This condition occurs where the metal around the penetration is forced into a leaflike or petal form.

(4) Punching: Punching is a condition of the plate where the impact and penetration of the projectile have caused a plug of metal, (the diameter of the projectile) to be punched out of the plate. Punching may be partial or complete. Of the two, complete punching is the more hazardous, since the metal piece ricochets within the vehicle, increasing the casualty-producing potential.

(5) Bulging: Impact of the projectile may also produce a condition called bulging or dishing sometimes accompanied by cracking of the plate.

(6) Fracturing: In some instances, the impact of the projectile may fracture the plate. In other words, the plate may crack, cleave, and/or part without punching, spalling, or dishing.

Armor-piercing projectiles of several types have been developed and used. Armor-piercing projectiles inflict damage through penetration of the plate and by ricochet within the target vehicle or structure. In addition to penetration, there is usually some damage from spalling. Research during the later stages of World War II indicated that a shot made of high density metal, within an outer sheath of less dense metal (which more or less prevents the core from shattering on impact and acts as a carrier) is extremely effective in penetrating armor plate. The hypervelocity armor-piercing projectile [HVAP] with tungsten carbide core is a result of such research.

Some types of armor-piercing projectiles are fitted with a cap in order to reduce the tendency of the projectile to shatter on impact with armor [known as Armor Piercing with Armor Piercing Cap, or APC]. Other types of armor-piercing projectiles are loaded with explosive and fitted with a delay fuse so that after penetration is effected, the resulting explosion produces blast and casualty-producing fragments within the vehicle or structure [known as High Explosive Antitank, or HEAT].

Despite its very thick armor, the Tiger I was far from being invincible. It was just as vulnerable to hidden antitank guns as were Allied tanks. In North Africa a small number of Tiger I tanks (thirty-four) were sent to support Rommel in late 1942. They did fairly well against Allied tanks and antitank guns in their initial combat engagements. However, on January 20, 1943, two Tigers unknowingly passed in front of a British antitank gun position and exposed their thinner side armor to the English gunners. A description of that encounter is included in a report from the Public Archives of Canada:

CANADIAN SCHOOL OF ARTILLERY (OVERSEAS)
BULLETIN NO. 5 - APPENDIX "B-5"
GERMAN HEAVY TANK Pz.Kw VI.

The following is a report by the US Army Observer on the Tunisian Front.

1. The first of the new German Heavy tanks to be destroyed in this theatre was accounted for by 6-pdrs (57mm) of the [unnamed] Antitank Bn. (British).

The emplaced 6-pdrs opened fire at an initial range of 680 yards. The first round hit the upper side of the tank at very acute angles and merely nicked the armor. As the tank moved nearer it turned in such a manner that the third and fourth shots gouged out scallops of armor, the fifth shot went almost through and the next three rounds penetrated completely and stopped the tank. The first complete penetration was at a range of 600 yards, at an angle of impact of 30 degrees from normal, through homogeneous armor 82-mm (approximately 3-1/3 inches) thick. Ammunition used was the 57 mm AP semi AP solid shot.

2. One element of this action contains an important lesson that should be brought to the attention of all antitank elements and particularly Tank Destroyer units:

(a) The British gunners did not open fire until the enemy tank was well within range.

(b) In addition to opening fire with their primary weapon—the 57 mm—the Antitank unit opened with intense light machine gun fire which forced the tank to button up and in effect blinded him. His vision being restricted to what he could see through his periscope, the enemy tank gunner apparently became confused and was actually traversing his gun away from the Antitank guns when he was knocked out for good.

(c) Once they opened fire, the British gunners really poured it in and knocked out one more heavy Mk VI tank and six Mk III tanks. Also, for good measure, one Armored Car.

3. Conclusions that may be drawn from this action.

(a) The unobstructed vision of the gunner in a tank destroyer gives him a very real advantage over his opponent squinting through the periscope or narrow vision slits of a tank.

(b) The tank destroyer unit must force the enemy tank to "button-up" by intense fire from every weapon he has, including machine guns, tommy guns and rifles.

The ability to destroy a Tiger I from other than the front is described in a wartime report from the 7th Armored Division while in Belgium in December of 1944:

While northern and eastern flanks had been heavily engaged, the northeastern section had been rather quiet. The only excitement there had been was when an M8 armored car from "E" Troop destroyed a Tiger tank. The armored car had been in a concealed position at right angles to run along a trail in front of the MLR. As the tank passed the armored car, the M8 slipped out of position and started up the trail behind the Tiger, accelerating in an attempt to close. At the same moment the German tank commander saw the M8, and started traversing his gun to bear on the armored car. It was a race between the Americans who were attempting to close so that their puny 37-mm would be effective in the Tiger's "Achilles heel" (its thin rear armor), and the Germans who were desperately striving to bring their "88" to bear so as to blast these "fools" who dared to attempt to fight a 60-ton tank with their little "runabout" and its "pop gun." Suddenly the M8 had closed to 25 yards, and quickly pumped in 3 rounds...the lumbering Tiger stopped, shuddered; there was a muffled explosion, followed by flames which billowed out of the turret and engine ports, after which the armored car returned to its position.

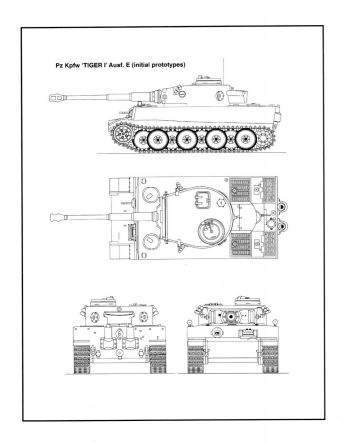

Pz Kpfw 'TIGER I' Ausf. E (initial prototypes)

Lt. Bud Pettet, who commanded a recon unit equipped with M8 armored cars in Europe, remembers:

I was an excellent shot in the Army. What I liked to do was find a covered position for my M8 about 300 yards away from a road that I knew German vehicles would pass. Since German tank commanders almost always had their heads sticking out of their turrets for better visibility, they made great targets. I used either my onboard .50 caliber machine gun or 37mm gun on them. As long as you nailed them on the first or second shot you were okay. If you missed, there was nothing worse than seeing the long barrel of an "88" being turned in your direction.

Dennis Riva, a fellow tank buff, remembers the wartime story of an M5A1 light tank veteran, whose vehicle came across a Tiger II tank traveling in a ravine between two small hills. The light tank was quickly moved onto the rise parallel and above the Tiger. The crew of the light tank then fired four to five rounds of 37mm ammo into the Tiger's thin upper rear engine deck. As smoke started to pour out of the Tiger's engine the German crew took flight.

These types of encounters with Tiger tanks were not recommended by the US Army. Normally, armored vehicles like the M8 or various light tanks were used in roles that would keep them out of the Tiger's path.

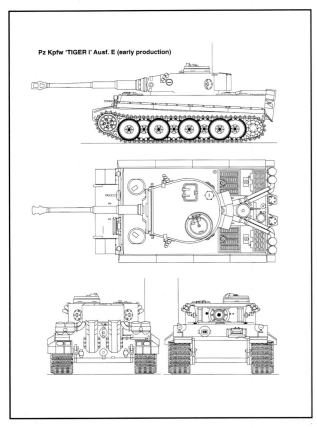

Pz Kpfw 'TIGER I' Ausf. E (early production)

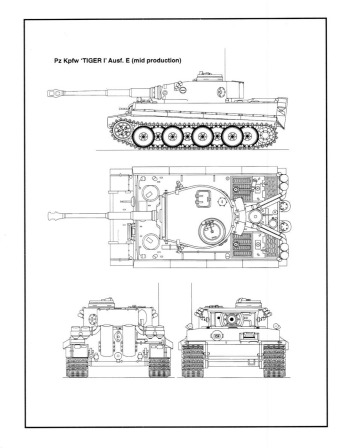

Pz Kpfw 'TIGER I' Ausf. E (mid production)

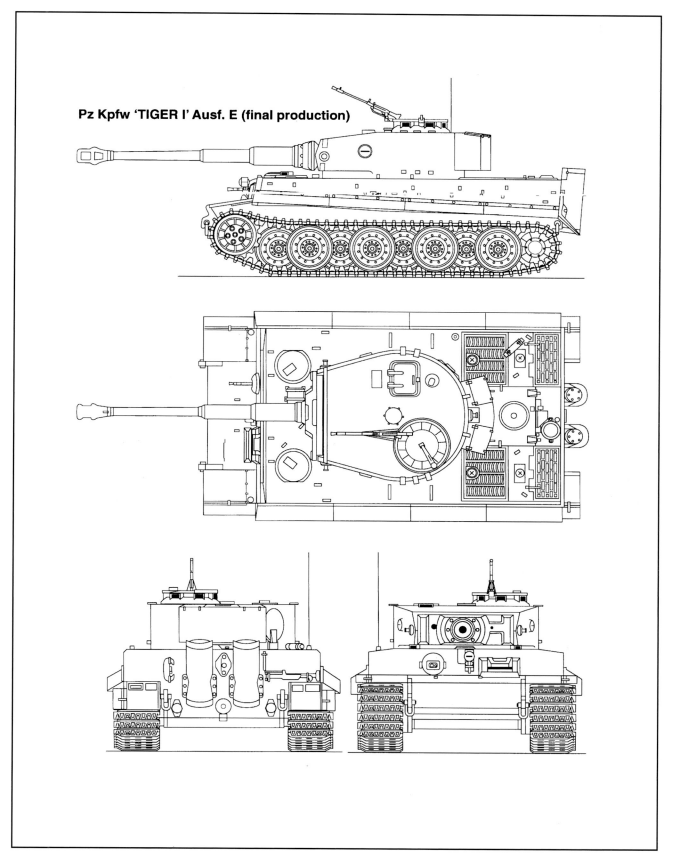

Pz Kpfw 'TIGER I' Ausf. E (final production)

Artillery versus the Tiger

The German military may not have always thought highly of American tanks during World War II, however Allied artillery (particularly American artillery) was always a serious threat to German armor and infantry. So accurate and fast was the American artillery in the battle for Tunis, North Africa, that captured German soldiers wanted to see the 155mm (nicknamed "Long Toms") automatic cannons.

An example of the successful antitank role assumed by American artillery during the fighting in North Africa (1943) can be found in a War Department citation describing the exploits of the 68th Armored Field Artillery Battalion:

> On the 15th, the combat command [from the 1st Armored Division], which the battalion was supporting, was attacked in the rear and flank by German tanks, at least sixteen of which directly attacked the battalion. That unit, however, remained in position, and by delivering direct fire on the tanks, the attack was broken and several Mark VI destroyed. On the night of February 16, enemy tanks again threatened the position of the combat command. Direct fire from the battalion was effective, repulsing the enemy with the loss of three Mark VI tanks and permitting the combat command to reorganize for further defense.
>
> The next day the battalion was given the mission of covering the withdrawal of the remainder of the division through Kasserine Pass. Through its direct fire it slowed the enemy advance and made possible the successful retirement of hundreds of men and salvage of

In response to the fielding of the Tiger I in early 1942, the Soviet military rushed into service as a stop-gap measure a specially-built tank destroyer armed with a fixed gun large enough to destroy or damage a Tiger tank with a single round. The official name for this vehicle was the SU-152. Armed with a ML-20 152mm gun-howitzer this vehicle first saw action against German Tiger Is during the large tank battles around Kursk in July 1942. During these battles the SU-152 destroyed at least a dozen Tiger Is. The photo of this massive vehicle comes from a German wartime manual. *British Army Tank Museum*

equipment, which otherwise would have fallen to the enemy. [Note: Their were never more then thirty-four Tiger Is in North Africa. Its highly unlikely that the 68th Armored Field Artillery Battalion destroyed ten Tiger I tanks in two days. More likely this was a case of misidentification rather then a deliberate exaggeration. Up until the end of the war, American soldiers were often confused over the many different types of German tanks.]

Between January 1944 and May 1944, the Anzio beachhead in Italy was a scene of continuous struggle between German forces (including Tiger I units) trying to wipe out the Allied beachhead positions and the Allied forces who wished to break out into the surrounding countryside. According to the official US Army history of that campaign, written by Martin Blumenson:

> Artillery was probably more important than tanks or tank destroyers in defeating the Germans.

From a US War Department Intelligence Bulletin (dated January 1945), comes the following conclusions from the 2nd New Zealand Division fighting German forces equipped with Tiger I tanks in Italy:

> The concentration of field artillery to counter Tigers is effective. Even if a brew-up [destroyed vehicle] does not result, the tank is invariably withdrawn. It appears obvious that the tank crews do not like the shellfire, as the possibility of damage to vital parts (tracks, suspension, bogies, wireless aerials, outside fixtures, electrical equipment, etc.) is always present.

In the March-April 1989 issue of *Armor Magazine*, Lt. General James Hollingsworth (Ret)., who saw heavy combat action during World War II, describes an incident in which American artillery shattered an attack by a formation of Tiger II tanks on units under his command:

> During the 16-19 November 1944 battles from the Worm River to the Roer River, the 2/67 AR (my battalion task force) faced 22 Royal Tigers (a Panzer regiment). A sergeant tank commander adjusted three rounds of 105-mm on the 22 tanks, followed by a 32-battalion TOT [Time-On-Target, which consisted of many artillery guns firing at once on the same targets.] of 105-mm, 155mm, 8-inch howitzers, and 240-mm guns. The 22 Royal Tigers vanished, leaving three tanks on the battlefield. Our 75-mm and 76-mm tank guns would not penetrate the Tigers. The 90-mm TD [tank destroyer] guns of the 201st TD Bn. also failed to penetrate. Thank God for the artillery.

Colonel Bill Hamberg, who commanded a Sherman tank battalion of the 5th Armored Division during World War II, remembers having up to twenty batteries of artillery guns (100 guns) on call to support his armor force. Bill recalls:

In an attempt to deploy a tank that possessed both a high degree of armor protection and a powerful enough gun to destroy both current and future German tanks, the Soviet Army fielded in early 1944, a new heavy tank known as the Ioseph Stalin 2 (IS-2). Based on a modified chassis, engine, and transmission of an earlier heavy tank design, the IS-2 turret was armed with a very long 122mm high-velocity gun fitted with a German type muzzle brake. The IS-2 pictured has been destroyed in combat and is being examined by a curious German soldier. *British Army Tank Museum*

While we often complained about the artillery fellows dropping a few stray rounds on our heads once in a while, in general we loved our heavy and fast artillery support. Be it a Tiger tank or a single sniper, if it fired at us, we would drop everything we had on it. I've seen entire wooded hillsides disappear in a cloud of explosions and smoke under one of our TOTs. The German artillery was in contrast, both slower and fairly inaccurate compared to our artillery units. That didn't mean they couldn't hit anything. They were still a threat to the end of the war.

During the early stages of the Battle of the Bulge, the 2nd Infantry Division managed to defend itself against the Panther and Tiger tanks of the 6th Panzer Army with a combination of infantry, tanks, tank destroyers, and artillery. According to the US Army's official history of those battles:

Artillery throughout this fight offered the first line of antitank defense, immobilizing many Panzers before they reached the foxhole line, leaving them with broken tracks and sprocket wheels like crippled geese in front of the hunter. The 155mm batteries were best at

Pictured taking part in a postwar military parade is a Soviet-built IS-2 heavy tank. The IS-2 was powered—like all Soviet tanks—by a large diesel engine. In addition to it's 122mm main gun the IS-2 was also equipped with at least three 7.62mm machine guns. German General Hasso von Manteuffel who fought against both the Western Allies and the Soviets considered the IS-2 the best tank of World War II. *Patton Museum*

In an continuous effort to stay one step ahead of German tank developments. The Soviet Army fielded a new heavy tank known as the Ioseph Stalin 3 (IS-3) during the very closing stages of World War II. Based on the IS-2, the IS-3 still mounted the same 122mm gun but it's armor arrangement was far superior in it's ballistic resistant shape. The well-sloped armor of the IS-3 can be seen in this picture of a captured post-war vehicle being driven in an 1968 Israeli military parade. *Israeli Army*

this work. The accuracy and weight of the defensive concentration laid on from Elsenborn ridge must also be accounted one of the main reasons the American infantry were not completely overrun during the night assaults of the 17th and 18th.

At the end of 1944, the German Army training staffs published a series of booklets for their troops, containing their official estimate of the American soldier and his equipment. While filled with much of the derogatory politico-military beliefs of the Nazi party, the booklets did describe those aspects of the American war machine that most impressed the Germans. High on their lists was the very effective cooperation between American infantry, tanks, and ground attack aircraft. American artillery earned the highest praise. According to the German Army:

It was distinguished by a very fast system of communication, accurate fire, a plentiful supply of ammunition, greater range then the German artillery weapons, skilled employment of artillery planes as aerial OPs, and extensive use of white phosphorus.

In the Soviet Army, artillery always played a very important role in their tactical plans. It was commonly referred to by the Russians as the "Queen of Battle." Every Soviet artillery piece also had a secondary role as an antitank gun when called upon.

An article written by Major P. Slesarev of the Red Army and originally published in the July 18, 1943, issue of the Soviet Army magazine *Red Star*, describes the Soviet use of artillery against German tanks:

Just as during the winter withdrawal, in counterattacks the Germans use primarily light and medium tanks (T-II and T-III) although the heavy, modernized T-IV with an additional side plate of armor is frequently used. Despite the fact that the additional armor plate is 20mm thick, our antitank and divisional artillery continue to pierce and burn the German machines, even at great distance.

The chief feature in the tank defense tactics of the Germans on the Orel sector is their relatively small concentrations. Groups of 25 to 30 tanks are typical, while only once were 80 brought into action.

Very characteristic is the method of German tank counterattacks. Rarely do their tanks move out ahead of their infantry more than 300 to 500 meters. Mostly they prefer operating by firing from the maximum distance of a direct shot. Just as soon as the tanks come within the range of the concentrated fire of our artillery, they immediately turn back. This indecisiveness on the part of the enemy tank crews is caused by the great amount of medium and heavy artillery in the immediate vicinity of the combat formations of the infantry.

In his 1960 book, titled *Tiger im Schlamm* (reprinted with the publisher's permission), Otto Carius describes what it is like to be caught in an Russian artillery barrage:

Shortly after daybreak, I was awakened more abruptly than I would have liked. The alarm clock this time was the Russians. Their methods were extremely disagreeable. Out of the blue, they laid down a barrage that left nothing to the imagination. It covered the entire front of our bridgehead. Only Ivan could lay down a barrage like that.

Even the Americans, whom I got to know later on the Western Front, couldn't compare with them. The Russian fired with every weapon they had, from light mortars all the way up to heavy artillery. They showed us that they had been doing everything but sleeping in the previous few weeks.

The entire 61st Infantry Division sector was covered with such a barrage that we thought all hell had broken loose. We were right in the middle of it and it was completely impossible for us to get to our tanks from the bunker.

Whenever we got ready to dash after one salvo hit, the whistling sound of the next one forced us back to the bunker entrance. Due to the intensity of the fire, it was impossible to tell where the main point of the attack was. After all, the fact that the Russians were attacking was no longer a secret. Naturally, the line to our supporting infantry was broken after the artillery fire had started. Everything was up in the air. We assumed that the Russians were attacking in our sector at Lembitu. But, we also had to count on the possibility of the enemy infantry capturing us before we even got to our tanks.

The Russians shifted their fire farther north after a good half hour, an eternity for us.

Allied Air Power versus the Tigers

During the battles in North Africa (1943), air power had not yet become a serious threat to German Tiger tanks. However, during the early stages of the Allied landings on the coast of France in June 1944, it was Allied fighter bombers armed with bombs and rockets that kept German tanks from overrunning the beachheads. Allied tanks had proved themselves unequal to the task when confronting Tiger and Panther tanks.

The most effective Allied fighter bomber was the single-engined British Typhoon and its three-inch rockets. American planes like the P-47 Thunderbolt and the P-51 Mustang tended to use their machine guns and 500 pound bombs when attacking German tanks. However, the Germans felt that rockets were a much more dangerous threat to their tanks. Because British pilots had more training than their American counterparts in attacking ground targets, they proved to be the top Tiger tank killers during World War II.

The memoirs of American Major General E. H. Harman describe a December 26, 1944, combat engagement between British Typhoons supporting the US Army's 2nd Armored Division and German tank units:

"A little later, American soldiers were treated to an odd spectacle. A squadron of Typhoons appeared in the sky led by one tiny, armored Cub. It was like a butterfly leading a squadron of buzzards. The Cub dived on Tigers and Panther tanks coming up the road towards Celles [Belgium] and then made tracks towards our lines. The Typhoons screamed down, rockets sizzling from their wing runners, and left devastation in their wake."

In a wartime report, Lt. Col. Wilson M. Hawkins commander of the 3rd Bn, 67th Armored Regiment commented: "Close support aircraft have helped in our advances by bombing enemy armor. I saw them work during the breakout at St. Lo and the advance across France. I saw them break up German tank counterattacks after we had secured Barmen, which is on the west bank of the Roer, north of Julich."

Lt. Colonel Bill Hamberg remembers: "As long as there were P-47 Thunderbolts flying in our area of operation, it was very rare to see any German tanks come out to do battle with us. I remember on one occasion seeing a crew of a German Panther tank abandon their vehicle and run for their lives after one pass by a P-47 Thunderbolt. While the Thunderbolt only used its machine guns on the first pass, it was probable that the German tank crew figured the Thunderbolt would drop its 500 pound bomb on their vehicle on the next pass."

Allied air power had also done much to destroy or damage almost everything related to Tiger tank produc-

One of the mainstays of the Soviet Army's towed antitank-gun fleet during World War II was the 76.2mm field gun. Seen here being towed into combat by a truck fitted with rubber tracks around it's rear wheels, the 76.2mm field gun was an excellent antitank weapon until the advent of the much thicker armor found on the German Tiger tanks. However, if used in ambush positions the gun could still destroy the Tiger I with hits to it's thinner side armor. *British Army Tank Museum*

One of the few Western-built Allied weapons that stood a chance in punching a hole through the frontal armor of a Tiger I was the British-designed-and-built "17 Pounder" antitank gun. Originally fitted on a towed mount as pictured, the gun was quickly fitted on a variety of tracked vehicles to give it more battlefield mobility. Against the frontal armor of the Tiger II even the 17 Pounder was at a dangerous disadvantage. *British Army Tank Museum*

The most numerous Allied tank to carry the British 17 Pounder into combat was the American-built Sherman tank which was supplied in large numbers to both British and Commonwealth forces. Unhappy with the low-velocity 75mm gun originally fitted to the Sherman, the British modified the vehicle to mount the much more-powerful 17 Pounder. One of the many modifications needed to adapt the Sherman to it's new role was the elimination of the hull-mounted machine gun which can be seen plated over on the Canadian Army tank pictured. *Canadian Army*

tion and getting them to the troops in the field. The most serious blow to Tiger II construction was a series of bombing raids on the factories involved in building the vehicle beginning in late 1944. These raids destroyed over half the Tiger II production run.

Because of Allied air attacks on the German railroad system, both in Germany and the occupied countries. German armored divisions had no dependable long-distance rail transport. Instead, they had to rely on long-route marches which wore out the Tiger and Panther tanks before they could even get to the actual battlefield. German wartime sources describe the roads leading to the Normandy front as being littered with broken-down and wrecked vehicles. The movement that was done was accomplished at night, and then only at a snail's pace.

So complete was the Allied control over the skies above the German forces during 1944-45, that the German troops joked that Allied planes were painted silver, while German planes were both colorless and invisible. The joke went on among German soldiers: "In the West they say the planes are in the East, in the East they say they're in the West, and at home they say they're at the front."

The Soviet Army had a large number of ground attack aircraft of varying degrees of effectiveness. The single-engine Ilyushin-2 "Shturmovik" armored ground attack aircraft armed with bombs and rockets was the best known and the most feared among German tankers. Over 35,000 were built during World War II. Early models were armed with two 20mm cannons in addition to it's normal complement of bombs and rockets. Later models were equipped with a single 37mm cannon. However, lack of accuracy with their air-to-ground weapons (especially unguided rockets) never allowed Soviet planes to pose the same level of threat to individual German tanks as those of the Western Allies. Despite overwhelming numbers by the closing stages of the war, the Red Army never managed to obtain the same level of cooperation between it's air and ground elements as the Western Allies managed to practice in their drive across Western Europe.

Soviet Tiger Killer

On the Eastern Front, the first production Tiger I's were sent into action at Hitler's insistence on August 29, 1942. During their first combat with the Soviet Army, three of the four Tigers employed had mechanical breakdowns. On September 21, 1942, these same four tanks were again sent into action, but their luck was no better. This time, all four Tigers were either lost to Soviet antitank guns (which blew off their tracks) or became mired in soft ground. The Germans managed to recover three of the four tanks. The single vehicle that could not be towed from the battlefield was destroyed in place to prevent it from falling into Soviet hands. However, on January 16, 1943, the Soviets finally captured an intact Tiger I tank.

A Soviet view of the capture of their first Tiger tank is recounted in an extract from an article by the military historian Dr. Giuseppe Finizio:

In Romanovsky's [A Soviet Lieutenant General] version published for the first time in *Operatsiya Iskra* (Spark), Lenizdat 1973 and reprinted in *Leningrad Does Not Surrender* by N. Kislitsyn and V. Zubakov, Progress, 1989): "I was informed that an unusual enemy tank was moving through the corridor. Our light guns fired at it, but even direct hits could not stop the heavy, obviously strongly armoured vehicle. The German tank was heading for Schusselburg and at the time our 18th Infantry Division was approaching the road. The tank came under heavy direct fire. The shells did not cause damage, but the driver, evidently taking fright, turned off the road and tried to get away towards Sinyavino. As it turned, the tank got stuck in a peat bog. The Germans got out and were all killed. An examination of the bodies showed that the tank had been carrying some German general [later found to be untrue], but he had no papers on him. But we did have the tank and it was undamaged. On January 18, Soviet tankmen headed by Col. G.A. Mironovich towed the tank to the army command post where K. Ye. Voroshilov, G. K. Zhukov and K. A. Meretskov ordered its immediate dispatch to Moscow. As it turned out the tank was the notorious "Tiger," on which the Germans had placed great hopes. In Moscow the Tiger was tested on the proving ground, and in May 1943 all units of the Red Army knew everything about it, particularly its vulnerable spots."

Despite the US Army's Tank Destroyer branch not wanting a large towed antitank gun (preferring a fully-tracked armored chassis instead), it was provided with over 1,500 3in towed antitank guns known as the M6. At 5,000lbs, the weapon was five times heavier then the old 37mm gun the Army started the war with. Because of it's size and weight it was extremely difficult to handle by it's crew. Protected by only a thin armored shield, the M6 proved highly vulnerable to enemy fire. The gun's biggest fault was that it couldn't penetrate the frontal armor of German tanks like the Tigers. This same gun was later mounted on a Sherman-based tank chassis and was known as the M10 Tank Destroyer. *Michael Green*

After studying their new prize, the Russians realized that much of their inventory of tanks and antitank guns were now obsolete. Extracts from an June 1978 article in *Military Review*, published by the US Army and written by Lt. Col. Charles M. Bartlett on *Soviet Self-Propelled Cannon Artillery* describes the Russian findings and their responses to the German Tiger tank:

When the Soviets captured their first German heavy tank in early 1943 and subjected it to various firing tests, the existing SU76 and SU122 [turretless self-propelled tank destroyers] had little effect at 1,000 meters. The weapons that did achieve some success were the 85mm antiaircraft gun and the 122mm corps [artillery] gun. Accordingly, the SU85 was introduced. This weapon was a combination of a modified 85mm antiaircraft gun and a T34 tank chassis. The earlier model SU122 ceased production when the SU85 appeared. [Note: In Soviet Army nomenclature SU (*Samakhodnaya Ustanovka*) meant self-propelled mount]

In late 1943, the SU152 was replaced with the JSU152 which was based upon the JS heavy tank chassis. This weapon possessed better armor protection and improved road performance. Because the demand exceeded the supply for the 152mm gun-howitzer used in the JSU152, a JSU122 mounting a 122mm corps gun was produced. Another model (JSU122A) using the 122mm tank gun also was produced.

It wasn't until the M36 Tank Destroyer was deployed to Europe in September 1944 that the US Army finally had a weapon that could occasionally punch holes in German Tiger tanks. The M36 carried a 90mm high-velocity gun, the same one that was later fitted to the M26 Pershing heavy tank. Being very thinly armored and open-topped, the M36 was not the perfect vehicle to duel it out with the heavier armored Tiger tanks. *US Army*

When the decision was made to refit the T34 tank with an 85mm gun, a similar decision was made to introduce an SU with a 100mm gun. This weapon underwent development, and, by September 1944, the SU100 was in full production. As sufficient models reached the field, the SU85 was retrograded and later refurbished and given to satellite countries. The Soviets felt that the SU100 was the best SU of World War II.

Throughout the war, the SU was in many respects a substitute for a tank. The SU, with the exception of some earlier prototypes, was limited in elevation (15 to 25 degrees) and traverse (10 to 30 degrees). Although capable of achieving ranges on the order of 10,000 meters (SU76) or 17,000 meters (SU122), there are only a few isolated inferences that the SUs were used in an indirect-fire role. By the time the SU became available, there was rarely a need for this capability. Towed artillery weapons, truck-mounted multiple-rocket launchers and infantry mortars provided the bulk of the indirect-fire support.

The tactical role of the SU was to support the infantry's and armor's advance on a narrow front, as well as act as the foundation of an active defense. The SUs followed the tanks in much the same manner as the modern overwatch technique. The Soviets believed (and still) do that the most expeditious method of conventional fire support at the least expenditure of ammunition was by direct fire. The traditional artillery preparation usually started and ended with a flurry of activity, the latter signaling the beginning of the attack. To offset this pattern, the Soviets employed the SU in the direct-fire role to maintain the tempo of firing until the actual moment of the assault.

Generally, the SU maintained a more varied selection of ammunition than the tank and was able to adjust its fire easier due to the nature of the projectile. Engagement ranges of the SU normally were further than the engagement ranges of the tanks it supported. Thinner armor protection limited the SUs engagement of tanks to special situations, primarily in prepared defensive positions or in emergency conditions.

Many German tankers that saw service on the Eastern Front during World War II, considered the Russian SUs more dangerous then any of their wartime tanks or towed antitank guns. In a 1949 article published by *Armor Cavalry Journal*, Soviet weapons expert Garrett Underhill describes the official Russian wartime view of

Coming into service during the last few months of World War II, the US Army deployed a small number of M26 Pershing heavy tanks. Armed with a 90mm gun and protected by steel armor up to 4in thick, the Pershing helped to even the odds between the German and American tanks. While a big improvement over the Sherman, the Pershing was still not an equal to the Tiger II. The Pershing's 90mm gun fired a 23.56lb round, seen here being loaded during a training exercise in 1951. *US Army*

their SUs: "The Soviets have stated that for antitank and assault gun infantry support work they preferred the SU's lower silhouette and larger gun. The silhouette afforded greater security through concealment, enabling surprise action. It also afforded less target to antitank guns. The gun affords greater hitting-power at maximum ranges, as well as more devastating HE effects against infantry weapons."

Otto Carius, a highly decorated Tiger I tank ace, racked up an impressive number of destroyed Soviet tanks during his time on the Eastern Front. Yet, it was a Soviet assault gun (German term for Soviet SUs) of an unknown type that almost did him in on April 20, 1944. In an extract from *Tiger im Schlamm* (reprinted with the publisher's permission), comes a description of that encounter:

The round which hit ripped off the cupola right at the weld line. I was lucky because if the round had hit somewhat higher on the hatch I wouldn't have got off so easily, despite the saving grace of the cigarette.

In order to finally get out of the Russian line of sight, we moved rapidly to Point 312 which meant that we were in the woods. I turned to the right to cover the path which ran into our road from the north. It was intended that the tank following me would provide security to the south. I immediately identified a Russian assault gun to the north and had my gunner take aim. Ivan [German slang for Soviet soldiers] bailed out of his vehicle when he noticed that we were laying our sights on him.

Kramer fired and at the same time another Russian assault gun hit us between the turret and the hull.

The following tank had not reached Point 312 yet. It remains a mystery to me how we got out of our Tiger. In any case, it happened as fast as lighting, we gathered in the ditch. I still had my headphones on, the only thing we saved from our tank.

The best-known Soviet SU from World War II and the most feared by the crews of Tiger tanks was the SU152. It was nicknamed the "Animal Hunter" or "Conquering Beast" by Soviet soldiers. The vehicle first saw action during the massive battle of Kursk in July 1943. The 152mm gun mounted on the SU152 fired a shell that weighted ninety-five pounds. What this gun lacked in muzzle velocity (less than 2,000 feet per second), it made up for in projectile mass. The Soviets built 704 of these tank destroyers during World War II. This SU and the many others types were designed by the Russians in a frantic effort to counter the continual upgrading of German tank armor during the war years. Because there was so little time to conduct elaborate research and development programs, the Russians were forced to mount a variety of existing guns on armored vehicles that might not have normally been built if more time had been available. Despite these disadvantages, the Russians still managed to field a tank in large numbers that could effectively engage and destroy the vaunted Tiger before the end of the war.

A 1949 article in *Armor Cavalry Journal*, by Soviet weapons expert Garrett Underhill, describes the background of the vehicle:

In this tank, Kotin's team [the designers] abandons the KV rectangular-type hull with uniform-thick-

Two American soldiers in a posed shot display one of the firing positions for the well known Bazooka. The Bazooka was a 2.36in smooth-bore rocket launcher. It could be fired from the shoulder in the standing, kneeling, sitting, or prone position to launch high-explosive rockets against tanks, armored vehicles, pillboxes, and emplacements. Against the thick armored hide of German Tiger tanks the Bazooka was not up to the job. *US Army*

The Soviet Army placed very little effort in the development of man-portable antitank weapons for it's infantry formations. Instead of rocket launchers, Soviet soldiers had to depend on very large and obsolete antitank rifles. Dropped from the inventory of all other armies by 1942, these guns fired a 14.5mm round, too small to do damage to a Tiger tank at almost any range or direction. *British Army Tank Museum*

ness plate (more fitted for production than for resistance to attack). They go in for ballistic form, including a shaped casting for the front top of the hull. The driver is placed in the front center, and the superstructure fared away either side of him. The sides of the superstructure slope, and the rear plate (with two transmission servicing hatches) slopes toward the front.

The big cast turret fares away toward the front, but its rather fat at the rear, where a DT machine gun is set in a ball mount on the left. The commander's cupola is also on the left. As on all Soviet tanks, a DT is mounted coaxially with the big gun, but for antiaircraft there is an innovation. A 12.7mm DShK is permanently mounted atop the turret in front of the cupola. It can also be used against disorganized personnel when the tank is passing through a breakthrough area, as well as against planes. Though the original Stalin may sound like a monster, its actually small and low—as low, if not lower, than a Sherman. The chassis width again permits saving on height, though by this time the Soviets felt that the chassis and suspension were due for some minor redesign. Armor on the front was upped to almost four inches. The Germans felt that it gained as much as 50% in impenetrability over the KV because of form. Sides of the original were around three inches, with the turret sides close to four. But Panther guns and late 88's could hole it anywhere at ranges up to 2,200 yards.

The ace in the hole was the new gun—a big, long 17-foot 122mm gun, tipped by a German-type double

The thick well-sloped frontal armor of the Tiger II was virtually impenetrable to most Allied antitank rounds except at very close ranges. Even the sides of the Tiger II turret and hull could stop most Allied guns under 85mm. This Tiger II took a high-velocity hit on the mantle that covers the hull-mounted machine gun. The hit failed to penetrate, but did gouge out a piece of the armor surrounding the machine gun firing port. Notice that this Porsche turret has one of it's sighting ports plugged, as it was fitted with the same single-lens sight found on the Henschel turrets. *British Army Tank Museum*

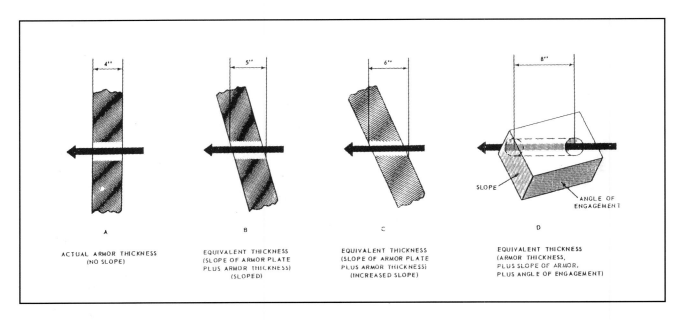

ACTUAL ARMOR THICKNESS
(NO SLOPE)

EQUIVALENT THICKNESS
(SLOPE OF ARMOR PLATE
PLUS ARMOR THICKNESS)
(SLOPED)

EQUIVALENT THICKNESS
(SLOPE OF ARMOR PLATE
PLUS ARMOR THICKNESS)
(INCREASED SLOPE)

EQUIVALENT THICKNESS
(ARMOR THICKNESS,
PLUS SLOPE OF ARMOR,
PLUS ANGLE OF ENGAGEMENT)

This line drawing from a postwar US Army manual. Shows how the sloping of armor plate on a tank can effectively almost double the ballistic protection afforded an armored vehicle. Normally the range and angle of impact are two important factors that will affect the degree of penetration possible with high velocity antitank rounds. The angle of impact is determined by the slope and shape of the tank armor being fired at. Also important is the angle of target engagement. Is the weapon being fired at the tank in question located above or below the target vehicle? For example, if a tank with sloped armor is hit by a gun above it's relative position, the advantage of sloped armor would be canceled

baffle muzzle-brake. (The 122mm caliber may be strange to the US, but it's a Russian caliber for 4.8 inches. Guns of such caliber have long been common in Russian field artillery.) A bracket is fitted to the rear of the hull to hold the gun steady for traveling.

[Note: The Joseph Stalin-2 (JS-2) tank went into production in late December 1943. Despite its use in this extract and others, the JS transliteration is technically incorrect and should read IS for Iosef Stalin.]

The IS-2 first saw action in February 1944 and became so effective against German heavy tanks that Tiger crews were told to destroy IS-2 tanks before engaging any other targets. The Soviets fielded about 3,500 IS-2 tanks during World War II.

Reprinted with the kind permission of Gregory T. Jones are extracts from his unpublished article on Karl Bormann, a Tiger II tank commander who saw combat involving Soviet IS-2 heavy tanks. Bormann comments: "I had missed the battle of the Kursk Salient and I was a relatively young tanker when I came to Armor via the Infantry in 1943. The Tiger Tank was a reliable weapon for us when <u>employed properly</u>. I served in both types of Tiger tanks. Both were too heavy for their motors and so not maneuverable enough. Because of their "lethargy," the old tankers who had participated in the development of the Panzer branch could not get very excited about the heavy tank. The best example to me of a maneuverable tank was the Russian T-34, and one with a good 76.2 mm (tank gun) on top of that!"

In February of 1945, after being thrown into action from Arnswalde in Pomerania, twenty-one of the precious combat-ready Tiger IIs of what was now titled the 503 SSPzAbt, divided into four quick response units to relieve infantry divisions in the area of the port city of Danzig, hard pressed by Soviet advances. "We weren't even numbering the tanks in our battalion, too easy for the enemy to find the platoon leader or company commanders through the numbers," Bormann said. Hordes of Soviet tanks were encountered and over a stretch of a month and a half, sixty-six Soviet tanks, forty-four cannon, and fifteen transport lorries were destroyed by Karl Bormann and his crew of Teitsch (loader), Hoffmann (driver), Bier (radio), and Reichel (gunner). "It is not just a question of the commander, but also, especially the driver and the gunner. For example, since we shot complete rounds as opposed to separate warhead and charge used with heavy Soviet tanks, my loader was quicker in reloading. The 88 was unbeatable!"

In response to the limited German success in the area, the Soviet 2nd Guards Tank Army brought in numerous Stalin (IS-2) Tanks; tanks whose 122mm cannon could disembowel German Panther Tanks and cause even the Tigers serious problems. A glancing blow from a "122" shell could produce concussion enough to disable a Tiger's turret mechanism. Bormann comments: "The Iosef Stalin (Tank) was without a doubt our best opponent, very difficult to knock out! However, as with most tanks, if you got them on the turret ring, then it was all over for him. With the Tiger II, I even knocked out a Stalin from the side at 1700 meters with its first round, 'GLUCKS TREFFER' (lucky hit)!! You really shouldn't underestimate just dumb luck. But for that chance alone I would give the Tiger II my preference over the Tiger I."

Otto Carius took a heavy toll of Stalin tanks on the Eastern Front. In July of 1944, Lieutenant Carius mounted his Tiger I accompanied by only one other Tiger tank from his unit and surprised an advance detachment of Soviet IS-2 tanks taking a break in a small Russian village. During the short engagement that followed, Carius managed to personally destroy ten of the IS-2 tanks. The following extract comes from a descriptive narrative of that event which was published in a German Army field newspaper [Note: it differs slightly from the combat report] on July 28, 1944. The author was German War Correspondent Herbert Steinert:

In each situation, Lt. Carius has known and felt how he had to employ his Tiger. He struck the enemy with his tank in such a manner that his thrusts surprised him and caught him unaware.

That was also the case yesterday. Accompanied by a second Tiger, this young tank commander was moving over the broad expanses of the highway in order to cover the road against surprise advances by the Soviets. He did not know that at the same moment the Josef Stalin Guards Tank Brigade, freshly brought in from Moscow to the critical defensive fighting in the Dunaburg area, had assembled for the decisive advance against the highway. The brigade, an elite unit of the Soviets, employed the latest models of tanks. While the bulk of the attacking brigade was dispersed and held up, the lead enemy armor elements succeeded in penetrating deeply into the defensive front.

Like all tanks, the Tigers were unsuitable for fighting in towns and cities. The limited visibility possessed by tanks makes them very vulnerable to even infantry tank-hunting teams in built-up areas. The biggest advantage of the Tiger tanks was their ability to engage and destroy the enemy at long ranges. Using a valuable vehicle like the Tiger in an urban setting is poor tactical judgment. The Tiger II shown in this picture has a very large hole on the side of it's turret. The weapon that made the hole is unknown. Note the size of the "88" round propped up on the side of the vehicle's turret. *British Army Tank Museum*

Believing in their material superiority, the Soviets felt secure on their march. Among the few huts of a village, the highway in arm's reach, the advance guard of the tanks conducted a short break for orientation. The latest types of Soviet tanks were now massed tightly together. Commanders and drivers lounged about, smoking cigarettes, bent over maps, in the turrets, while a few tankers strolled through the barnyards on the prowl for something to eat.

Coming over the small rise, Lt. Carius' two Tigers collided with the Soviets at the shortest range possible. The young tank officer felt his throat get tight. He counted a total of 17 Soviet tanks! Two Tigers against them! The fight would be hard. Whoever was defeated would die. But, there was no turning back. Attack! The main guns of the two Tigers roared in a primordial manner. The Soviet tanks swung their turrets. The 17 lumps of iron raced through a grain field to the protective cover of the woods. Their main guns flashed. Muzzle reports. Impacts. The dirt shot up a few meters high around the Tigers. Their motors howled crazily. They pursued the enemy. Tank tracks. The impacting rounds ripped deep scars into the earth.

One fireball after another followed from the powerful barrel of Lt. Carius tank. Whatever he shot at, he hit, wherever he rolled, he broke the resistance.

After 20 minutes of wild firing, the advance guard of the Josef Stalin Tank Brigade had been shattered and destroyed. The mangled remains of the latest Soviet tank models lay smoking, smoldering, and burning between the highway and the woods.

Despite Otto Carius' luck that day in catching the Soviet IS-2 tanks by surprise, he considered the IS-2 the equal or better of the Tiger I due to its better ballistic shape.

In his 1949 article, Mr. Underhill goes on to describe an improved Stalin tank which came into action near the very end of World War II in Europe:

After some minor hull modifications, Kotin undertook a complete redesign of the Stalin for production in 1944. His original Stalin seemed to be a little too big and thus too heavy for the basic suspension and horsepower units derived from the KV. The weight was close to that of the big KV-2 when the Stalins were combat loaded, and a drastic redesign was called for if speed and "passability" were not to be sacrificed.

The result was the Joseph Stalin III, which appeared in action in 1945. Troops aptly called it the "Pike" because of its sharp angled nose of plate. For the first time in Soviet tanks the front plates (which join in verti-

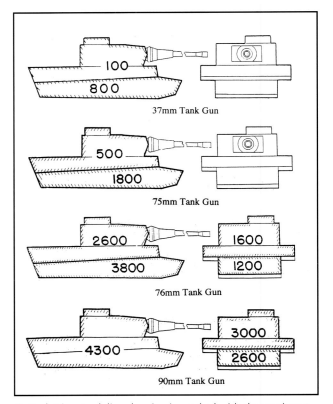

37mm Tank Gun

75mm Tank Gun

76mm Tank Gun

90mm Tank Gun

Prepared by the Technical Intelligence Section of the US Army's Ordnance Branch in January 1945, these line drawings of both the Tiger I and IIs show their vulnerability—or lack of—to a number of American tank guns used during World War

II. Each Tiger-tank line drawing is marked with the maximum range in yards at which penetration of different plates is likely to occur. The ranges shown were computed on the basis of zero angle of attack.

The Tiger II pictured, fitted with a Henschel turret, is on display at the Royal Military College of Science located at Shrivenham, England. The Tiger II is one of a handful of armored vehicles within the College of Science's private collection used to demonstrate important trends in tank development. To the right of the Tiger II is a Soviet-designed T-34 medium tank armed with an 85mm gun. This particular Tiger II is covered in Zimmerit. The use of Zimmerit was discontinued on Tiger IIs built after September 1944 because of an unfounded belief that it could catch fire after taking shell hits. *Wheels & Tracks Magazine*

cal center line, sloping off to the sides sharply) aren't pierced for the driver. He sits with his head almost right under the turret, on a seat that can be raised or lowered as on US tanks. His periscope is in the cover hatch. The rest of the chassis is more or less like the original Stalins. The other big change is in the cast turret, which has been squashed down and made round, with sides sloping sharply upward and in. At the edges, they actually overhang the superstructure sides. The commander's cupola is dropped. The turret carries the radio, which has a buggy whip antenna on the left. A 12.7mm DShK machine gun is mounted in front of the right turret hatch. There are plenty of hand-holds for the tankborne troops considered as a necessary escort for heavy tanks.

With this tank, the last redesign in six years of work, Kotin proudly proclaims himself a genius like Morosov. His acknowledged co-designer of the KV, N.L. Dukhov, doesn't share honors with him this time; instead it is Shashmurin and Rybin who are cut in on the prize. Whoever is really responsible, they enable a claim

to be made that the weight of the Soviet "heavy" is back to what the engine and suspension were designed to handle back in 1938-39—50 tons. Kotin proudly writes that his tank scales at a third the weight of the German Royal Tiger—and packages more power. (It also packages the crew like sardines, but then comfort has always ruthlessly been sacrificed for combat capability in Soviet tanks. The "unnecessary" comfort built into British and American tanks is what Soviet tankers single out first for criticism.)

But all that glistens is not gold—especially in Russia, where it has always been unwise to judge by appearances.

This wonderful tank mounts a gun which should have its ammunition power-rammed—but has no rammer. Its 122mm rounds have to be loaded in shell and cartridge case components, as on the standard wartime US Navy 5-inch 38s. This hardly makes for speed in getting in the first few rounds in one of the main missions the Soviets give a heavy—tank vs. tank fighting. The size of ammunition and gun makes for less ammunition storage capacity.

Why did the Soviets jump from an 85 right to this 122? Why did they not, like the Germans, beef up their heavies' power by a super-velocity 85—for the Germans were very satisfied with their Royal Tiger's Model 1943 88? How come they didn't shift back to the fine 100mm gun, when that became available? Why did they put a 122 in a tank, when in 1943 they were already mounting the long-range 122mm M1931/37 field gun on a well-armored KV chassis?

These questions suggest that wartime Soviet armor cannot be considered without the background of Soviet tactics—for attempts to gauge any piece of foreign armor by trying to fit it to one's own concepts, is likely to produce wrong conclusions. Recalling Stalin's known direct interference in KV development, in aviation details, and in artillery design, the question is raised as to whether he (like Hitler) was the one who preferred big things better than ones less striking but more efficient. Wartime reduction of tank materials quality suggests that the qualitative reduction of ammunition, consequent upon fantastic quantitative production to meet the needs of gigantic armies and air forces, may have had something to do with the selection of such a big piece over a smaller one. Recollection of how Kotin himself blandly confesses to slipping one over on the Red Army—by "just happening" to have a design that Stalin at once liked—raises the issue of whether bureaucratic intrigue played its role.

Thus folk who seek to compare the Stalin tank to American ones should not think just in terms of comparative weights and powers—but of missions. The German Panther had the weight of the new Stalin, but it was a medium tank for armored force duties, while the Stalin was built for the missions implied in the Soviet definition of heavy tank. Moreover, the Stalins were and are part of a team—one which in Soviet divisions include heavy and medium tanks, heavy fire support self-propelled guns and tank destroyers.

As the Germans proved by their brilliant victories and their stupid failures, in war as in sport, it's the team that counts—and not the apparent stars.

Other than tanks and various self-propelled tank destroyers (SUs) the Soviet Army also had an entire range of towed antitank guns. The guns themselves varied in size from 45mm to 100mm. While lacking the mobility of a self-propelled chassis, they could be most effective in destroying German armored vehicles of all types, including Tiger tanks. Michael Wittmann, World War I's most well-known German Tiger tank commander, described in an August 3, 1944, issue of an "SS" newspaper why antitank guns were such a threat to his vehicle: "The antitank gun is harder to spot than the tank; it's able to get to get off more rounds before [I] can find it."

Otto Carius, describes his impression of antitank guns in an extract from *Tiger im Schlamm* (reprinted with the publisher's permission)

The destruction of an antitank gun was often accepted as nothing special by lay people and soldiers from other branches. Only the destruction of other tanks counted as a success. On the other hand, antitank guns counted twice as much to the experienced tanker. They were much more dangerous to us. The antitank cannon waited in ambush, well camouflaged and magnificently set up in terrain. Because of that, it was very difficult to identify. It was also very difficult to hit because of its low height. Usually, we didn't make out the antitank gun until they had fired the first shot. We were often hit right away, if the antitank crew was on top of things, because we had run into a wall of antitank guns. It was then advisable to keep as cool as possible and take care of the enemy, before the second aimed shot was fired.

When the Tiger I came into service, the Soviet Army already had a super-hard subcaliber tungsten-core round for its 45mm antitank gun (copied from a German round). While the round tended to be very inaccurate, it could occasionally penetrate the driver's front vision port on the Tiger I. The Soviets later developed a similar round for both their 57mm and 76mm towed antitank guns. To improve the effectiveness of its smaller caliber antitank guns, the Soviets copied another idea from the Germans. This involved the grouping of antitank guns under a single commander who could concentrate the mass fire of as many as ten guns on a single tank at a time. Individually, these guns might not be able to destroy a Tiger on its frontal arc. But, acting together, even the thick armor of a Tiger I could be broken down. During the famous July 1943 battle of "Kursk," which involved thousands of German and Soviet armored vehicles, dug-in Soviet antitank guns protected by huge minefields defeated three German armored vehicles for every antitank gun lost. The famous German Tiger ace Michael Wittmann, who took part in the battle, managed to destroy thirty-six Soviet antitank guns and twenty-eight tanks in five days of brutal fighting. [Note: Only 146 Tiger I tanks took part in the battle of Kursk.]

The Soviets built over 100,000 various types of tanks and SUs during World War II. These figures are in sharp contrast to a German World War II total of tank and self-propelled gun production of roughly 25,000 vehicles. Of these 25,000 AFVs, only a little more then 2,000 were Tiger tanks. Numbers alone show that the legendary Tiger, despite the higher level of proficiency among it's crews when compared to Soviet tankers, never stood much chance against the overwhelming Soviet quantitative advantage in manpower and material.

American and British Tiger Killers

On the Western Allies side, the only really effective antitank gun capable of taking on the Tiger I tank was the British 17 pounder. First entering service in 1942, the towed version of this gun proved to be both too large and unwieldy to be fully effective in the role in-

This set of two US Army photos shows the same Tiger II from two slightly different angles. Picture on the left has an American soldier with his hand marking the spot where a 90mm round fired from an American Army M36 Tank Destroyer punched a large hole through the vehicle's front track and running gear. Picture on the right shows the other American soldier on the top of the Tiger's hull pointing out to the photographer were another 90mm round penetrated the side of the turret. Also very noticeable is the Tiger's right side track which has been cut by American fire.

tended for it. However, since it proved to be the only antitank weapon the British had that stood a chance against the Tiger I, it was quickly fitted to a variety of armored tracked vehicles. The British, however, still did not have complete faith in the 17 pounder. A 1945 British Army report describes the vehicle-mounted 17 pounder in action against German tanks like the Tiger: "It was suicide deliberately to try to engage in a battle of fire and movement with an enemy tank."

The best known vehicle to mount the 17 pounder was the US-built Sherman tank, which had been supplied in large numbers to the British and Commonwealth tank units. In British service it was nicknamed the "Firefly" by the troops. But, like the Tiger, there were never enough to go around.

It was a British Firefly that brought about the demise of the Tiger tank ace Michael Wittmam in France, August 8, 1944. The Firefly was hidden in an orchard when Wittmam's Tiger along with three others passed the vehicle's position. Because the Tiger's thinner rear and side armor was now exposed, the British crew destroyed the Tigers in quick order.

The British military also modified a number of American-supplied M10 Tank Destroyers to mount a 17 pounder, instead of their normal three inch guns. In this configuration they were nicknamed the "Achilles."

During World War II the American Army had a number of towed antitank guns ranging in size from 37mm to 57mm to three inch. Unfortunately, none of them really proved effective in the roles they had been designed for. According to the official history of the US Army in World War II: "The 57mm battalion antitank guns, and their crews, simply were tank fodder [during the Battle of the Bugle]. The mobility of this towed piece, which had been a feature of the gun on design boards and in proving ground tests, failed in the mud at the forward positions. Only a very lucky shot could damage a Panther or Tiger, and at the close of this oper-

ation both the 2nd and the 99th Divisions recommended the abolition of the 57mm as an infantry antitank gun."

The towed three inch antitank gun of the US Army also performed very poorly during the Battle of the Bulge. According to the official history of the US Army in World War II: "The experience of the 801st Tank Destroyer Battalion, a towed outfit, was markedly different [from that of a self-propelled tank destroyer unit]. Emplaced close to the infantry line, its three inch guns were brought under intense shelling and could be moved only at night. During attack, bogged in mud and unable to shift firing positions, the towed tank destroyers quickly fell prey to direct fire or infantry assault. Between 17 and 19 December [1944] the 801st lost 17 guns and 16 half-tracks. Indeed, the greatest combat value of the towed battalion came from the mines carried on the half-tracks which were used with effect by adjacent riflemen and the employment of the gun crews as infantry."

Only the 90mm antiaircraft gun (fielded in 1942) showed any promise as a gun that could destroy a Tiger I. However, tests conducted in the US showed that it took too long for the 90mm gun crew to emplace the weapon into a position to fire at ground targets. The Army therefore, concluded that the gun on its original mount was unsuitable in a towed antitank role. Despite this official Army conclusion, General Omar N. Bradley ordered eight battalions of the 90mm antiaircraft gun into the front lines shortly after the invasion of France as a backup for his outgunned Sherman tanks. A few 90mm antiaircraft guns were also used by the US Army during the Battle of the Bulge as antitank guns and did account for a few German tanks. Despite these examples, work on the development of a towed antitank carriage for the 90mm gun never resulted in a product. The US Army later mounted the 90mm gun on both a fully-tracked chassis known as the M36 Tank Destroyer and on the M26 Pershing heavy tank. In combat, the 90mm gun proved to be somewhat of a disappointment. In a wartime report S/Sgt. Harvey W. Anderson, a medium tank platoon leader stated: "I believe the 90mm gun on the T-26 [M26] is almost comparable to the 88mm on the Mark VI but does not obtain the necessary muzzle velocity to penetrate the Mark V or the VI from the front.

"I have actually seen the 90mm Armor Piercing Cap bounce off a German VI at about 1400 yards. In turn I have seen a German Mark VI with an 88mm KO [knock out] an American M4 at 3300 yards with a ricochet hit through the side."

The 90mm M3 shell fired from the M36 tank destroyer and the M26 Pershing heavy tank weighed twenty-four pounds and had more striking energy than the 88 round fired from the Tiger I's gun. But, since the quality of the steel used in its construction was inferior to what the Germans used, its final performance fell far short of the German round.

Charles Geissel, who served as a lieutenant in the 628th Tank Destroyer Battalion during World War II, recalls: "Our unit was one of a very few to be equipped with the M36 Tank Destroyer armed with a modified 90mm antiaircraft gun. Most other tank destroyer units had the M10 armed with a 3 inch modified naval gun. When we first received our M36's in England we were told in classes that the 90mm gun mounted on our vehicle was far superior to the German 88mm gun. Yet, on my unit's first encounter with a Royal Tiger, our 'B' company found their 90mm armor-piercing rounds wouldn't penetrate the turret armor of the German tank. It wasn't until a 90mm shell hit near the top of the vehicle's turret that a penetration was obtained. This round managed to set off a fire in the German tank and the crew then abandoned it. If I remember right ' B' company suffered several causalities during that brief shoot-out. Our unit encountered only one other Royal Tiger before the war ended. It also proved very difficult to destroy."

The M26 tank was the culmination of a long-range program initiated by the US Army in the spring of 1942 to originally develop a new medium tank to replace the M4 Sherman tank series. Because the Sherman was considered an adequate weapon (until the first few weeks after the invasion of Europe on June 6, 1944), the development of the M26 was given a very low priority. When the Army realized it needed a tank with more firepower and better armor protection to match the Tiger I, the M26 had already been fitted with a 90mm gun and had grown to a weight of forty-six tons. Because of its weight, the M26 was designated as a heavy tank. In contrast, the Sherman medium tank weighed roughly thirty-four tons.

The US Army had always recognized that heavy tanks had superior firepower, heavier armor, and greater crushing power. Against these were the disadvantages of higher cost, lessened speed and maneuverability, lower reliability, transportation problems, and the general difficulties involved in operating and maintaining such unusually large land vehicles. The Germans had suffered from all these problems and more in building and using the Tiger tanks. So acute were these problems that many German soldiers and officers even today question the wisdom in having built the Tiger tank at all. Most American tankers who fought against both the Tiger and the Panther medium tank considered the Panther a better all around tank. For the time and effort expended to build one Tiger, two Panthers could have been produced.

In February 1945, the Army rushed twenty of the M26's to Europe. As the Army had foreseen, the M26 was difficult to get into battle because it could not cross the old narrow bridges that dotted so much of Europe at

From the photo collection of Michael V. Altamura—who saw action with the US Army's 750th Tank Battalion—comes this somewhat grainy picture of an abandoned Tiger II somewhere in Belgium, in December 1944. Michael still remembers how massive the Tiger II was compared to their standard Sherman tank. At one point during the war, a single Tiger II on the edge of a open forest meadow had blocked his unit's advance. When the Colonel in charge radioed up to the lead tank to why they didn't rush the enemy tank, he was told in a firm but polite manner that his men would follow him anywhere, as long as he led the charge. Eventually, the Tiger II was outflanked by a platoon of Shermans that managed to destroy it with a number of rounds to it's thinner side-hull armor. *Michael V. Altamura*

A disabled Tiger II, fitted with a Porsche turret, shows many of the upper turret details. At the top of the picture is the Panther tank type commander's cupola, which is missing it's hatch. Underneath the commander's cupola is the loader's hatch opening, which is also missing it's hatch. Right behind the loader's hatch opening is the smaller opening for a multipurpose grenade launcher that could fire smoke, signal, or anti-personnel rounds. Above the grenade launcher is a ventilating fan outlet. Behind the ventilating fan outlet is the opening for tossing out empty shell casings. *British Army Tank Museum*

the time. It was also too wide to be shipped by European railroads. It needed its own special tank transporters to move it from one battlefield to another. The M26 also caused heavy damage to the Army's existing portable bridges. Since the war in Europe was quickly coming to an end, the M26 tank only saw limited combat action against the Tiger. One of the few encounters involving both a Tiger tank and an M26 Pershing occurred on February 25, 1945, near Elsdorf, Germany, and is recounted in Richard Hunnicutt's book *Pershing* (reprinted here with permission): "The tank [M26] had been positioned behind a roadblock to watch for enemy movement. This turned out to be a poor location with the fires burning in the vicinity. In the darkness, flames from a burning coal pile silhouetted the turret which was exposed above the road block. A German Tiger tank [Tiger I], concealed behind the corner of a building, fired three times at the turret at a range of about 100 yards. The first 8.8cm shot penetrated through the coaxial machine gun port, spun around inside the turret killing the gunner and the loader. The second hit the muzzle brake

and the end of the gun tube jarring off the round that was in the chamber. The discharge of this shell caused the barrel to swell at about the halfway point even though the projectile went on out the tube. A third shot glanced off the upper right-hand side of the turret tearing away the cupola hatch cover which had been left open. The Tiger then backed up, immobilizing itself on a pile of debris and was abandoned. The loader of the Tiger was later captured and confirmed that his tank had done the firing."

Since the M3 90mm gun mounted on the M26 tank could not effectively deal with the thick sloped frontal armor on the Tiger II, the American Army mounted an improved 90mm gun, known as the T15E1 on a single M26 and called it the "Super Pershing." The T15E1 gun was the equal to the Kw.K 43 gun mounted in the Tiger II. This single example of the "Super Pershing" was rushed to Germany in the very closing days of the war, in hopes that it could find a Tiger II to fight it out with. However, the war came to an end before such a fight could be arranged.

US Army Heavy Tanks

The Germans were not the only ones to develop heavy tanks during the early years of *World War II*. Even before the Germans started to build their first Tiger tank prototypes, the US Army had already formally inaugurated in May 1940 the development of a new heavy tank weighing up to sixty tons. Studies leading toward this project had been made as early as September 1939. However, it wasn't until February 1942 that the Army had a vehicle ready for testing at Aberdeen Proving Ground. Weighting roughly fifty-five tons the test vehicle was 23ft 1in long, 10ft 2 2/3in wide, and 10ft 3in high.

Known as the M6, the vehicle was at first equipped with both a three inch and a 37mm gun mounted together coaxially in the turret. Later models were fitted with a 90mm gun when fears arose that the three inch gun was not up to destroying German heavy tanks. Additional armament consisted of a number of .30 and .50 caliber machine guns.

The M6 heavy tank had a cast steel armor hull, being five inches thick on the front. The sides and rear of the hull varied from two to two and one half inches. One inch armor was used for roof and floor, and in addition, a one inch side skirt served to support the suspension system and to provide some protection for the track itself. There was also another test model of the M6 with a welded hull known as the M6A1.

The maximum vehicle speed was approximately 37mph on level ground. The design in theory would permit crossing a trench eleven feet wide, fording to a depth of four feet, and climbing a ten degrees slope at 15mph.

Testing of the M6 and M6A1 heavy tanks ended in April 1942. In July 1943 the Army issued a report listing a number of significant shortcoming in the design of these vehicles. (1) The firepower was not commensurate with the weight and size of the vehicle. (2) The fire control equipment was obsolete. (3) The crew was unable to man the armament because of the location of the controls. (4) The turret had insufficient ventilation. (5) The transmission was unsatisfactory and would require a complete redesign to obtain satisfactory shifting.

(6) The accessories requiring daily or more frequent maintenance were inaccessible.

In a letter dated August 12, 1944, the President of the US Army Armored Board wrote to the commanding general of the Army Ground Forces. In his letter, he expressed doubts that the M6 heavy tank would ever be of much use in combat. It was too heavy to ship and could not be counted on to make it to a battlefield under its own power.

Since the Army was not interested in seeing the entire vehicle redesigned. It was recommended that the M6 and M6A1 heavy tank project be canceled. However, before this could occur, the Chief of the Army's Research and Development Service proposed in August 1944 that fifteen of the forty-four M6 series of heavy tanks be modernized and armed with a high-velocity 105mm gun. It was felt by some that a heavy tank mounting a gun having great penetrative power would be needed as American soldiers advanced further into German defences. Even a tentative designation M6A2E1 was assigned to this proposed vehicle.

General Eisenhower was contacted as to his views on such a tank. On August 18, 1944, he cabled: "We do not want at this time the 15 tanks M6 that were offered, as they are not considered practicable for use in this theatre now."

In December 1944, heavy tanks M6 and M6A1 were declared obsolete. Although they were never in combat, their development contributed a number of important mechanical principles that were applied to other American-built vehicles, resulting in improvements in both light and medium tanks, and leading to the development of the M26 Pershing heavy tank.

Hand-Held Antitank Weapons

The best known hand-held antitank weapon used by American soldiers during World War II was the famous "bazooka." Invented by a Colonel Skinner of the US Army, the bazooka fired a 2.36 inch rocket which was propelled by its own recoil consisting of a discharging jet of gas to the rear of the long open barrel that basically made up the weapon.

The first bazookas were built in June 1942 by the General Electric Company. Although originally designed as an antitank weapon and despite what Hollywood war movies portrayed, by the time it reached US troops in the field, it was already obsolete because of the thicker armor on German tanks.

Tests conducted by the 702nd Tank Destroyer Battalion (US Army) in July and November 1944 showed that: "The bazooka could not penetrate the front of the Mark V (Panther) or Mark VI (Tiger) tanks nor the side of the Mark VI, but could penetrate the side and turret of the Mark V."

As claimed by an US Army Ordnance observer (during the fighting for Sicily in 1943), an American bazooka destroyed a Tiger I tank with a lucky hit to the driver's vision slot. Because of the very short effective range of the bazooka (100 yards), it was very hard to find many American soldiers willing to stand in front of any German tank and try to duplicate this feat.

During the American Army's struggle to breach the German Siegfried Line in November 1944, a battalion of the 112th Infantry battalion was attacked by German infantrymen of the 1055th Regiment and at least ten tanks and assaults guns of the 16th Panzer Regiment. The American soldier's experience with the bazooka are recorded in the Army's official historical records of World War II: "As the German tanks clanked methodically onward in apparent disdain of the exposed mines strung across the hard surfaced roads, the defenders opened fire with bazookas. At least one scored a hit, but the rocket bounced off. The German tanks came on, firing their big cannons and machine guns directly into foxholes and buildings. Reaching the antitank mines, the tanks merely swung off the roads in quick detours, then waddled on. Such seeming immunity to the bazookas and mines demoralized the men who saw it."

Bill Gunther, who was assigned as an infantry replacement to the 84th Infantry Division in December 1944, remembers having a choice between being a point man for his company or the unit's bazooka man. Choosing the lesser of two very dangerous jobs, Bill started to lug a bazooka across Western Europe. Bill recalls: "Most American soldiers by that time of the war already knew that the bazooka was useless against most German heavy tanks, especially Tiger tanks. I had heard these stories in England, even before I was sent to my unit in Belgium. Having no wish to become a dead hero, I worked out an arrangement with the guy who carried the rockets for my bazooka, a nice Jewish kid from the South. We agreed that if a Tiger tank was coming our way, we would make damn sure that neither of us would be found together. As things turned out, the first time we ran into a German tank, we were caught by surprise. The entire company ran for its life to the protection of a nearby wooded area. It think it was a Tiger tank, but I was so scared at the time and it was so long ago that I can't be positive anymore."

Some American soldiers were not discouraged by the inability of their bazookas to penetrate the frontal armor of German tanks like the Panther or Tiger. Private Eugene Hix of the 22nd Infantry (fighting in France in July 1944) reported to his superior officer a very colorful description of how he destroyed a German tank: "Colonel, that was a great big son-of-a-bitch. It looked

A close-up look at the tank commander's cupola of the Tiger II. This type of cupola was fitted with seven episcopes intended to give the tank commander some form of all around vision. The design wasn't perfect, it had a number of blind spots that the tank commander could not observe. The most forward looking episcope had a crude aiming point fitted in front of it. The cupola also had a pivoting circular hatch that could be raised and then swung to one side as shown. In combat conditions the hatch, which was mounted on a vertical shaft, could be lowered over the commander's head by means of a hand wheel. On top of the cupola was an attachment rail for the mounting of a MG34 or MG42 machine gun. *Tank Magazine*

like a whole road full of tank. It kept coming on and looked like it was going to destroy the whole world." Private Hix therefore fired his bazooka three times at the front of the German tank which kept on coming. Hix then decided to wait until the German tank passed, he then disabled it with one round from behind. Hix was later (posthumously) awarded the Distinguished Service Cross (DSC) for destroying three German tanks with his bazooka in three days.

During the Battle of the Bulge, a disabled Tiger II tank was set upon by American infantrymen armed with bazookas at close-range. Despite numerous attempts, the crew compartment of the tank proved imperious to bazooka rounds. So Cpl. Charles Roberts and Sgt. Otis Bone drained some gasoline from an abandoned vehicle, doused the tank, and lit the whole vehicle on fire with thermite grenades.

The British Army had been offered the bazooka, but decided it was unsuitable for their needs. Instead, they fielded a hand-held antitank weapon known as the "Projector, Infantry, Anti-Tank" (PIAT). Unlike the bazooka, which fired a small rocket containing an explosive charge, the PIAT was nothing more than a hollow tube with a large 200 pound firing spring (which had to be cocked by hand) and a long steel rod. When the trigger was pulled, the spring pushed the steel rod forward. A fairly large bomb would then be hurled

through the air at an enemy tank. The bomb itself was fitted with a tail, which contained a small cartridge that went off when it was hit by the steel rod. The force of this cartridge going off pushed the steel rod and spring back to the cocked position so the weapon could be reloaded. Because the PIAT had a larger warhead than the bazooka, it was a slightly more effective in the antitank role.

The Soviet Army was much less concerned with providing their infantry with a portable antitank weapon than the Western Allies were. Soviet soldiers had to depend on obsolete antitank weapons like the PTRD41 or the PTRS41, which were nothing more than oversized rifles. They measured up to six feet long, weighed over forty pounds, and fired a 14.5mm tungsten core round which lacked the size and punch to do much damage to a Tiger tank. They could, however, damage a Tiger's suspension system, optics, and engine compartment if hit in the right spot. From an extract from an after-action battle report in the personal collection of Otto Carius comes this description of the large Soviet antitank rifles: "The Russian Model 42 antitank rifle obtained penetrations up to 17mm, as measured on the front of the driver's position. This rifle was encountered quite frequently and can be recognized by its prominent muzzle flash."

It wasn't until near the end of the war, when Soviet infantrymen started to use captured German *Panzerfausts* (German recoilless antitank weapons) that they began to pose a real threat to Tiger tanks. The Soviet Army wasn't the only army to use captured German *Panzerfausts* to defend themselves from Tigers. Bill Gunther, an American bazooka man remembers on one occasion in Europe: "Our unit was told that an attack by German Tiger tanks was coming our way. My commanding officer detailed me and another soldier to take up a defensive position in a bombed-out building near a road that the German attack would come from. Knowing that our bazooka would have little effect on Tiger tanks, I took with me a number of captured German *Panzerfausts*. Luckily for me the German tank attack never came."

Ken Hockman, who served as a driver of a US M5A1 light tank during World War II, remembers: "We had a few captured German *Panzerfausts* in our unit. Unfortunately, after one of them blew-up in the face of a soldier who attempted to fire one, everybody quickly lost interest in ever using one in combat."

Very popular in Hollywood war movies and comic books, hand grenades are seen by many without a military background as an excellent antitank weapon. In real life, their limited explosive content and range confines them to the antipersonnel role. This doesn't mean that a Tiger tank couldn't be destroyed by a grenade. Dave Jones, remembers as a thirteen year old kid, trading baseball cards with his best friend for his father's captured enemy medals. The medals were supposed to be from a dead German tanker. The story as told to Dave by his friend's father as how he acquired the medals dates from the Battle of the Bulge. Cut off from his infantry unit

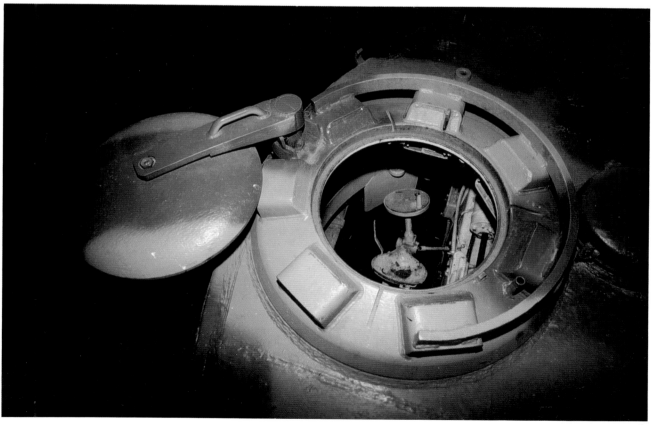

with two fellow soldiers, cold, wet, and hungry, he and his friends found themselves at the side of a Belgium road hoping to hitch a ride. At the roadside, they were surprised to find the tanks racing past were German and not American. Before running for cover, they noticed a parked German tank farther down the road. Being young and foolish they decided to sneak up on it. When close enough to what they believed was a Tiger tank [Note: Most American soldiers called every German tank they met a Tiger] they found the vehicle's commander taking a cigarette break. Opening fire with their rifles, the German tank commander was killed. His body slumped half in and half out of the tank's cupola. As they scrambled up the sides of the tank, the German crew frantically tried to pull the body of their commander into the turret so they could close his hatch. There then occurred a gruesome tug-of-war as the American soldiers tried to pull the body out of the cupola to toss a grenade down into the tank's turret. The Germans lost the tug of war and their lives.

For the typical American infantryman of World War II, confronted with an oncoming German Tiger tank without any antitank weapons handy, the one tried and proven method of dealing with it according to Don Bourne, a platoon leader in the 44th Infantry Division, was to either "run like hell" or "find someplace to hide." According to Don, the German Tiger and Panther tanks were scary things to see in combat: "They were huge when compared to our Sherman tanks. Their large muzzle brakes sticking out from a woodline or from behind a building send shivers down my spine. Terror was a constant element in the lives of any infantryman, tanks like the Tiger just raised the terror factor a few notches higher."

One of Don's scariest encounters with a Tiger tank happened in November 1944, in a tiny French village of less then eight buildings, his platoon of roughly forty men heard the unmistakable roar of a Tiger engine start-

ing up: "Not wasting any time I ordered all my men into the basement of the nearest building. As we hide, the German Tiger came right up to the building we were in and fired point-blank into it. The entire building then collapsed on top of itself. Fortunately for us, the German tank crew was unsure what building we were hiding in. He then processed to destroy every building in this small village. It wasn't until we heard him drive off that we dug ourselves out of the rubble that we were buried in."

Tiger II Armor Protection

Unlike the Tiger I with its flat box-like armored shape, the first prototype of the Tiger II accepted by the German Army in November of 1943 featured highly sloped armor. This followed in the footsteps of the Panther medium tank, which had, in turn, been copied by German tank designers from the Russian T-34 medium tank.

The Russians were not the first to apply sloped armor on their fighting vehicles. The famous pre-war American tank designer J. Walter Christie had built a number of prototype light tanks that featured some sloped armor. However, it was the Russians who first applied sloped armor to a mass-produced tank.

The reason sloped armor was adopted by the Russians and later copied by the Germans was because sloping surfaces increased the effectiveness of a given layer of armor. The sloped surface improved the armor in two ways. First, it increased its thickness when measured from a horizontal plane (a measurement known as the *armor basis*), and second, it offered a less favorable surface for attack because projectiles were more likely to bounce off than penetrate. The value of sloped surfaces on armored vehicles was dramatically illustrated by test results from the United States, which proved that at identical optimum obliquities (angles) the average resistance to penetration of purposely selected plates of both good and poor quality varied very little.

The well-sloped armor arrangement of the Tiger II is described in a US Army wartime report dated September 13, 1944:

Thicknesses and angles to the vertical are as follows:

Plate	Thickness in mm.	Angle to vertical in degrees
Turret, top front	42 (1.6 inches)	78
Turret, top centre	42 (1.6 inches)	90
Turret, top rear	42 (1.6 inches)	82
Turret, side	80 (3.1 inches)	25
Turret, rear	80 (3.1 inches)	25
Turret, front	80-60-50 rounded	(3.1-2.3-1.9 ins)
Gun mantlet	80-100 (3-4 inches)	irregu-lar
Front glacis plate	150 (5.9 inches)	50
Front nose plate	100 (4 inches)	55

From the personal photo collection of Karl Brommann comes this picture of him sitting on the barrel of his Tiger II somewhere in Eastern Europe. His success in battle is shown by the number of kill rings on the barrel of his Tiger's main gun. After the war Brommann became a dental laboratory technician at a university clinic in Germany until his retirement. *Dr. Gregory T. Jones*

Side superstructure	80 (3.1 inches)	25
Side hull plates	80 (3.1 inches)	90
Superstructure, top front	42 (1.6 inches)	90
Superstructure, top rear	42 (1.6 inches)	90
Belly plate, front	42 (1.6 inches)	90
Tail plate	80 (3.1 inches)	25

The effectiveness of the thick frontal armor on the Tiger II is described in a 1945 wartime report by Sgt. Clyde D. Brunson—a tank commander in the 2nd AD: "One day a Royal Tiger tank got within 150 yards of my tank and knocked me out. Five of our tanks opened up on him from ranges of 200 to 600 yards and got five or six hits on the front of the Tiger. They all just glanced off and the Tiger backed off and got away. If we had a tank like the Tiger, we would all be home today."

In the American Army, it usually fell to the Sherman medium tank to battle it out with the Tigers. Unfortunately the Sherman's standard M61 armor piercing round for its 75mm gun just bounced off the Tiger I and Tiger II frontal armor and sometimes its side armor. Even the up-gunned Sherman with a 76mm gun couldn't penetrate the front armor of either Tiger model, except at ranges under fifty yards. The ineffectiveness of both the 75mm and 76mm guns is demonstrated in the following wartime report in which Sgt. Steward B. Olson describes a fight with a Tiger tank:

During the fighting for the town of Freialden-hoven, Germany, the latter part of Nov. 1944, the task force under Capt. Chatfield was stopped by a minefield near Ederen, Germany. The two leading tanks were knocked out by mines, both in positions where they overlooked the road between the two towns.

A Tiger tank coming down from Freialdenhoven to Ederen was spotted by the knocked out, but still manned, mediums (one 75mm and one 76mm). They opened fire at approximately 1000 yards, and the Tiger swung to face it. Both tanks got ricochets and direct hits on the Tiger, as proved later. The Tiger swung back on the narrow road and proceeded about 50 yards, then swung his tail to the two tanks. He was then knocked out by an AP through the back plate into the motor. 24 hours later, I had the opportunity to observe the burned Tiger and found the results of the fire.

Several scars were visible on the slope plate [front hull] and around the hull, but the one hit that stood out was a direct hit by an AP to the upper left of the sight opening in the gun shield. The shell had penetrated about five inches straight into the steel and dropped out, doing no damage to the Tiger.

The frontal armor on the Tiger II was invulnerable to penetration by any Allied tank or antitank gun that it met. Because the frontal armor on the Tiger II was designed to be softer than Tiger I armor, it was not as brittle as the Tiger I's frontal armor and was not so prone to crack.

Strangely enough, when the West German Army was formed in the mid-1950s, and its military leaders started to think about designing a new tank, they decided on a fast highly mobile tank that weighed no more than thirty tons. This was in sharp contrast to the fifty-six ton Tiger I and the seventy ton Tiger II. The West Germans had gone over the combat records of the Tigers and decided that any advantage their heavy armor provided them was far outweighed by their limited mobility and poor automotive characteristics. Another factor in the West Germans' decision to build and deploy a very thinly armored tank was their conclusion that new generations of cheap antitank rockets, which could burn through the thickest steel armor, made the type of armor found on the Tiger tanks worthless. When the West Germans finally fielded their new tank, known as the Leopard 1, its frontal armor was proof only against rounds up to 30mm. In later years they changed their view on the value of armor protection and slowly upgraded their fleet of Leopards.

German Armor Plate

During World War II German tank designers and the manufacturers of armor plate were in a constant race to keep at least one step ahead of the armor piercing rounds being used by the Allies. An interesting look at how the Germans put their Tiger tanks together can be found in portions of a British Army report and dated May 15, 1944:

The introduction of plate interlocking by German AFVs is worthy of note because it has begun in this new range of vehicles where plate thickness has been considerably increased. Hitherto no German AFV has employed armour of greater single thickness than 50mm and even this thickness has been used in only limited positions. In the above vehicles the bulk of the armour varies between 60mm and 100mm in thickness.

All operational German AFVs have been welded since 1935, except in the joints between the sub-assemblies; nevertheless, considerable care has been exercised in joint preparation and there seems to have been no attempt to reduce machining. The joints have been stepped with a view of producing a system of construction which will avoid shock loading of the weld under attack. Most extensive machining has been involved in this procedure, and it is quite definite that Germany has not benefited in a reduction of machining time by the early introduction of welding.

The use of plate interlocking, in addition to stepped jointing, is of special interest as it calls for an even greater amount of machining and this is unlikely to have been introduced without some definite object in view.

The origin of the idea of plate interlocking is difficult to trace, but it is worthy of mention that it is used extensively in naval construction and also in the construction of heavy engineering equipment such as heavy fabricated machine tools, i.e. large hydraulic presses, etc. This being the case, German AFV designers may have adopted the idea from one or other of these sources.

In conclusion, it appears that plate interlocking is merely a development of previous German practice, modified to allow the employment of thick armour with a high standard of hardenability and its attendant poor welding properties.

German AFV welding has always followed a different train of thought from British and American practice in that no effort has been made to simplify armour plate machining problems through the use of welded construction. Allied welding practice has been partially adopted with a view to eliminating machining and the weld itself has been developed to attain good physical and ballistic properties.

The German welding is inferior compared by Allied standards, but a creditable job in light of the armour plate analysis and the type of welding rod used. The stepped jointing and more latterly the plate interlocking combined with stepped jointing for heavy thicknesses enables the welding to meet German field requirements and in production, assembly is facilitated at the expense of extensive machining.

This late-model Tiger I was responsible for the destruction of the first American Army M26 Pershing tank during a nighttime operation in February 1945. Hidden behind the corner of a building within the town of Elsdorf, Germany, the crew of this Tiger I spotted an M26 tank with its turret silhouetted in front of a burning coal pile. With the first shot the Tiger crew killed both the gunner and loader on the M26. Their second shot destroyed the M26's muzzle brake. The third shot and final shot from the Tiger ripped off the M26's cupola hatch. While attempting to change position the Tiger tank backed up on and immobilized itself on some rubble and was then abandoned by its crew. *Dick Hunnicutt*

The 90mm gun on the standard M26 Pershing was not able to penetrate the thick, well-sloped frontal armor on the Tiger II. In an attempt to deploy a version of the M26 tank that could match the hitting power of the KwK43 gun as fitted to the Tiger II, the Americans mounted a longer and more powerful 90mm gun on an M26 and called it a "Super Pershing". Because the gun was so heavy it was necessary to attach two large coil springs on top of the vehicle's turret to help balance the gun (this was done away with on latter prototypes of the vehicle). To increase the existing armor protection of the only Super Pershing to make it to Europe, US Army troops cut off the frontal armor plate from a captured Panther tank and attached it to the front of the vehicle, as seen in this photo. *Dick Hunnicutt*

CHAPTER 4

MOBILITY

Mobility is almost as important as firepower and armor protection to a tank's success on the battlefield. Mobility includes *strategic mobility* (the ability to move rapidly into a zone of operation), *operational mobility* (the ability to move rapidly around a zone of operation once it has gotten there), and *tactical or battlefield mobility* (the ability to move quickly to firing positions and evade enemy fire).

A crucial factor of battlefield mobility is a tank's endurance. This includes both operating range (fuel capacity and consumption) and operating distance between breakdowns (expressed in statistical terms as *mean miles between failures*).

Endurance is based largely on the moving parts in the propulsion system and running gear. These compo-

Like all tanks, the top running speed of the vehicle is not as important as it's endurance, or how long will it run before it breaks down. This was always the Tiger's biggest weak point. While the Tiger's thick armor and powerful gun provided it a big advantage in tank-versus-tank combat. The heavy weight of the Tiger's steel armor also caused automotive problems which resulted in constant mechanical breakdowns. To help prolong the life of the Tiger's automotive components the Germans always preferred shipping the vehicle by rail as often as possible. *Private collection*

Weighing in at about fifty-six tons, the Tiger I was powered by a large water-cooled gasoline engine that gave it a top speed of 24mph. This top speed may not compare well with some modern tanks which can attain speeds of over 55 mph. However, most World War II tanks could not travel much faster than 35mph. The American Sherman tank had a top speed of only 26mph. The Russian T-34 was a little faster with a top speed of 31mph. The Tiger Is pictured somewhere in the vast open plains of Russia are obviously traveling in an rear area were air or ground attack is not a problem. *Private collection*

nents naturally include the engine, transmission, tracks, track drives/supports, and wheels.

All World War II German medium and heavy tanks were propelled by Maybach aircraft engines which were specially modified for tank usage. These water-cooled gasoline-powered V-12 engines were produced in several power ratings. Early model Tiger I tanks had a Maybach HL210 21-liter engine rated at 650 horsepower. This engine was soon upgraded in production by the HL230 23-liter engine rated at 700 horsepower. The HL230 was later fitted in both the Panther tank and the Tiger II tank. (Details of the HL230 engine and other major sub-systems common to both the Tiger I and Tiger II will be described in the section on the Tiger II tank).

In their study of an early model Tiger I tank, the British were most impressed with both the compactness of the engine and its finish and workmanship. In service the HL230 was not completely trouble-free. Early models of the engine were rushed into service before all the bugs could be worked out. Extracts from a captured German document (translated by the US Army) dated September 26, 1944, stated:

1. Pz. Kpfw. Tiger with engines HL230P45 and numbers ranging from 61001 to 61281 and 61359 to 932401 should no longer be used by the field forces. Special attention should be given by the troops to the Pz. Kpfw. with these numbers. If troubles increase they should be exchanged for the better model.

2. For engine HL230P45 (Tiger) up to number 932723, the governor should be set at the maximum rate of revolutions of 2500 rpm with full engine load, conformable to the Army Bulletin 43 No. 477.

3. Motors with higher numbers than the ones given in (2) can be installed without additional work. Motors outside of the range given in (1), having the marking "M" on the right valve cap over the shield with the engine number have been upgraded and can be installed immediately.

Tiger Automotive Systems

In any tank design, maintenance issues play an important role. Fuel lines, hydraulic lines, mechanical linkages, and power cables must be easily accessible. Component parts should also be designed so the vehicle's crew or maintenance personnel can replace them in the field.

A cover letter and extracts from a translated German maintenance manual gives a comprehensive overview of many of the automotive components found in the Tiger II tank. These components are merely improved versions of those found in the last production version of the Tiger I (Model E):

SUBJECT: Tiger II Tank Instruction Manual
To: Chief Ordnance Officer, HQ., COM. Z. (Fwd)
ETOUSA, APO 887, US. Army

1. Transmitted herewith is the translation of Maintenance Manual for the Tiger Model B (Tiger II) tank. It was taken from a tank having serial No. 28101.
2. The manual identifies the engine as the HL 230 P30 and lists the horsepower as 600hp at 2600rpm. This is 92 Horsepower below previous listings on the same type engine so it may indicate that for this tank, some modification has been made to limit the engine horsepower in order to possibly increase engine life.
3. General data as extracted from the enclosed manual is as follows:
a. Engine - HL 230 P30
b. Combat weight - 75 tons
c. Fuel capacity - 203 gallons (US.)
d. Fuel consumption Roads 1.91 gal/mi
   Cross country - 2.67 gal/mi

A British technical team who examined a captured an early Maybach 210 engine considered it to be a generally excellent design, achieving small size yet high output. This overhead picture of a Tiger I 's HL 210 engine shows the unit in it's rear hull compartment. The engine itself was 4ft long, 3ft 2in wide and 3ft 1in tall minus its air cleaners. The air cleaners are visible on top of the engine in this photo. *US Army*

Early production models of the Tiger I were powered by a Maybach HL 210 twelve-cylinder gasoline engine as pictured. The HL 210 engine was regarded by British technical personnel as a scaled up version of the Maybach engines used to power the Mark 3 and 4 medium tanks. Because the Germans felt the HL 210 was under powered for the Tiger I's weight, they quickly switched to a larger version of the same basic engine known as the HL 230. *British Army Tank Museum*

e. Fording - 5'9"

f. Vertical step - 2'10"

g. Maximum gradient - 35°

h. Ammunition stowage - Manual lists stowage for only 48 rounds.
   However, tanks examined have had stowage for 70 rounds with 22 rounds being stowed in the rear of the turret.

i. Transmission - 8 forward - 4 reverse speeds.

j. Maximum speeds - 25.8 mph. Reserve - 2.1 mph.

k. Speed on roads: 23.6 mph, cross country: 9.3 to 10.4 mph.

l. Radius of action - Roads - 106 mi.
   Cross country - 74.4 mi.

m. Track—Two tracks are listed as being used: The normal combat track 31 1/2" in width and a transport track 26" in width. No tanks have been located however, with the narrow track fitted. Ground pressures with the two are as follows:
   Combat track————-14.3 psi
   Transport track——17.5 psi

For the Ordnance Officer:
GEORGE D. DRURY

Description and Service Chart
for Panzerkampfwagen Tiger Model B
Chassis No. 280101 MAH 119

Technical Data:
Engine

Type - - - - - - - - - - - - - - - Maybach HL
- - - - - - - - - - - - - - - - - 230 P30 (High Output)
Stroke - - - - - - - - - - - - - - 145 mm
Bore - - - - - - - - - - - - - - - 130 mm
No. of cylinders 2x6 V-shape - 12
Piston displacement - - - - - - 23 Liters
Compression ratio - - - - - - - 6.8 to 1
Power output - - - - - - - - - 600hp at 2600rpm
Ignition - - - - - - - - - - - - 2 magnetos with built in distributor
Distributor - - - - - - - - - - Automatic
Fully advanced ignition through centrifugal governor (measured to position of crankshaft) - - 30°
Firing order of cylinders - - - 1-8-5-10-3-7-6-11-2-9-4-12
Lubrication - - - - - - - - - - Pressure lubrication with geared pump
Cooling system - - - - - - - - Circulation pump cooling system
Oil system - - - - - - - - - - - Water cooled
Oil cleaner - - - - - - - - - - FAUDI - Large surface filter
Carburetor - - - - - - - - - - 4 Solex double air chute down carburetor
(cross country) Type 52 G. - FF 11 D
Air cleaner - - - - - - - - - - 2 cyclone oil with bath air filter

Revolution indicator- - - - - Speedometer with red marked Danger point
Revolution control- - - - - - Governor
Starter - - - - - - - - - - - - - Bosch 6hp, 24 Volts
Generator - - - - - - - - - - - Bosch 700 Watt
Weight of power unit - - - - - 1300kg

Suspension
Type of suspension - - - - - - Overlapping
Type of bogie wheels- - - - - - Steel, rubber (damped)
Number of bogies - - - - - - - 9 each side
Diameter of bogie wheels - - - 800mm

Transmission
Type MM OG 40 12 16 B
Number of speeds - - - - - - 8 speeds forward,
- - - - - - - - - - - - - - - - 4 reverse

Speed at 3000rpm [engine speed]

Gear Range Miles/hour		Kilometers/hour
1	2.54	1.68
2	3.83	2.38
3	5.62	3.5
4	8.33	5.1
5	12.75	7.9
6	18.95	11.8
7	27.32	17.0
8	41.5	25.8
Reverse	3.39	2.1

Steering system- - - - - - - - Type: Two-radius steering System L 801
Number of steering ratios - - 2
(Note: This is thought to be a system similar to the Tiger I.)
Smallest turning radius - - - - 2.08m
Maximum turning radius- - - 114m
Brakes - - - - - - - - - - - - - Disc-Brakes LB 900-4
Material for Brake lining - - - Cast-iron
Diameter of Brake discs - - - - 565mm (outer)

Speed versus Maximum Range:
a. Roads: 38kph (23.6mph) /170km (106mi.) range
b. Cross country: 15/20kph (9.3 to 10.4mph) /120km (74.4mi) range

Gasoline consumption
Number of containers - - - - - 7 with total capacity of 860 Liters

Consumption for 100 km
a) Roads: 500 Liters (133 gal.)=0.465 miles per gallon
b) Cross country: 700 Liters (185 gal.)=0.335 miles per gallon

Liquid capacities
Water, cooling system - - - - - - - - - - - 114 Liters

To give the Tiger I sufficient mobility over soft ground, the Germans had to provide it with tracks wide enough to lower the vehicle's ground pressure. Unfortunately, the 28.5in tracks designed for this task were to wide to allow the Tiger I to be shipped by rail. The maximum width of any vehicles transported by European railroads is 10ft 4in. To overcome this logistic problem, the Germans found that it was necessary to give the Tiger I a second set of narrower tracks (21in wide) for transport and traveling on good roads. The Tiger I pictured on a Gotha 80 ton transporter trailer is fitted with the narrow transport tracks, while the wider combat tracks are stored under the vehicle's front hull. *British Army Tank Museum*

Oil

a) Motor oil
Motor - - - - - - - - - - - - - - - - - - - 25 Liters
Cyclone air cleaner - - - - - - - - - - - - 5 Liters
b) Lubricating Oil
Transmission
Steering - - - - - - - - - - - - - - - - - -30 Liters
Two final drives - - - - - - - - - - - - - - 14 Liters
Turret drive- - - - - - - - - - - - - - - - - 4 Liters
Fan drive, each side - - - - - - - - - - - - 3 Liters
c) Special oil
Shock absorber - - - - - - - - - - - - - - 7 Liters

Fuel

Total: 7 containers capacity - - - - - - - - 860 liters
1 container rear side: - - - - - - - - - - - 85 liters
2 containers upper left and right: - - - - - 290 liters
2 containers lower left: - - - - - - - - - - 80 liters
2 containers lower right: - - - - - - - - - - 65 liters
2 containers in fighting compartment: - - 340 liters

Automatic fire extinguisher extinguishing fuel: 3 liters

Fuel tanks

Fuel is stored in 7 tanks with total capacity of approximately 860 liters:
One fuel tank with filling tube in upper rear side in motor compartment, capacity approximately 85 liters
Two fuel tanks on upper left and right side of motor compartment, which will be submerged when tank crosses water, capacity approximately 290 liters

Two fuel tanks at left and right of bottom in motor compartment:
capacity of right tank - - - - - - - - 65 liters
capacity of left tank - - - - - - - - - 80 liters
Two fuel tanks at left and right side in fighting compartment underneath ammunition boxes capacity approximately 340 liters.

All fuel tanks are connected with another in such a manner that they can all be filled through one fill pipe which is located in the center of the engine compartment. With the help of a battery of valves it is possible to empty all the tanks in three phases. All fuel tanks can be emptied through a drain plug in the hull floor. All tanks are interconnected with an air vent system.

Fuel pumps

Two mechanically driven fuel pumps which are located on the left side of the motor housing, pump the fuel from the main fuel line into a fuel line which leads to the carburetor and fills the float chamber. The fuel line is routed so that its highest point is above the level of the fuel in the fuel tank. An air vent system to the fuel tank prevents a siphon effect in the fuel inlet pipe.

The fuel pumps are of the membrane type, driven by a push rod. If the float chamber is full, the fuel pump idles.

Like the British military the American Army was also interested in evaluating captured Tiger Is found in North Africa. In the US Army it was the job of the Foreign Materiel Branch at Aberdeen Proving Ground—home of the Ordnance Corps—to collect technical intelligence on enemy equipment. To receive information on enemy equipment as fast as possible, the Ordnance Corps and other technical services set up Enemy Equipment Identification (EEI) units to travel to combat areas to view and study captured weapons and equipment. The picture shown is from one of their reports and shows the foot of an American soldier on the combat track of a Tiger I. *US Army*

The HL230 engine is not equipped with an electrical fuel pump, but has a small hand pump with which it is possible to pump fuel into the carburetor, thereby avoiding the mechanical pumps. The pump handle is located under a flap in the bulkhead.

Turret drive

The turret traversing mechanism housing contains a clutch system for the two main drive shafts from the engine to the transmission. Turret traversing torque is derived from the main drive shaft in the housing, connecting through a drive gear to a fluid drive on the turret ring. The traversing mechanism idles until the fluid drive is engaged.

Brakes

The disc brakes are engaged either by the brake pedal or brake levers. The levers can be locked to serve as parking or emergency brakes. The brakes must not be used for steering — they should only be used for steering purposes in an emergency.

Width of brakes (disc and lining) – – 66mm
Permitted minimum width – – – – – 58mm
Clearance of brakes can be measured through small holes in brake housing each side
– 0.5-0.7mm
Free travel brake lever – – – – – – – – 13° - 45mm

The brake lining is only loosely in contact with the brake discs. The process of braking is mechanical. Braking torque is exerted by 29 ball bearings which are located between the brake discs. Tightening of discs is effected with the help of 6 springs. The brake rod to brake lever linkage has a length adjustment at the lower eye.

After the brake lining has been worn, the linkage of the brake lever has to be shortened. If the width has been worn to less than 58mm the brakes must be replaced.

Final drive

The final drive is located at the front of the hull on a strong support. Sprocket power is transmitted from the steering gear through two power transfer shafts to the right and left. The gearing is a double herringbone reduction set which compensates for any longitudinal misalignments.

The two final drive housings are symmetric and interchangeable between the left and right sides of the vehicle. Lubricating oil is fed through a feeder line from the crew compartment. The final drives can be filled by using a funnel through inlet tubes located to the right and left of access hatches. The cap of the oil gauge pipe should be taken off to allow the air to escape while filling. Otherwise, the oil will flow very slowly through the feeder line.

The side shafts of the steering gear are flanged and connected to the pinion of the final drive. Speed reduction is accomplished by a large spur gear and a planetary gear set. The sprocket carrier is bell-shaped. It is fastened with 10 screws and 3 bolts. Oil is contained by gaskets and a labyrinth seal on the roller-bearings. The final drive shaft is sealed by two packing rings and labyrinth seals. If leaks occur, grease can be forced through fittings in between the two packing rings. Dirt and water is prevented from entering through two center rings on the sprocket wheel.

The final drive gearing is oil spray lubricated. The oil is sprayed into the housing and runs over the hub of the large gear into the bottom of the housing near the oil drain plug.

From an 1943 US Army technical intelligence report, comes two pictures showing some of the components that make up the Tiger I's water-based engine cooling system. The picture on the left shows one of the vehicle's two radiators, while the picture on the right shows one of the vehicle's two pairs of fans. The radiators and fans were found on either side of the Tiger I's engine in separate compartments. The entire system was considered most unusual by Allied military personnel when first examined. The onboard water in the system was circulated by a centrifugal pump. *US Army/US Army*

This photo shows what is left of an early model Tiger I after British military personnel have torn it apart in an effort to understand all of it's technical features. The photo dates from early 1943 and clearly shows the vehicle's steering unit in the very front of the hull compartment. Due to the heavy weight of the Tiger I, the Germans used a fairly complex and expensive power-steering system in it. This was in sharp contrast to the much simpler and cheaper clutch-and-brake system used in most Allied tanks. The large circular object located on the far left of the steering unit is one of two disc-brake drums. *British Army Tank Museum*

Suspension

The overlapping suspension consists of 8 inner and 10 outer bogies. Each side has 9 wheel arms, 5 outer, and 4 inner bogie wheels. Each wheel arm is connected with the hull through a torsion bar which fits into a pressure lubricated housing. All bearings are greased by use of a grease gun. Bearings are lubricated from central lubricating positions. One lubrication position is located behind the radio operator and driver's seats underneath the floor; the other one is located beside the fuel tank on the floor of the crew compartment. The grease is contained by two packing rings which are arranged to allow grease under pressure to escape through the outer flange (relief valves).

Bogie wheels are composed of strong sheet steel discs which press upon two rubber rings which hold the outer rim. The bogie is fastened to the hub by two conical rings which are divided and held together by a thumbscrew (SW 17mm).

Hubs for inner and outer bogies are different, but both have Timken-type bearings. It is very important to avoid over tightening of bearings. If the bogies are removed, the hub remains on the wheel arms.

The torsion bars on the first and last wheel arm have a higher spring rate. All have the same type splined ends.

[NOTE: In contrast to the Tiger I, which had interleaved road wheels, the Tiger II had an overlapping wheel arrangement. With nine axles, wheels were placed alternately on the outside or inside of the tank track. Previously, each single alternate wheel had rotated be-tween two wheels to its front and rear. That earlier arrangement had caused ice, rocks, and other obstacles to jam the track mechanism. While the overlapping wheel arrangement on the Tiger II was an improvement over the earlier system on the Tiger I, overlapping wheels place a potentially damaging twisting load on tank tracks. Because of this problem and the fact that the interleaved and overlapping wheel arrangement systems are heavier than the more typical double road wheels as found on most World War II tanks, they were never used in any other postwar tank design.]

Shock absorbers

The two front shock absorbers are attached to the forward wheel arms beside the driver and radio operator. The front shock absorbers can easily be lubricated with a grease gun. The two rear shock absorbers are attached to the rear-most wheel arms beside the lower fuel tanks. The rear units must be lubricated through the fittings at the rear central lubricating position.

The shock absorbers resist wheel arm motion only on downward wheel strokes. The absorbers are filled with a thin special oil. The downward stroke is limited by a rubber bump stop which is impacted by the arm at motion extremes. The shock absorber clevis pins are removed by a special tool. Tightening of the union nuts of the shock absorber arm is done with C-spanner 155/165 (Special tool).

Track

a) Cross country track: 800mm. Ground pressure with special track is 1.02kg/cm^2.
b) Transport track: 660 mm. Ground pressure with special track is 1.23 kg/cm^2.

This overhead photo is of the rear engine deck of the Tiger II located at the Patton Museum. In the center of the engine deck is one of two ventilating fan covers located on the engine access hatch. The other ventilating fan cover is hidden by the rear of the Henschel turret. On either side of the engine access hatch are the radiator fan covers. Behind the radiator fan covers are the exhaust outlets. The large circular cover located on the rear of the engine deck is for the Tiger II's deep fording equipment, which was never fitted except for early testing purposes. *Michael Green*

Pictured is the removal of the Maybach HL 230 engine from the Tiger II located at the British Army Tank Museum. The engine is to be restored to running condition. It will then be placed into the hull of the museum's Tiger I, which now lacks it's original engine. The museum's plan is to eventually restore the Tiger I to fully operational condition. The decision to restore the Tiger I to running condition and not the Tiger II is based on the fact that the Tiger I saw combat with the German Army. The museum's Tiger II was only a prototype vehicle that never saw combat. *British Army Tank Museum*

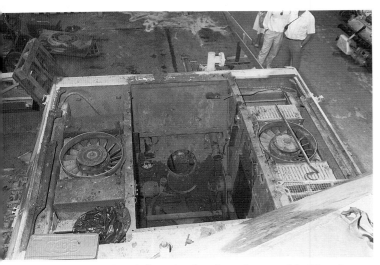

This overhead photo is taken from the top of the Tiger II prototype tank on display at the British Army Tank Museum. The view is of the vehicle's rear hull compartment. The vehicle's entire rear engine upper deck has been removed as well as it's gasoline-powered Maybach HL 230 engine. Visible on either side of the now-empty engine compartment are the vehicle's twin radiator fan blades. The HL 230 engine could produce up to 700 metric hp. Most modern main battle tanks are powered by high-powered diesel engines that produce up to 1,500hp. *British Army Tank Museum*

The cross country track is too wide for railroad transport and must be replaced by the transportation track when shipped by rail.

The cross country track has 46 double shoes which are connected by track pins. These pins are equipped with a head on the inside and a locking ring on the outside which in turn is secured by another pin which fits through a hole in the track pin.

The transport track is the cross-country track for the Panther and has split rings instead of locking rings to secure the track pins.

To improve traction, grousers can be attached to the track shoes. Eight spare track shoes are fastened to the turret.

Weight of a double shoe cross country track: 62.7 kg / transport track: 42.9 kg.

Track tension is adjusted at the rear idler by means of a wrench.

Rear Idler

The rear idler is mounted to a crankshaft having two sets of ball bearings. The idler arm passes through two pressure lubricated housings. Both bearings are lubricated through a grease fitting. Grease is pressed from the outer bearing through a tube to the inner bearing. Both rear idler ball bearings are lubricated through a grease fitting on the outside.

The track tensioner is adjusted by means of double box spanner.

Ventilation of fighting compartment and exhaust pipe

A blower behind the engine forces air from an opening on the deck through a duct to the bulkhead and from there into two smaller ducts which lead to both sides and finally into a duct surrounding the exhaust pipe. After cooling of the exhaust, the air is taken up by the radiator cooler.

Cooling of transmission

Transmission oil is cooled by a flexible pipe which leads through a water filled cooler in the crew compartment. The oil circulates under pressure from the transmission oil pump. Cooling water can be replaced from the fighting compartment whenever the glass indicator gauge shows the water level in the water tank to be low.

In cold weather, the water will freeze if it is not drained. The water can be drained through a drain plug under the transmission housing in the hull floor.

Ventilation of engine compartment

An air intake duct opens through the left side of the engine compartment to ventilate this compartment.

Ventilation of Cyclone Air filter

On each side of the Cyclone Air filter is a small cavity for trapping dust particles. This dust trap is connected with the vent by a flange and flexible tube.

Exhaust pipe

The exhaust system leads from the engine to the exhaust pipes in the side of the hull. The engine and exhaust system are connected through a double ball and socket joint so the engine can move independent of the exhaust system. The two exhaust pipes in the rear are heavily armored and are equipped with a sheet metal heat shield.

Electrical equipment

Generator

When the engine is running, the generator supplies all electrical accessories and also charges the batteries. A voltage regulator keeps generator voltage constant regardless of engine speed. The regulator also adjusts the output voltage depending on the condition of the batteries to avoid overcharge. The generator commutator, which is subject to overheating, is equipped with a vent.

The regulator is installed separate from the generator unit. It has an automatic switch which connects the battery with the generator as soon as the voltage output is sufficient to charge the batteries. If the voltage output decreases, it breaks the circuit to the battery.

Starter Mechanism

The Bosch-start VP is a "Hauptstrom" electromotor with adjustable armature. The starter requires 24 volts. A switch system connects the two 12-volt batteries in series to power the starter when the starter button is pushed. The starter shaft/pinion are connected through a clutch that disengages the starter when the engine starts.

Wiring System

Two batteries of 12 volts each are connected in parallel. When the starter button is pushed, a battery switch (SF/Se8) connects both batteries in series and increases the voltage to 24 volts.

Storage battery

The master switch which disconnects the entire electrical system is located on the bulkhead and can be reached from the crew compartment. All electrical lines are fused. On the panel are two fuse boxes with eight fuses of 15 Amps each and two fuses of 40 Amps each. The same panel is equipped with a connector for an extension headlamp (Magneto lamp). All lamps use 12 volts.

Electrical Heater

A 100 watt battery-powered electrical heater can be used in cold weather. A special hot-plate with a capacity of 300 watts with an extension plug is provided for cooking purposes. A pilot light indicates when the current is turned on.

Automatic Fire Extinguisher System

The fire extinguisher system controls fuel fires at the carburetor and fuel pumps. It uses spray "CB" and sprays through four nozzles. The three liters of extinguishing fluid are sufficient for five discharges. Heat sensors are connected to electrical valves with nozzles located in potential fire areas. If the temperature reaches 120°C, the valves open and discharge the fluid for seven seconds. If the fire is not extinguished by then, a timer will open the valves for another seven seconds and so on.

Cranking system.

A cranking system is installed just above the electrical starter and connects with a pinion which fits into the flywheel gear. The engine crankshaft is equipped with a dog clutch into which the crank fits. The starter linkage is used to push the pinion through until it fits into the flywheel gear while the engine is at a standstill. This way the flywheel can be turned by hand crank. As soon as the engine starts, the pinion disengages itself. If

This rear view of a Tiger II fitted with a Porsche turret, shows the dual engine exhaust pipes located at the rear of the vehicle. Both the Tiger Is and early prototypes of the Tiger IIs had upright jacketed exhaust pipes. Field experience showed that hot exhaust gases were being sucked into the Tiger's cooling system causing numerous engine problems. To prevent this problem on the production models of the Tiger II, new unjacketed exhaust pipes—which were bent to direct the hot exhaust gases away from the vehicle's air cooling intakes— were fitted. The crew of the vehicle pictured have added what looks like a Tiger tank fender as an additional way of deflecting exhaust gases away from the engine cooling intakes. *British Army Tank Museum*

the motor does not start, repeat the same process. Under no circumstances should the pinion be engaged while the engine is running.

Note: For engine HL230P30 (Pz.Kpf Tiger Model B), the hand crank is found at the right side behind the engine oil tank through which the crankshaft passes.

The hand crank fits into a small opening at the right side of the hull just below the exhaust pipe. The opening is protected by an armor plate.

Crankshaft Gasoline Starter

A large opening covered by armor plate is located behind the center of the crankshaft and is equipped with two brackets for the gasoline starter. The large cover remains in place at all times; to insert the hand crank, just remove the small plate covering the hole in the large one. The starter rests on both brackets and must be secured against movement. The claw of the hand crank fits into the claw of the crankshaft.

Prior to the 1930's, tank turrets were turned by manually operated hand cranks. As newer tanks were designed with larger and heavier turrets, it was necessary to provide them with a powered traverse system. There are two types of power-operated turret traversing systems; electric and hydraulic. The Tiger I and II were both fitted with a hydraulic turret traverse system, plus the standard manual controls. The bottom shows the hydraulic unit on the turret floor of the Tiger I. The top shows the hydraulic unit of the Tiger II located underneath the gunner's manually-operated elevating handwheel. Right behind the elevating handwheel in both pictures can be seen the gunner's firing handle for the "88". Both photos were taken from the loader's positions in their vehicles and in both pictures the gunner's seat can be seen. *British Army Tank Museum / Tank Magazine*

General Dwight Eisenhower walks past an overturned Tiger II somewhere in France in 1944. General Eisenhower was very upset when he found out how poorly American tank and antitank guns performed when placed up against German Panther medium and Tiger heavy tanks. Besides the various service openings visible on the bottom of the hull there can be seen the Tiger II's emergency exit hatch opening in the bottom left hand side of the picture. Also shown to good effect is the Tiger II's overlapping wheel arrangement. *British Army Tank Museum*

Tiger II Driver's Manual

Another interesting Tiger II wartime manual (translated into English by Mr. Charles Lemons of the Patton Museum) is the *Handbook For the Tank Driver* dated September 1, 1944:

This Handbook for the Tank Driver serves as an aid for the training, driving operation, and maintenance on the Tiger Model B. It covers a range of subjects for use by driver's school classes on the Tiger Model B, as well as serving the driving instructor as training reference and the driver as a reference book.

The handbook covers the necessary driving operations in a short and concise manner in order that, through correct and considerate use and appropriate maintenance, the tank will remain ready for service. Only those subjects concerning the operation of the tank by the tank driver are discussed.

The vehicle maintenance schedule is to be left in the tank. The instructions contained within are to be followed completely.

Operating Instructions (Transmission)

1. Starting:

Set the direction selector to "LEERLAUF" (neutral). Step on the clutch pedal and start the engine. While the engine is running, let out the clutch. This will allow the transmission to warm up. If the vehicle has been sitting for a time, especially in cold weather, the transmission must be warmed up until it is warm to the touch. Only after it is warm, is the oil in the transmission thin enough for the gearshift and steering to work satisfactorily.

2. Driving:

Step on the clutch pedal to release the primary clutch. Set the direction selector from "LEERLAUF" (neutral) to the desired position (RUCKWARDS - reverse, or VORWARTS - forward). Push down on the accelerator until the engine rpm's are about 1600 and slowly release the clutch.

3. Shifting while driving.

To select the desired gear on the shift handle, push the handle to the right and back into the gear position you want. Use of the clutch pedal is not necessary.

Notice:

Direction selection and gear shifting are two separate and independent processes. To get the shift handle out of gear, it must be depressed until abrupt resistance is felt. During cross country or labored road travel, one or more gears can be skipped. It is, however, always best to shift whenever the vehicle speed changes through either braking, coasting, or acceleration, to the gear most appropriate to the speed.

Chart of Vehicle Speed per Gear at 2500 RPM (maximum engine RPM)

1st Gear	2 km/h	1.24 mph
2nd Gear	3 km/h	1.9 mph
3rd Gear	4 km/h	2.5 mph
4th Gear	7 km/h	4.3 mph
5th Gear	10 km/h	6.2 mph
6th Gear	16 km/h	10.0 mph
7th Gear	23 km/h	14.0 mph
8th Gear	34 km/h	21.0 mph
1st Gear (Rev)	3 km/h	1.9 mph
2nd Gear (Rev)	4 km/h	2.5 mph
3rd Gear (Rev)	7 km/h	4.3 mph
4th Gear (Rev)	9 km/h	5.6 mph

Notice

To avoid severe transmission damage, you should follow the gear/RPM chart at all times.

The best speed for the engine for upshifting is about 2300 RPM and for downshifting about 1700 RPM. For all shifting the engine speed must be above 1600 RPM, otherwise there will not be enough oil to operate the internal clutch or main clutch. Consequently, the clutch would interfere with the shifting of gears and result in severe transmission damage.

Starting

To unclutch, brake, or downshift in any of the first four gears, you put the direction selector into "LEERLAUF" (neutral) and let in the clutch. The direction selector cannot be shifted to "LEERLAUF" (neutral) when a gear higher than 4th gear is selected. In order to stop quickly while driving in one of the gears 5th through 8th, you must push in the main clutch and operate the brakes until the tank stops. You will then have

The Tiger II's suspension system consisted of eight inner and ten outer bogies (road wheels). Each side had nine wheel arms for five outer and four inner wheels. Each wheel arm was connected with the hull through a torsion arm which fitted into a pressure lubricated housing. At the front of the hull was the final driving sprocket, at the rear of the hull was the rear idler. Many of these features can be seen in this picture of the Tiger II now on display at the British Army Tank Museum. This particular photo shows the vehicle shortly after it's arrival in England. This vehicle is the second Porsche turreted prototype which came to England without a main gun. The large gun barrel behind the Tiger II belongs to a captured Jadgtiger armed with an 128mm gun. *British Army Tank Museum*

to hold the clutch in until one of the lower gears (1-4) is selected, at which time you can put the direction selector into "LEERLAUF" (neutral).

Reverse Travel

You can drive in reverse only in 1st, 2nd, 3rd, and 4th gear (5th - 8th gear are locked out). These four gear ranges should be used for cross country or heavy laden road travel. With the clutch in and the direction selector set to "RUCKWARTS" (reverse), you give it the gas and slowly release the clutch. For long distance reverse travel, 4th gear should be used. In reverse, you must steer opposite to the direction you wish to travel.

Turning In Place

Turn the steering wheel in the desired direction left or right, push in the clutch or put the direction selector into neutral and give it the gas. One track will travel in a forwards direction, the other track will travel in reverse.

Instructions for the Operation of the Tiger II Heavy Tank

Startup

a. Before starting on every trip:
1) Check the fuel supply and replenish as needed.
2) Check the oil level in both cooling fans and replenish as needed.
3) Check the oil level in both of the side reduction gear boxes and fill as needed.

4) Is the track damaged? Are any of the track blocks broken?
5) Any track pin keys missing?
6) Are the screws/bolts on the drive and road wheels tight?
7) Does the internal communications equipment work properly?

b. Starting the engine:
NOTE: A cold engine should only be started by hand crank or by external starter motor.

1) Open the fuel flow valve.
2) Switch on the master battery switch.
3) Switch off the air fans (only in cold weather).
4) Using the hand pump, fill the fuel lines and carburetor by pumping towards the furthest fuel tank to push out any blockages in the line.
5) Insert ignition key.
6) Work the starter carburetor.
7) Push in the clutch.
8) Insert the hand crank or attach the external starter motor, both of which are to be operated by the radio operator and loader.
9) When started, disconnect the starter apparatus and step on the gas.
10) Let the engine warm up and set the direction selector on the transmission to "LEERLAUF" (Neutral). When the water temperature reaches 50 degrees centigrade, the engine should idle at about 1000-1200 rpm's.
11) Turn on cooling fans.

A picture of the Tiger I driver's controls. Above the steering wheel is the driver's laminated glass vision port in the front hull plate. Vision through the port is controlled by the small hand wheel on the upper right of the steering wheel. The hand wheel lowers or raises an exterior sliding armored shutter. Two spare vision blocks can be seen in this picture, stored above the driver's instrument panel. Under the instrument panel is the pre-selector lever for gear changing. The driver on the Tiger I was also provided with an fixed periscope mounted in the hatch above his head. *British Army Tank Museum*

c. While the Engine is Running:
1) Check the oil level with the engine at idle.
2) Check the fluid level in the transmission with the engine at idle.
3) Check the oil pressure. With the engine at 2000 RPM, the pressure must be a minimum of 3.5 atm (52 psi). If not, the engine must be shut down and the source of the problem determined.
4) Did the battery charge warning light go out at about 1000 RPM?
5) With the engine running and the vehicle at rest, CARE MUST BE TAKEN THAT THE STEERING WHEEL IS NOT DISTURBED FROM THE MIDDLE POSITION DURING THE EXIT OR ENTRY OF THE DRIVER. Also ensure that the direction selector on the transmission is set to "LEERLAUF" (Neutral) to keep the vehicle from moving.
6) Test the hand and foot brakes by moving the vehicle a short distance backwards and forwards.

Driving
While you are driving, be sure to pay attention to the following:
1) Tachometer: It should remain outside of the red areas.
2) Oil Pressure: At 2000 RPM, it should not go below 3.5 atm (52 psi).
3) Water Temperature: Should remain between 80-85 degrees C.

a. On the Road:
1) Disengage the hand brake.
2) Start on the level in 3rd gear.

Driving and Shifting:
1) For a smooth acceleration of the Tiger, make timely gear shifts.
2) In every gear, you should keep the rpm's between 1800-2000.
3) Up shift with rpm's at 2300 and downshift with rpm's at about 1600-1700.
4) While driving, DO NOT RIDE THE CLUTCH!

Braking and Stopping:
1) Brake with either the foot or hand brakes (or both).
2) Shortly before stopping, disengage the clutch.
3) Shift the direction selector to "LEERLAUF" (neutral) and set the hand brake.

b. Cross Country:
Starting:
1) When starting on an upward slope, release the hand brake, and at the same time let out the clutch and give the engine gas. When starting on a downward slope, use the hand brakes.
2) When starting on upward slopes, start in 1st and 2nd gear.

Driving and Shifting:
1) DO NOT OVER-REV THE ENGINE. WATCH THE TACHOMETER! The maximum of 2500 RPM must not be exceeded.
2) Before driving on a slope, downshift to a lower gear.
3) Drive downhill in the same gear which you would use to drive up the same slope.

An interior view of the driver's position in the Tiger II, now on display at the US Army's Patton Museum of Cavalry and Armor located at Fort Knox, Kentucky. Unlike the box-like hull of the Tiger I, the Tiger II had a well-sloped frontal armor plate. The only hatch-down vision the Tiger II driver had was provided by a rotating periscope mounted in front of his hatch. The driver's seat was adjustable for both forward and backwards movement. The seat could also be raised or lowered, along with the steering wheel and accelerator when the driver had his head out of his hatch. The leather cushions for the driver's seat are missing from this vehicle as well as the driver's rotating periscope. *Patton Museum*

4) While driving downhill and using the engine as a brake, use the hand brake as needed.
DO NOT OVER-REV THE ENGINE!
The engine speed governor does not operate going downhill.

5) Avoid steering on slopes. Drive perpendicular to the incline and wait until the vehicle is on a level before beginning to steer.

Braking and Stopping:
1) For stopping, either the foot or hand brake can be used.
2) To stop the vehicle, you should shift to 1, 2, 3, or 4 gear and you do not want the direction selector in "LEERLAUF" (neutral).
3) Push the clutch in and put the direction selector in "LEERLAUF" (neutral). If you are going to park the tank, shut off the motor and shift the direction selector to "VORWARTS" (forward).

Stops on the March.

While stopped on the march, the Tiger should be checked using the following plan.

a. Checks for the Suspension and Track:
1. Track Pins, Track Pin Retainers, and Track Blocks.
2. Nuts and bolts on the road and drive wheels.

b. Checks for the Engine
1. Locate/identify the causes/origin of unusual or abnormal conditions (engine noises, dense, or excessive exhaust, etc.).
2. Cleanliness of the Engine Air Filters.
Knock out the dust every 50 kilometers.

Shutting down the Motor and Work Needed after the Trip.
1. If the engine is hot, let it cool for a few minutes at standstill and in neutral before shutting it down.
2. Withdraw the ignition key.
3. Upon every shutdown of the engine, turn the fuel shutoff valve to off ("zu").
4. Turn the master switch to off.
5. Top off the fuel tank.
6. Check the Tiger, assessing all damage. Make your reports to your superiors.
7. Put the vehicle back into order, with the driver and the "I-Dienst" (2nd echelon maintenance personnel).

Tiger Combat Mobility

Many people perceive the Tiger I and Tiger II as being slow and unwieldy because of their size and weight. This was not completely true. For their day and the roles they were designed to fill, the Tiger tanks did fairly well in some circumstances when compared to many Allied tanks. Capt. Henry W. Johnson, of the 2nd AD, stated in a wartime report: "The wider tracks of the Mark V and the Mark VI enables it to move much better cross-country and in muddy or snow-covered terrain, than the narrow tracks of the Sherman tank. The field expedient of duck bills added to widen the Sherman tread aids, but does not effect the advantage the German Mark V and Mark VI tanks have. It is my opinion that the Mark V and Mark VI enemy tanks are far superior in maneuverability to our Sherman tanks.

"The slow cruising speed of the German tanks enables them to move into position and to slip up on our tanks much easier than the loud noise of our own motors will enable us to move."

S/Sgt. Alvin G. Olson, a tank platoon leader, stated in a wartime report: "At Freialdenhoven, Germany, I saw a Mark V and Mark VI tank scarcely dig into the plowed field while the tracks of our M4 tanks were often deep enough in the same field to show the marks of the tank's belly dragging."

The capability of a tank to traverse soft soils without sinking depends on a number of interrelated factors. The most important is ground pressure. The heavier a tank becomes, the wider and longer its tracks need to be. The weight of the tank divided by the area of track on the ground is called *ground pressure*. Therefore, tank designers design for the lowest ground pressure (the widest and longest track footprint possible). The objective is to

The recovery of any large and heavy tank is an awkward and difficult job even under non-combat conditions. Tankers in all armies spend a lot of training time learning how to recover their vehicles from both man-made and natural obstacles. German tankers of World War II were no different. With the very poor automotive characteristics of the Tiger tanks, breakdowns were a normal occurrence. The heavy weight of the Tiger tanks was a serious problem since the only other German vehicle really able to recover a Tiger easily was another Tiger. This type of activity was frowned upon by the Germans since it placed both a heavy strain upon the vehicles involved and took an important weapon out of action. The two late-model Tiger Is pictured are somewhere in Russia. The stuck Tiger is being towed out of a ditch by a fellow Tiger. *Private collection*

distribute the weight over a large enough area to allow the vehicle to "float" on soft terrains. Tiger tracks were wide, and the vehicle was long, so it had relatively low ground pressure.

Another factor that contributes to soft soil mobility (part of what is now called *trafficability*) is the weight distribution. Excess weight in the front, back, or either side of the vehicle raises the ground pressure at that location and can cause a corner of the vehicle to "sink" in mud or other very soft terrains. The vehicle can be immobilized if this happens. The Tigers were fairly well balanced.

A third factor is traction. Tank tracks are designed to aggressively clutch the ground so that they do not slip.

Finally, a lot of power is required to displace mud and soft sand at high speeds. The power-to-weight ratio and design details of the Tiger suspensions allowed them to traverse muddy European fields at much higher speeds than the lighter-weight Allied tanks. The Tigers constantly surprised American tankers who were unable to cross muddy European fields that the Tigers seemed to glide over with the greatest of ease. The Tigers' advanced (for their day) torsion bar suspension provided plenty of roadwheel travel. Cross-country speed capability was also enhanced by the vehicle's long hull.

Mobility Problems

The Tiger I and Tiger II had their automotive weaknesses. These were more pronounced in the Tiger II because of its greater weight. The Germans were always less concerned with mechanical reliability than the US Army and, as a result, were always in desperate need of replacement tanks. They tended to rush their tanks almost straight from the drawing board to the battlefield. Hitler's personal interest in the Tiger tanks and his demands that they be fielded quickly also caused problems. This policy resulted in numerous automotive teething problems in the field, which, in turn, required an almost continuous series of minor modifications to keep the vehicles running properly.

Colonel William A. Hamberg, who commanded a tank battalion from the famous 5th AD during World War II, remembers: "Almost half the Tiger tanks we ran into during our drive across Europe were abandoned either due to mechanical problems or lack of fuel."

The range of most German tanks, including the Tiger I and Tiger II, was limited to roughly eighty-five miles because of their weight, powerful engines, and limited fuel tank capacity. When traveling cross-country, the range of the Tigers could drop to forty miles or less. Franz Kutz, who fought on the Russian front as a German infantryman recalls: "I was always very happy to see our tanks, especially Tigers. The only problem was their very short range, which meant they would always leave us when we needed them the most. When in battle with Russian tanks I always preferred the support of our 'Sturmgeschutz' [infantry support vehicles often used as

An overhead picture of the driver's compartment of the Tiger II currently on display at the French Tank Museum. Both the vehicle's driver and bow gunner had identical pivoting hatches which folded neatly on the upper hull when not closed down. In front of the open hatch can be seen the top of the driver's rotating periscope. Directly above the driver's open hatch can be seen the small opening for the gunner's TZF9d monocular sighting telescope. *Tank Magazine*

tank destroyers] who almost always stayed with us."

From an article by Lt. Colonel Albin F. Irzyk (US Army) that appeared in the January 1946 issue of the *Military Review* comes these comments: "It might astonish some to know that prisoners of war [Germans] claimed that some of their large tanks had a running time of a mere two and a half hours on a full vehicular load of gasoline. Thus, the tanks did not have the endurance nor the cruising ranges of our tanks [Shermans]. Therefore, in many instances they had to be transported by rail virtually to the front lines, unloaded, and put into the battle. How far could we have gone with our tanks if we had had to follow a procedure like that?"

The very short operational range of the German tanks was shared by many Allied tanks of World War II. Space under armor is very limited in a tank, and fuel

 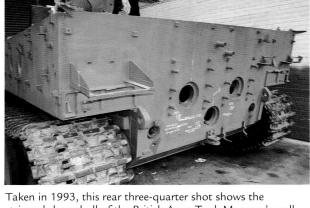

This interesting picture of the Tiger I located at the British Army Tank Museum, shows to good advantage both the box-like hull of the vehicle and its interleaved road wheel arrangement. The picture was taken in 1993 and shows the vehicle in a maintenance bay of the museum. In order to restore this vehicle to operational condition after so many years required that the tank be stripped down to its basic components and basically rebuilt from the ground-up. Notice the Tiger's turret has already been removed as well as all the exterior fixtures. *Jacques Littlefield*

Taken in 1993, this rear three-quarter shot shows the stripped-down hull of the British Army Tank Museum's well-known Tiger I which is being restored to operational condition. Visible in this picture are three rear engine access holes. The two holes at the mid-line level of the rear engine armor plate are for the muffler exhaust pipes. The two smaller holes on either side of the rear engine armor plate are for making adjustments to the vehicle tracks. The larger hole in the lower middle section of the rear armor plate is for the hand operated inertia starter. *Jacques Littlefield*

takes up a lot of room that is better utilized for battle. Also, large onboard fuel stores are dangerous if the armor is pierced. Thus, it is critical that large amounts of fuel be available near the front lines to support the tanks. This was a problem for the Germans; their logistical support units were under continuous air attack for much of the later part of World War II. The best tank in the world becomes nothing more than an expensive bunker without an uninterrupted flow of fuel.

Tanks have a short life span. Owing to their heavy armor and the necessity to use small lightweight engines, suspension components, and running gear to conserve space for potent weapons and onboard ammunition, the automotive components and running gear are always under high stress. Even in peacetime it is not unusual for a tank to require major overhaul after less than six thousand miles of use.

The German Army was well aware of the limitations of their Tiger tanks. Special instructions were issued to upper-level German officers to remind them that the Tiger tank could turn the tide of battle in their favor as long as they used them sparingly. For example, forced marches were taboo, since they placed undue

strain on the engine, transmission, and suspension systems. (Tiger tank tracks, which were made of cast-manganese, had a life span of less than 500 miles when subjected to hard use.) When Tigers were forced to move from one battlefield position to another, the instructions suggested that they travel individually. Traveling alone, a tank can be driven at steady speeds with minimal use of the clutch and brakes, thereby saving wear and tear on critical components. Because of their size and weight, the route of Tiger tanks had to be planned very carefully. Terrain features, bridges, manmade structures, and, of course, minefields all had to be taken into account. A number of postwar memories by German officers mention the necessity of changing their battle plans to accommodate the tactical and terrain limitations of the Tiger tanks.

An extract from an after-action battle report in the personal collection of World War II Tiger ace, Otto Carius, describes the problems encountered when Tiger tanks were overused: "As a result of continuous movement and the subsequent heavy stress on the running gear and motors, plus the lack of time available for maintenance service, damage results which causes the Tiger unit to break down when they are most needed."

CHAPTER 5

AMERICA'S ONLY TIGER

On October 10, 1992, Sgt. Chris Koski, a Track Commander with HHT, 5/15 Cavalry, led his crew, consisting of SPC George Bayer (driver) and PFC Anthony Nanney (assistant driver), on a mission which added another footnote to the history of the Armored Force.

In their M88A1 Armored Recovery Vehicle, they towed one of the last surviving German King Tigers into shelter at Trover Hall at Fort Knox, Kentucky. Home of the US Army Armor Center, Fort Knox is also home for the world famous Patton Museum of Cavalry and Armor, which was formally established in May of 1949. The museum itself was formed around a group of captured vehicles and equipment which arrived at Fort Knox in late 1946 from the US 3rd Army. The Tiger II, although not part of the Patton Museum's original collection, has been part of the US Army's historical collection since its transfer to the US Army Ordnance Museum in the late 1950s. Its arrival at the Patton Museum was part of a decision by the US Army Center of Military History to shift historic artifacts between the two museums, with an MBT-70 being transferred to the Ordnance Museum.

Charles Lemons, curator of the Patton Museum, talked about the background history of their Tiger II (vehicle number 332), which is now on display for the public inside the Museum. The following is an abstract of my interview with him:

The vehicle was built by Henschel in early September 1944 and was originally intended to be issued along with eleven other Tiger II tanks to a German Army Heavy Tank Battalion number 509. At the last minute, the Patton museum's Tiger along with the eleven other tanks were transferred to a Waffen SS Heavy Tank Battalion number 501. This unit formed an important part of the infamous "Kampfgruppe Peiper" which saw heavy action during The Battle of the Bulge. The vehicle was abandoned by its crew near the small Belgium village of Trois Ponts and captured intact by American soldiers on December 24, 1944. The fellows who recovered the tank remember it was just sitting beside the side of

the road, gun pointed down range. From the wartime pictures we have seen, it appears that the crew took all the vehicle's machine guns with them. However, the tank was still in perfect running condition went they left it.

In setting up our original exhibit I had assumed that it had run out of gas, but a veteran of the 463rd Ordnance Evacuation Company said "No, no, it wasn't out of gas." Asking him what he meant, he said "Well, we got in it and started it. It started, but it wouldn't move. It was frozen to the ground." It may very well be that is why the German crew walked away from it. It had sat there for so long that when the German crew started the engine up, it wouldn't move. A more likely answer is that the tank had nowhere to go anyway, since the only bridges across the Amblève River were in American hands, and they were tightening the noose around the Germans.

A Tiger II—abandoned for lack of fuel by it's German crew—is being gassed up by a number of American G.I.s. The tank, numbered 204, was part of Colonel Jochen's Peiper's 1st SS Panzer Regiment, which in turn was part of the 1st SS Panzer Division. This unit saw heavy action during the German's Ardennes offensive. After being refueled, the Americans drove the tank a couple of miles before it's engine caught fire and burned. *British Army Tank Museum*

Unsuccessful in their effort to return Tiger tank 204 to an area were it could be recovered by technical personnel from Aberdeen Proving Grounds. The G.I.s who managed to block a main road with Tiger 204 eventually pushed it off and down the steep hillside slope to the right of the vehicle. Tiger 204 had been part of an SS task force commanded by Colonel Jochen Peiper, famous for his role in the Malmedy massacre. Peiper himself, who had won a reputation as a tough and ruthless tank commander on the Eastern front, believed the Tiger tanks were too slow and under powered to be of much use in offensive actions. *British Army Tank Museum*

As it was, the American soldiers took some fuel and poured gasoline all around the outside of the vehicle and then lit it on fire. When the ground melted, they were able to drive it away under its own power. Now I don't know exactly why they then put it on a forty-five ton trailer, but I've got a good guess. Have you ever seen the book *Battle of the Bulge, Then and Now*? You may remember the pictures of Tiger number "204" in that book. One photo shows Tiger 204 sitting on a little narrow road with a whole bunch of people standing in front of it, trying to figure out how it works. Those soldiers standing and kneeling in front of the tank are the same men who recovered our tank, and the fellow kneeling in front of the vehicle is Gordon Love, whom I interviewed about Tiger 332. They drove Tiger 204 to that spot, then the engine caught fire and that was the end of that. The engine caught fire and burned and they couldn't get it restarted. It had to be rather embarrassing, since they had stuck a sixty-eight ton tank in the middle of a lane and a half road, which was the major roadway for that area. What they ended up doing was pushing it

off the road, literally into the valley below. After that experience with Tiger 204, they got smart. When they found Tiger 332, they loaded it on a trailer instead of trying to drive the tank anywhere. They took it to Spa, and that is where you see it in another picture. Later on, the guys from Aberdeen found it and decided that it would be shipped back to Aberdeen Proving Ground, Maryland, for technical tests.

General Impressions

Now as far as the vehicle itself, it was built by Henschel, the turret is made by Krupp, the gun by Dortmund-Hoerder. The whole thing's really rather an interesting vehicle. It had a lot of safety features in it. The Germans apparently put a lot of work into figuring out what was going to work well. It did have some major problems; the reduction gears on the sides were apparently too weak for full service. That tended to be where they would break. Another thing that we do notice is that the "teeth" on the drive wheels have slight bends in some of them where you can see that the torque of actually having to move the vehicle along has bent them slightly backward.

There's just some very silly things about the Tiger that, on the surface, didn't make a lot of sense to me. For example, the electrical system is 12 volt, but the starter is 24 volt. That's why you didn't start the Tiger using the electric starter unless you already had the engine warmed up. You either started it with a hand crank, which took two people, or you could start it with a "pony" motor. With a crank starter, you would spin the centrifugal starter up and then pull on the ring on the back of the vehicle, which would engage the starter and the tank would, hopefully, start. The "pony" motor could either be hooked to the two studs on the rear of the tank, directly into the crankshaft, or you could hook up a Kubelwagon or Schwimwagen with a short shaft, to the crankshaft.

The engine is a V-12 gasoline, made by Maybach. There's seven fuel tanks inside: two inside of the actual hull, and the other five are scattered around the interior of the engine compartment or next to the radiators. You also have four radiators, which apparently made for sufficient cooling, and then you had the fans. The fans are driven off of the engine and apparently also were used to force air through the air filters to supply air for the engine. The fans are two speed, which could be changed with a slide handle and gear. You pull it one way, and you drop the gear down one more and it would increase the fan speed, and you could also control the cooling by opening and closing vents over the radiators, which makes a lot of sense. There's a centrifugal clutch on the fans too, which also meant as the engine speeds up, the fan speed would also increase. You could actually spin the fans with the engine at rest. You had cooling that ran all the way through the thing.

As I said, the fans that cool the engine are not only used to do that, but they also help to draw clean air through the air filters and force the air down. It doesn't necessarily force the air into the carburetors, but it does force outside air into an area where the carburetors can get it. So, that means that they are dual purpose. It drags the air not only through the radiators, but it also drags air through the air cleaners. There's two types of air cleaners; an oil bath type and a dry type. In fact, when it's done, the fans force the dirt that is collected in the dry filter back out, so it's a rather interesting setup.

The other interesting thing is the way the filters are made on these vehicles. You don't have filters that you replace. All the filters in here are self-cleaning, or can be cleaned in place. Your fuel controls and everything are up by the driver...makes it real interesting. Your drains and everything are down underneath of the tank, where they're fairly easy to get to.

The hatches are very nice on this tank. The interesting thing is that your main hatch on your turret does not seem to have any gasketing. It's metal to metal almost, so I'm not sure how well that works. It's a rather interesting concept.

On Driving

The transmission is semi-automatic, as well as pre-select. Select a gear, push the handle to the right, push it up to the next gear notch, and back into the gear position. You have just changed gears. That's basically it. Direction selection and the gear shift are separate. In starting the vehicle, you place the direction selector into neutral. Because of the cross-drive type final drive, whenever the engine's running, you've got to keep your hands away from the steering wheel. If you don't, this thing will neutral steer, so you have to be very careful about what you do. If the engine is running and you turn the wheel, you are going to turn, and the driver's manual even warns you to please keep your hands off the steering wheel at all times if the engine is running. You would then push in the clutch, select either forwards or backwards, and then select your gear. Your gear selection choices - 1st, 2nd, 3rd, 4th, 5th, 6th, 7th, 8th. You're normally going to start somewhere between 1st and 4th gears, low, depending on what type of ground you're on. If you're on a hillside, you are going to start in 1st. If you're on a packed road, you start in 4th.

Let's say you set it in fourth. That's okay. The direction selector is in neutral. You push in the clutch pedal, set the direction selector to forward, and press on the gas. You let out the clutch and away you go. From that point on, you don't have to use the clutch pedal. You simply get up the rpm, let off the gas and quickly

Having learned their lesson from trying to drive Tiger tank 204 on the local Belgium roads, a search for another Tiger II was conducted in the general area of La Gleize by the same American soldiers who found Tiger 204. A Tiger II almost completely intact, numbered 332, was soon found sitting abandoned on the side of a road. Unlike Tiger tank 204, Tiger tank 332 was not out of fuel. The Americans who recovered the vehicle believed the tank tracks had become frozen to the ground, causing the German crew to quit the vehicle. After pouring gasoline all around the outside of the tank, the Americans lit a fire which thawed the ice in and around the tracks. The vehicle was then loaded on a trailer. *Patton Museum*

take the thing out of gear, slide the shifter up to the next gear, and put it back into gear. You're set, you're ready to go, and you can now increase rpm again until you are ready to shift again. You would downshift in the same way. There is a way of emergency gear shifting, which is a little more complicated, but it does work. Again, that's all in the manual.

Crew Positions

I've sat in the tank. The steering, all your gearshifts and everything is close at hand, although some of them are down a little bit. There's really no floorboards in the hull. There's only one escape hatch, and that's on the bow gunner's side. Your torsion bars are rather visible up near the front and you've got that huge shock absorber on either side of the vehicle inside. Your heating and cooling selector for the engine is also

set right next to the driver. All of your gauges are there to the right, and they are moderately well lit. They're only lit by internal gauge lights, but there's also one or two external lights that light them up. With the interior of the tank being painted dunkle gelb (dark yellow), I would assume that it would be fairly light inside as it is.

Your radio rack is there above the final drive and behind the driver's gauges. Although there is a built-in area for a ventilator between the driver and radio operator, there had never been a ventilator installed. The vent cover just hangs out there in the middle of nowhere, but there was no gasketing, nothing. In fact, there's no way of actually hooking up anything to it, so that's always confused the heck out of me as to why they bothered to install it. You have sheet metal covers on your transmission, I would assume, to keep yourself from getting burnt. They are stood off probably about an inch away from the transmission, so I believe they are heat shields. The controls for the fuel tanks are behind and to the right of the driver's seat. A tool box, with hinged lids, is directly behind the seat. Although there is a mount for the navigation compass, one was never installed. The driver's periscope mount is painted black, and has three spring loaded turn positions, as well as being designed to retract into the hull for changing periscope heads. Spare heads are stored in a simple mount on the left hull wall, very near the tubular "Atemschlacht" container for a breathing tube. However, the driver's position has the only truly adjustable seat. It's got a back to it, can fold down and raise up and does all kinds of neat things.

The radio operator's seat is basically a pad sitting almost on the deck. It sits on a little box-like structure and there's a folding backrest for it. As I said before, the radio racks sit between the operator and the driver, directly over the final drive and transmission. The ma-

These three pictures taken by the American soldiers who recovered Tiger 332, show the vehicle loaded on top of an M9 forty-five ton twelve-wheel trailer. The Tiger II, with a width of 12ft 3in and a weight of almost 70 tons, badly overloaded the trailer. In comparison, the M4 Sherman tank was 8ft 9in wide and weighed in at about 35 tons. In transporting Tiger 332 to a rear area shipping point, most of the tires on the M9 trailer burst into flames under the massive weight of the vehicle. *Patton Museum*

Tiger 332 was shipped by sea to Aberdeen Proving Ground, home of the US Army Ordnance Corps. At Aberdeen, a detailed analysis of the vehicle was conducted by the Foreign Materiel Branch to understand it's technical capabilities. Sometime shortly after World War II, Tiger 332 was sectionalized for display purposes along with a number of other historical armored vehicles. The entire right side of the vehicle's turret and a good portion of it's right hull were removed. *Ordnance Museum*

chine-gun mount and a large circle around the mount base is painted black. The radio mounts are gray, with the cabling being unpainted steel wire mesh covered. To the radio operator's right is main gun ammunition storage with a small double rack for spare periscope heads mounted on the lower wall. There is also a storage rack for two machine gun barrel carriers, which are angled backwards at about a 60 degree angle. Under the deck, just behind the radio operator's seat are the mounts for the radio power supplies and dynamotors. There is no machine gun ammunition storage in the radio operator's position, all of the ammo bags being stored in racks around the turret ring base or on the cross beam just forward of the turret. On the forward side of the same crossbeam is a circular strap mount, but I have no idea what was stored there, as it was too small for the standard gas mask container. As with the driver's position, there is also a tubular container for the "Atemschlacht."

Getting in and out of the driver's and the bow gunner's positions into the turret is not something I'd wish on very many people. The bow gunner's position is much easier to get out of, but if you try to leave the driver's position with the turret facing forward, it is nearly impossible. You almost have to turn the turret to one side to get from one position to the other because of the placement of the gunner's seat and the traversing handle. The fact that there is a shield that comes within 18" of the deck at that point basically blocks you from even getting up in there. If you turn the turret, ... say 90 degrees to either side, you can get into the turret. But with the turret facing forward, the driver really does not have

very many options. If you tried real hard, I think you could probably get out. The main weakness is the fact that, if the driver got into big trouble and really needed to get out using the escape hatch, the driver's a dead man - literally. If the gun is facing forward, he'd better be real thin and real agile, or he's never going to get out of that position. Everybody else can get out of the escape hatch except for him.

The most crowded person in the tank is actually the gunner. He's kind of packed in there. The gunner's

In 1957, Tiger 332—along with a large number of other historical vehicles—were forced from the building they had been stored in since World War II. They were then placed in an outdoor storage area. Tiger 332 did have it's exposed sides covered with thin sheet metal. However 24 years of East Coast weather took a heavy toll on the vehicle's internal and external components. *Richard Cox*

got a lot of stuff for him to look at. Of course, our original gun sight is missing, but you can see where the gun sight would have been suspended from the ceiling and the front of the turret. Between the gunner's knees is the traverse handwheel, and off to the right, well within reach, is the elevation handwheel. The elevation on this thing is air assisted which, again, is another interesting concept. It's powered by air, and when it is operational, you could take two fingers and elevate that gun up and

down...beautiful. Your power traverse is right at your feet, and it has a lock that you can use to lock it, so as not to accidentally turn the turret. The firing mechanisms are well within reach. You're kind of far down but, of course, your sights are internally lighted, with the power coming from a small junction box mounted on the roof that you plug your sight into. The gun is to your right, with the traverse power pack (pump and motor) directly underneath the gun. A small box mounted

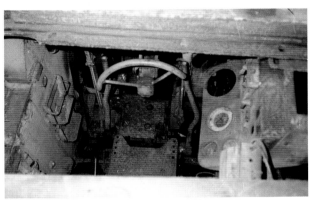

In 1992, a transfer was worked out between the US Army Ordnance Museum located at Aberdeen Proving Ground, Maryland and the US Army's Patton Museum of Cavalry and Armor located at Fort Knox, Kentucky. In exchange for an early prototype MBT-70 tank located at Fort Knox, the Ordnance Museum would allow the Patton Museum to restore and place Tiger 332 on display indoors. With the assistance of both staff and volunteers the difficult and time-consuming task of repairing 24 years of neglect began. This overhead picture shows the driver's position in the vehicle when it first arrived at the Patton Museum. *Patton Museum*

Looking into the rear hull section of Tiger 332, the bulkhead wall that separated the crew compartment from the engine compartment is visible to the right of the picture. To the left of the bulkhead wall is one of two hull ammunition racks located on the right side of the hull. Already removed from Tiger 332 was the vehicle's turret. The opening in the upper hull for the turret basket is clearly visible. *Patton Museum*

Looking into the forward hull compartment of Tiger 332, what is left of the driver's instrument panel is visible in the center of the picture. To the lower left of the instrument panel can be seen the top of the steering wheel. Directly above the steering wheel is the metal framework for mounting the driver's rotating periscope. The rectangular opening above the driver's compartment is normally covered by a large armored cover plate. In field use, the Germans used this opening to get at the transmission and steering unit. *Patton Museum*

This picture, taken from inside the hull of Tiger 332, shows the bow gunner position. The bow gunner was also responsible for operating the vehicle's radio equipment—which is missing from this particular vehicle. When fitted, it was mounted to the left of the bow gunner on top of the gearbox. The leather pad that the bow gunner sat on is also missing from this vehicle. However, the bow gunner's fold-away backrest can be seen in the lower right hand corner of the picture. Where the radio operator's feet would be located, are components from the vehicle's final-drive gear housing. *Patton Museum*

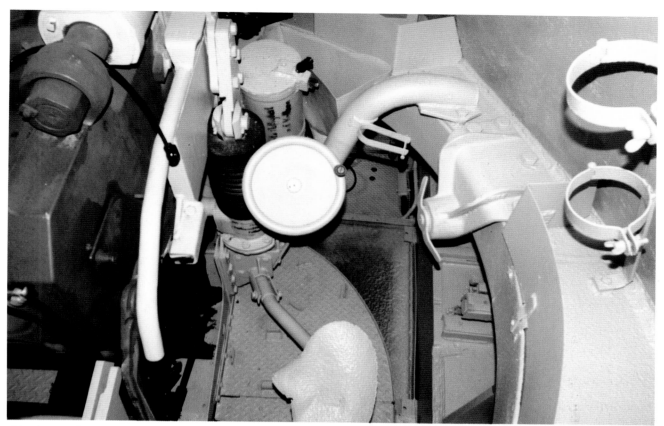

This picture taken inside Tiger 332 at the Patton Museum, show the loader's position. The loader sat on the right side of the main gun which can be seen on the left of the photo. Visible at the bottom of the picture is the loader's seat which could be folded upwards. Above the loader's seat is the auxiliary turret-traverse hand wheel. The only view the loader had outside of his vehicle when buttoned up, was a small overhead periscope fitted in the roof of the Tiger's turret. *Jacques Littlefield*

at eye level on the gun mount is hooked to the firing circuit, and lights up when the gun is ready for firing. To the gunner's left, mounted on the turret side, is an inter-communications box, where he and the tank commander plug in their headsets. The gunner's seat sets directly on an open box, which covers a small air pump powered by the traverse power pack. The seat pad is leather and padded with horsehair. The back of the seat is set on a bar bolted to the turret just above the turret ring and incorporates a footrest for the tank commander.

Close behind the gunner is the tank commander's position. His seat is bolted to the turret, just above the turret ring, and has a footrest just behind the gunner's seat. Directly above the commander is the main turret hatch, with its opening hand wheel at the commander's left. The commander has 360 degree vision due to the episcopes mounted around the cupola.

The loader has a bicycle type seat that sits real low on the right hand side of the turret. It doesn't look particularly comfortable. A helper handwheel for the traverse is mounted in the loader's position. Forward, along the right side of the main gun, is the coaxial machine gun, which is serviced by the loader when he's not

busy loading the main gun. The storage on the turret side next to the loader includes the 25mm flare gun and flares, as well as grenades for the smoke projector, which is mounted in the turret roof above the loader. The loader has a single small episcope for vision, which is restricted to the front of the turret. Looking at the bullet bag storage around the turret, it is obvious that the loader was responsible for getting the radio operator the necessary ammunition for the bow machine gun. The loader's hatch is rectangular and spring loaded to open quickly. It has a cable and "D" ring for pulling the hatch closed. The only other thing of consequence in the loader's position is the loader's safety switching box, mounted on the right side of the gun mount. It is with this box that the loader can safe the gun prior to or after loading.

The Gun

As I said, the gun was made by Dortmund-Hoerder, and is the final version of the tank mounted 88mm guns. The gun is electrically fired and, as such, incorporates a multitude of safety features. The gun can be electrically isolated from the tank's electrical system at two different points - the gunner's position and

The loader's hatch on the Tiger I and Tiger IIs were identical. The hatch itself was rectangular in shape and was hinged at the front. This picture shows the loader's hatch of Tiger 332 at the Patton Museum. The interior of the vehicle has already been cleaned of rust and been given a primer coat. The upper portion of the hatch—as well as the uncovered ventilating fan seen to the upper left of the photo—shows the rust which had begun to eat away this historical vehicle. *Patton Museum*

The turret of Tiger 332 was removed at the Patton Museum to allow easier access to the vehicle's hull during the rebuilding process. The Henschel turret—as fitted to Tiger 332—was a little over 7in thick on it's front plate. The turret sides were about 3in thick, with the roof of the turret being a little less then 2in thick. Unlike the fifty Porsche turrets which mounted a monobloc (one-piece) barrel, Henschel turreted tanks had a two-piece barrel which was easier to build. *Patton Museum*

the loader's position, by simply pulling a push-in plug. One safety is a pressure switch mounted in the recoil mechanism, and which will close only when there is sufficient oil pressure to stop the recoil of the gun. Another micro-switch, connected to the gun mount, closes only when the gun tube is run completely forward into battery. A second micro-switch, mounted to the left rear of the gun mount, will not allow the gun to fire if the loading tray is left in the upper position. The gunner's safety switch is very important in the chain of safety devices in the gun. This safety is also used in the Panther tanks and, in fact, they are identical. It has an arm, with a roller, projecting out of the left side of the box and which rests on a rail attached to the gun on the right hand side. A simple plunger projects from the front of the box, and a small flip handle projects from the left side. Once the loader has loaded a round, he "slaps" the plunger in, closing the firing circuit and lighting the ready light next to the gunner. The firing of the gun trips the switch open via the arm and roller, so that it must be reset by the loader after each firing. The switch may also be tripped by using the flip handle on the side of the box. A small window on the front of the box will either show "S" for sicher (safe), or "F" for fuer (fire), depending upon the position of the switch. If for some reason the loader decides that he needs to do something, or needs to step behind the gun, he can flip a switch on the side of the loader's safety box, which pops the plunger out, disabling the firing circuit. To fire the gun, the gunner simply closes the firing circuit mounted on the elevation handwheel. In case of electrical failure, the gun can be fired by using the manual blaster.

Basically, you would just track your target and just squeeze the hand wheel. Now if it fails to fire, directly in front of you and slightly to your right is something we've mentioned before, a manual blaster switch. It has a shield over it, so you just lift the shield and you can actually pick up the switch by giving it a twist to the right and lifting up. It will come out of the mount and then you can just "pop it" between your hands to fire it.

You could disable the gun firing mechanism several ways. The gunner can pull the plug on the thing. The power cord comes out of a small power box, mounted on the roof. It goes down and has several interlocks in it which I've mentioned before. The gun will fire only electrically. It is not a percussion fire gun, which makes it rather interesting. It means you don't have to worry too much about accidentally dropping the rounds and having the thing go off. Then again, if you lose your electrical power, you're dead. You are not going to have any power at all, which is why you've got that manual blaster.

So the loading procedure is something like this. Load: The loader brings the round up, either out of the turret rack or out of the hull rack, loads the thing into the gun. The breech closes, and he now steps off to the side and pushes the plunger on the safety box in with his hand. That lights up the ready light for the gunner, who now knows the gun is ready to go. The gunner can train the gun on target - whatever he needs to do. He fires. Immediately the gun goes into recoil. The safety switch automatically switches the firing circuit off. When the gun is halfway back in recoil, an air valve is actuated which allows high pressure air into the tube through the breech-ring, forcing all of the smoke out of the tube prior to the casing being ejected. As the gun begins its return to battery, the breech block opens, ejecting the spent case into the turret. The gun then returns into full battery, ready for another round. Because of their size, I doubt if you would fire very many rounds before stopping to toss the empties out of the turret.

The air used to purge the gun is being continually generated by the small pump underneath the gunner's seat, which operates as long as the engine is running. A small air flask is mounted in the turret floor, and is continually being replenished by the pump. This air could also be used to run a spray gun for painting or for filling tires for other vehicles, cleaning equipment, etc.

There is a small circular opening in the top of the turret which is closed by a hinged door, probably seven inches across, and it locks from the inside. I believe that it is probably the ejection port for casings. You flip it open from the inside and you can take one of those empty casings, push it up, and just give them a good heave upwards through that thing, and they'll drop to the outside and on to the ground. You could also probably leave the rear door open. I understand that if you fire that gun level, you could probably eject one of those rounds right straight out the rear door. For obvious reasons you really don't want to do too much of that. The rear door, you'll find, has one main use, and that is to load the ammunition from the rear. It is the only door big enough to really do that.

The Turret

The turret itself moves very smoothly, but not very fast. You have a two-speed hydraulic motor and pump to turn the turret. Now these are run off of the engine, and the system for doing this is pretty intelligent. The Tiger II does not seem to be as over-engineered as the Panther was. In the Panther you've got a lot of heavy gears and stuff. The Tiger seems much more circumspect in the way they did it. The traversing gear actually seems to take up less room inside the Tiger than inside the Panther. The storage inside seems to be fairly well laid out, except for the fact that everything seems to be reversed. These German loaders had to have been left handed, because that's the way you had to load; from the right side of the gun, whereas the Americans load from the left side of the gun. The turret is laid out to allow 22 rounds of main gun ammunition to be stored at the rear, 11 rounds on either side. With the aid of the roller mounted at the center, it is comparatively easy to load the main gun from there.

The construction seems to be very good, considering that it was made in late 1944. The roadwheels are in good shape, and the vehicle itself rolls very easily. The

brakes (on our vehicle) still worked when we got it. The emergency brake is designed to only lock the left track. You do have laterals, and you can steer the vehicle using them, but the manual says that it's not a good idea to do so. I think it's rather obvious if you're used to using that steering wheel, which actually turns the tank more like the M60 series or M1 tanks than it does anything else. If you start using the laterals, it will screw your mind up, because you won't be able to make the corners that you are used to when using the wheel.

The Germans tend to over-engineer stuff. They put a lot of protective systems in the oil system. You've got fairly high oil pressure. There is no splash, it's all pressure fed. In an American vehicle, your rods and bearings and stuff like that are normally splash lubricated. This engine has a ring at the very front of the crankshaft that has an oil line attached to it so that, no matter what the crankshaft is doing, it is always receiving

After being reassembled by the staff and volunteers of the Patton Museum, Tiger 332 was painted in a camouflage pattern similar to the one it had when it was found by the American Army in January 1945. After being placed on display within the museum building, Tiger 332 has quickly become one of the most popular exhibits in the Patton Museum. The museum is open year-round and is located at the entrance to the US Army Armor School at Fort Knox, Kentucky. *Patton Museum*

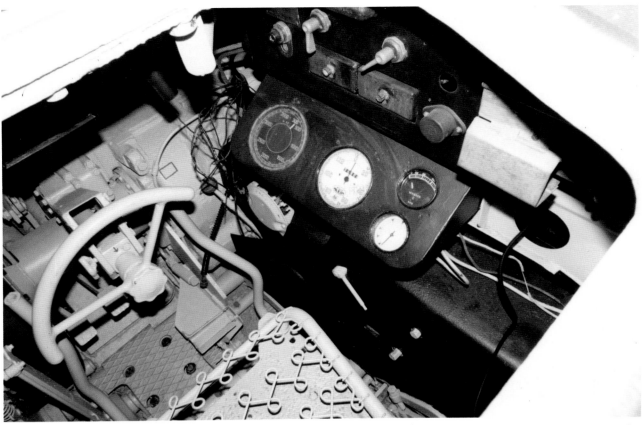

Looking down into the driver's compartment of the Patton Museum's semi-restored Tiger II, you can see the driver's instrument panel to the right of his seat. On either side of the steering wheel are the emergency steering levers. Because the Tiger I and Tiger II had power steering, they were easier to drive in some regards then most Allied tanks. However, a lack of skilled Tiger drivers was always a serious problems for the Germans in the last year of the war. Due to both a lack of fuel and extra Tiger tanks to train drivers on, many drivers arrived at their units without ever having driven a Tiger tank. *Jacques Littlefield*

oil. The crankshaft is hollow and it pressure oils all of the bearings, ...which I feel is rather a neat invention. Oil does leak out, and what oil does drip, drips into the oil pan. The pan is only there to collect the excess oil which has dripped off of the crankshaft. There are two pumps in the pan, and they are designed to return the oil to an oil reservoir, not the engine. From the reservoir, it is pumped into the engine and other mechanical devices. So you've got two scavenger pumps and a single main oil pump, which actually supplies the pressure. When you check the oil, you don't check it in the engine, you check it in the reservoir. The engine itself has other protective systems, such as the pressure activated valve which controls fuel flow to the carburetors. If the engine oil pressure drops below a certain level, this valve closes, shutting down the engine.

Paint

I kind of like the way they painted it, even the interior of this one. We did a much better paint job than the Germans did. When the Germans construct vehicles, all of their ferrous metals are painted in a red lead based

Taken inside Tiger 332 at the Patton Museum, this close-up picture shows the loader's periscope and mounting bracket. This fixture was mounted in the roof of the vehicle's turret. Above the periscope is a soft, shaped brow pad for the loader's forehead. Directly above the loader was another soft leather pad to protect him from banging his head on the roof. Also very visible within this picture are the welding marks that join the turret together. *Jacques Littlefield*

primer. There are a lot of parts that are painted at the various factories prior to installation, but when they start out, the vehicle itself is in red lead. Before they installed the electrical wiring, they painted the vehicle inside and out in dunkel-gelb. Whatever was covered up didn't get painted. The transmission is a dark gray color; gray or gray-black, and the steering mechanism is dark gray. The control panel is gloss black, but your upper panel, where all of the electrical switches are, was painted wrinkle-finish black. The radio racks are in dark gray, as are the radios. The plastic tubing which contained all of the lighting circuit wiring is a dark yellow plastic. Since all wiring was installed after painting, there is no overspray. Much of the wiring is contained in woven metal sheathing, silver in color, with the exception of the lighting circuits. When you get into the vehicle, you get the impression of somebody being very meticulous. All of the electrical wiring and electrical devices were installed after painting so that you don't get an overspray. Everything under the deck plates, on the other hand, is in red lead, because the deck plates were installed before they painted the interior. The seat frames are dark yellow, but the seat covers are made of black leather and stuffed with horsehair. Even that late in the war, they were still using leather stuffed with horsehair.

What stenciling there is, is done in black. It's very readable but there actually wasn't much stenciling. From what I can tell, the only thing they actually stenciled were warnings and notices, so that you knew if you did something, something might go wrong. A sign told you what the air pressure was inside the system, so you didn't do something stupid with the system. A couple of the switches that were on the firewall had "on" and "off" markings and then, of course, you had small data plates and stuff. Actually, that is about the extent of all the markings.

General Thoughts

There are two machine guns, but we haven't been able to find any place where they would have stored the machine pistols or their ammo. There is still a lot of stuff inside that confuses me, but I still like the way it's laid out. It actually makes a lot of sense. The radios are in one place; the intercom system seemed to work quite well, and all of the electrical power comes up through your slip ring. It's a very, very simple set up when you really get down to it. Just as American vehicles are simple, the German vehicles are even simpler. The Americans probably had no problems at all figuring out what was what, once you understood. You could get into this thing and drive it. If you couldn't figure how to drive it with the steering wheel, you could always drive it with the laterals. The clutching system probably drove them nuts though. They (the Americans) probably used that improperly until they got it to Aberdeen, unless they'd

already been briefed about the automatic transmission. They probably never shifted gears. As I've said, it's an interesting system, and even I have a hard time getting used to the way that thing works. If it wasn't for the problem of getting only 85 miles travel on 250 gallons of gasoline, and the problems with the steering gear, this thing is a fairly maneuverable tank.

If it neutral steers, it's maneuverable. I mean, you can't say that it isn't maneuverable. The fact that it would go across open fields where other vehicles would bog down is impressive. That gun would certainly kill anything on the field, and I can't see an American tank even laying claim to damaging one of these things except by getting very, very close. I'd have rather driven one of these things than a Sherman.

If the Germans had done a bit more, such as using better metal for the final reduction gears, they may have been able to do something. The big problem with the tank is that it is HUGE - 68 to 70 tons. I mean this thing is just gigantic. It was a sitting duck every place. Of course, most tanks are.

The vision for your bow machine gun is really not very good. I don't know why they even bothered. Your driver, on the other hand, could take quite a bit of a look around, and since he had a steering wheel, it was much easier for him to do that. Your tank commander's vision was pretty good, but he has blind spots close in and, of course, behind the tank there are big blind spots. Your loader, they give him an episcope, which is a small periscope, but it's really not worth while. Of course your gunner, he has his telescope, but there is really not much else for him to look out of.

In general, this was one dangerous vehicle. For its size and weight, it was much more maneuverable than most Allied tanks, and was capable of handling any vehicle sent against it. Mechanically, it had some major problems, which could have been solved had time been available. The final drives on each side were its Achilles' heel, and many of them had to be abandoned because of it. Its other problems would include things which you normally wouldn't think of or directly connect to the vehicle. Support, in the form of transport and recovery, was really lacking. The only vehicle capable of recovering a Tiger was another Tiger. It had problems in rail transportation, and many small bridges could not handle the weight. This severely restricted where the vehicle could go. On the road, it was slower than the mediums, but not that much slower. It was because the vehicle required special considerations when crossing bridges that columns were slowed by it. Fuel consumption was excessive and, basically, the vehicle was under powered for its weight. Fire control and sighting was superior to the Allies, and if infrared sighting had been introduced, it would have made the vehicle even more dangerous on the defensive.

CHAPTER 6

VARIANTS

Most armies, including the Germans, based a number of special-purpose variants on their standard tank chassis. Since there were so few Tiger tanks built, only a small number were ever modified to serve alternative roles. The following excerpts from an article on German armor written by Garrett Underhill and published in the 1949 September/October issue of *Armored Cavalry Journal* shed some light on the wartime context in which Tiger variants were deployed:

> During World War II and the 1920s, many armies experimented with various types of self-propelled guns. By the 1930s, the Allied powers of the West were broke, and the Germans were concentrating on tanks.
>
> Nevertheless, the German Artillery (could they have been empire building?) had the idea before the war

During World War II the Germans deployed a number of Sturmhaubitze (assault howitzers). Based on an older-model tank chassis, the assault howitzers provided the German tank formations mobile artillery fire-support. Because of combat experience in Stalingrad, the Germans mounted a small number of 150mm howitzers in a heavily armored vehicle known as the *Sturmpanzer IV* or *Brummbaer*. No more then sixty of these vehicles were built. This picture shows a *Brummbaer* somewhere in Italy during World War II. *Private collection*

> for a special armored support vehicle—which they called the assault gun. When it came out, Von Fritsch—still Army chief—assigned it to the Infantry. The Artillery continued to supply the crews and, through the war, ran the Assault Artillery School. The assault guns were first used in breaking through the Ardennes and smashing through the French positions on the Meuse in 1940.
>
> Properly speaking, the assault gun was an outgrowth of the light 75mm infantry howitzer. As such it had its roots in German World War I experience. Essentially different from infantry accompanying tanks of other powers (both in appearance, and in the fact that it relied wholly upon its shell-firing armament), it had very special tactics. It was the German version of an infantry-accompanying tank.
>
> As a result of war experience, a terrific expansion of assault artillery took place in 1942. Organizationally, assault artillery battalions remained GHQ [General Head Quarters] troops, being assigned to divisions for operations. SS Panzer divisions had integral assault gun battalions up to the end.
>
> As the war progressed, assault artillery *(Sturmartillerie)* developed. The original assault gun (actually a howitzer) blossomed into a family which was made up of *Sturmgeschütze* (assault guns, armed with *Sturmkanone*) and *Sturmhaubitze* (assault howitzers). The latter used the 105mm light field artillery howitzer in the light model. In the heavy model, the 150mm heavy infantry cannon was mounted. This latter was named the *Brummbär* (Grizzly Bear).
>
> The German system was to mount low in the front of a tank chassis a gun with very limited traverse. The front was well armored. In the original *Sturmgeschütz*, the top was protected only by folding plates. However, in the 1942 expansion, the IV's long 75mm was fitted along with the Mark IV's commander's cupola. The hull and fighting compartment were armored all over.
>
> Generally speaking, by avoiding a turret the Germans were able to mount in the chassis of any given tank the gun carried by the next larger tank.

Based on older-model tank chassises, the Germans developed a number of self-propelled or *Sturmgeschütz* (assault guns). With a high-velocity gun mounted in a hull-mounted superstructure and a non-traversable turret. These vehicles could be build both in large numbers and far more cheaply than the much more complex and expensive tanks like the Tigers. The vehicle pictured is an *Sturmgeschütz* 40 Ausf G armed with a 75mm gun and based on a Mark III chassis. *Jacques Littlefield*

When the long 75mm was fitted to the original *Sturmgeschütz* chassis, the improved assault gun had a weapon that could fight armor. This capability resulted in a metamorphosis; beginning in 1943, the original assault gun type became a hybrid assault gun tank destroyer.

The new models took the name of tank destroyer—*Panzerjäger*, or *Jagdpanzer*.

The armored force, which had jurisdiction over tank destroyers, objected to the limited traverse of the gun. The artillery and infantry overruled them. They preferred the added security afforded by the silhouette of the turret-less vehicle. They did not think that the added utility of a turret—which the armored force thought useful to engage targets of opportunity in proper armored force and tank destroyer missions—outweighed the proven value of the original squat silhouette design.

But the development of this type of armor—apparently not too well understood outside Germany and Russia—is a story in itself. Assault artillery might be termed an armored force trained for and assigned to the infantry. Assault artillery units were in a different class from breakthrough and other tank units which had, as part of their training, practice in tank-infantry teamwork.

The German Infantry and Artillery arms were much satisfied with their version of assault artillery. They effected no basic changes in tactical doctrine during the war; they only expanded basic principles, and added the AT function. The priority these senior arms attached to assault guns is well demonstrated by production records. While Germany was turning out 23,000 odd tanks in the war years 1939-44, she also turned out over 10,000 pieces of assault artillery.

The ultimate in assault weapons was the great *Panzer-Sturm-Mörser Tiger*— a 380mm (15in) rocket projector mounted on the very heavily armored *Jagdpanzer* edition of the Royal Tiger. [Note: The chassis was actually that of a Tiger I.] Eighteen of these monsters were built as a result of the slow progress the Germans made in the Stalingrad street fighting. Hitler felt that the five-foot long, 761-pound projectile this weapon fired could blow apart entire buildings. The hull could carry 12 of these rounds, which could be reloaded from the inside, and which could be fired to a range of 6,000-odd yards.

Essentially the *Pz.Stu.Mrs.* (assault mortar) was built to perform the same function as the British R.E.M.E.'s exterior-loaded "Flying Dustbin" as fired from a Churchill tank. But 6-inch armor sloped at 45 degrees gave the assault mortar even better frontal protection than was afforded its hybrid TD edition, and a greater degree of invulnerability than the Churchill.

The assault mortars appeared when the war was going the wrong way. Their only useful deed (in Nazi eyes) was their assist in the demolition of the Warsaw ghetto.

Extracts from an American Army report dated March 18, 1945, goes into some depth in discussing the various features of a captured German assault mortar based on a Tiger I chassis:

A 38cm (15in) rocket projector mounted on a modified Tiger I Chassis has been examined in the Ninth US Army area. Although the German nomenclature for this equipment is not known, it may be the ve-

Because of combat experience gained during the fighting for Stalingrad, Hitler had a special-purpose assault vehicle designed that could effectively destroy enemy pillboxes or fortified buildings at close range. The weapon picked for this job was a 380mm (15in) rocket projector. Because of the weapon's great size and weight it was decided to mount it on the chassis of the Tiger I tank. Only eighteen of these vehicles were built during World War II. To the Germans they were known as the *Sturmmöser* (Assault Mortar) Tiger. The *Sturmmöser* Tiger pictured is currently on display in a German Army technical museum located at the city of Koblenz. The vehicle was originally captured by the American Army in 1945. A number of years later it was returned to the West German Army for display purposes. *Paul Handel*

hicle referred to in German documents as the *Panzer-Sturm-Mörser Tiger*.

The vehicle projector is radically different in design and construction from any weapon previously examined. The propellant gases are deflected between the tube and liner by an unusual obturator, and escape through a perforated ring at the muzzle. The splined projectile fired by the projector is approximately five feet long and weighs 726 pounds. An unconfirmed report states that the range of the rocket is 6000 meters (6552 yards). The same source reports that the vehicle has a crew of seven, including a tank commander, a forward observer and five men to operate the vehicle and rocket projector.

The suspension, power train, engine and hull are those of the *Pz.Kpfw.* Tiger, Model E (Tiger1). The normal superstructure and turret of the tank have been replaced by a heavy rectangular superstructure of the type used on the *Panzerjäger* self-propelled guns. The superstructure is made of rolled armor plates and is of welded construction with the side plates interlocked with the front and rear plates. A heavy strip of armor is used to reinforce the joint between the front plate and glacis plate on the outside.

A ball-mounted machine gun, MG34, is set into the front plate on the right side.

A rectangular loading hatch, 62 inches long and 19 inches wide, is located in the center rear of the top plate. It is closed by two doors, one forward and one to the rear. The rear door can be opened independently of

the forward one and mounts a smoke projector, which has 360° traverse, in the center. The door is spring balanced and is hinged at the rear to open outward. A loading crane is mounted on the right rear corner of the superstructure.

The driver is provided with a double periscope mounted in the superstructure front plate. An opening directly above the driver's periscope permits the use of sighting equipment for the rocket projector. This opening can be closed off on the inside by means of an armor plate moved vertically by a rack and pinion arrangement.

A periscope with 360° traverse is mounted at the rear of the superstructure top plate.

The Mount

The mount consists of a large cast bracket extending through the front plate of the superstructure and welded to the inside. The inside of the bracket conforms to the spherical casting which acts as a cradle. The cradle is mounted to the bracket by horizontal trunnions.

This German Army picture from an instruction manual shows the manner in which the 380mm (15in rocket) was loaded onboard the *Sturmmöser* Tiger. Because the projector weighed over 700lbs and was 5ft long, it was necessary to provide each vehicle with it's own small crane. The vehicle could carry thirteen of these large rocket projectors when fully loaded. Once the rounds were inside the *Sturmmöser* Tiger, there was a folding loading tray with rollers that enabled the crew to place the large and heavy projectors into the breech of the rocket launcher. *British Army Tank Museum*

The tube is mounted in a spherical cradle supported by vertical trunnions. In elevation, the cradle and tube elevate together; during traverse, the tube pivots in the cradle—the cradle remaining stationary.

a. Elevation

Elevation is from 0° to approximately 85°, and provides the only means of regulating the range of the projectile. The elevating mechanism consists of a worm, wormwheel, and an arc and pinion on the left side of the projector and is operated by a handwheel. The elevating arc is bolted to a bracket which projects from the rear of the spherical cradle.

The projector and cradle are extremely well balanced and can be elevated with ease, with or without a projectile in the tube.

b. Traverse

Traverse is approximately 20° (10° right and left of center). For greater shifts in traverse, it is necessary to move the vehicle.

The traversing mechanism consists of a handwheel, worm and wormwheel, and a pinion and rack. The rack is bolted to the top of the rear bracket, and the other components are bolted to the top of the tube. A traverse indicator is graduated from 0 to 200 mils (10°) to the right and left.

c. Sight Bracket

The sight bracket is bolted to the front plate of the superstructure and is linked to the left trunnion. No range drum or scale was found in the vehicle examined. The azimuth indicator has a micrometer drum which is graduated from 0 to 100 mils and a hundred-mil scale graduated to 2 on each side of the 0 line.

Loading Arrangements

An ammunition loading tray is supported by tubular supports which fold into the floor when not in use. The tray is fitted with six rollers to assist in the manual loading of the projectiles.

A hand-operated winch on overhead rails is fitted to the roof of the superstructure. The rails run the entire width of the superstructure. The winch is used to place the projectiles in the storage racks and to carry the projectiles from the racks to the loading tray.

Ammunition Stowage

Ammunition racks are provided within the vehicle for twelve projectiles. One projectile may also be carried in the projector tube. Six racks are on each side of the fighting compartment.

Operation

The projectiles are placed on the loading tray by means of the winch and are then loaded by hand with the projector at 0° elevation. A plunger, fitted to the inside of the tube at the rear end, drops behind the projectile to prevent it from slipping back from its firing posi-

Always short of mobile-antitank vehicles, the Germans modified close to a thousand obsolete Czech-made light tanks into fairly effective *Panzerjägers* (tank hunters) by mounting in an open-topped superstructure, either captured Soviet 76mm antitank guns or German-made 75mm antitank guns. In it's final production form as pictured, the vehicle was known as the Marder III. Far from perfect, these make-shift vehicles served a useful purpose until replaced by newer generations of *Panzerjägers*. *Private collection*

Before tanks like the Tiger I could be built in large numbers, the Germans needed to field vehicles carrying enough firepower to destroy heavily-armored Soviet medium and heavy tanks. In an attempt to deploy the 88mm gun on a fully-tracked chassis as fast as possible, the Germans developed a self-propelled tank destroyer known as the *Hornisse*. Based on components of both the Mark III and Mark IV medium tanks, the *Hornisse* housed the very potent 88mm gun in a fixed mount, lightly armored, open-topped superstructure. Carrying forty rounds of main gun ammunition, the *Hornisse* had a four man crew. Later renamed the Nashorn, the Germans built over 473 during the war. The *Hornisse/Nashorn* pictured was captured by Allied troops. *British Tank Museum*

Shown here on display at the US Army Ordnance Museum, is one of only two surviving World War II era Panzerjägers (tank hunter) Tigers, originally nicknamed the *Ferdinand* by the Germans, after the designer Dr. Ferdinand Porsche. Subsequently, this was changed and the vehicle was nicknamed the *Elefant* (elephant). These vehicles were based on the chassis of the canceled Porsche Tigers, ninety of which were available when the Henschel design was chosen because of its better overall performance. Despite their poor automotive characteristics, Hitler wanted them armed with the 88mm gun and placed into service as fast as possible as tank destroyers. The vehicle pictured is a final production model featuring both a hull-mounted machine gun and a commander's cupola. *Michael Green*

As the war progressed, the Germans improved upon the assault-gun or tank-destroyer concept. Gone were the tall, open-topped, thinly armored vehicles like the Marder II and the *Nashorn*. Instead, the Germans deployed new vehicles based upon the chassis of the Czech T-38 light tank, the Panther medium tank and the Tiger II heavy tank. This head-on view of a *Jagdpanzer*, located on display at the US Army Ordnance Museum, shows the well-sloped frontal armor and the semi-fixed '88'. The gun itself could only be turned twenty-six degrees either way. However, designed as a defensive weapon that would lie in wait for targets, the lack of a tank's typical 360 degree traverse was not seen as a big handicap to the Germans. *Michael Green*

Somewhere in Russian lies this abandoned German Army *Elefant*. The missing track on the right side of the vehicle indicates that it may have run over an antitank mine. The lack of a hull-mounted machine gun shows this vehicle to be from the original production batch. The *Elefant* first saw combat during the July 1943 battles around the Russian town of Kursk. Even though it was armed well with the powerful '88' and protected by very thick armor plate, the *Elefant* proved to be an automotive failure. Difficult to drive and prone to constant mechanical breakdowns, the vehicle was greatly disliked by it's crews. *Ordnance Museum*

tion, 5 inches in front of the breech plate, when the tube is elevated.

As the breech plate is closed, the camming groove of a bracket, screwed to the top of the breech plate, cams a lock over the plunger.

The firing mechanism is then slid upward in a bracket which is screwed to the rear face of the breech plate and an igniter is inserted into the holder in the breech plate.

The firing mechanism is then slid down into the firing position and the projector is laid for elevation and azimuth.

When the lanyard is pulled, the flame from the igniter flashes across a gap to the igniting primer of the projectile. The propellant gases pass through the rear opening between the tube and liner, through the space between the tube and liner, and out through 31 holes of the perforated ring at the muzzle end.

Projectile

The projectile consists of a three-piece steel body: the nose, which contains the explosive charge and makes up approximately 60% of the total weight of the projectile; the tail, which contains the propellant charge; and the base plate . The sections are screwed together and are held in place by two locking screws.

America's Super Heavy Tanks

The Germans were not the only ones to design and build super heavy tanks during World War II. The American Army had as early as September 1943 initiated studies to develop a heavily armed and armored combat vehicle that could be built in time for the invasion of Europe. Unlike the German *Jagdtiger*, which was primarily built as a tank destroyer, the Americans were looking for an armored vehicle to attack heavily fortified areas like the German West Wall.

After different design concepts were considered, the Americans set about building the heaviest and biggest armored vehicle ever to be seen in the US Army. Known originally as the T28 heavy tank, it was later redesignated the "105mm gun motor carriage T95." A few months later it finally became the super heavy tank T28. This ninety-five ton vehicle built by the Pacific Car and Foundry Company was thirty-six feet six inches long, fourteen feet eleven inches wide, and only six feet eleven inches high without its machine gun mount. This very low height was achieved by doing away with a turret and mounting the T28's 105mm high velocity gun in the front hull. This meant the main gun could be traversed only about ten degrees either right or left. The vehicle carried sixty-two rounds of 105mm ammo.

Armor protection was up to twelve inches on the gun mantle, with decreasing amounts on other parts of the vehicle. The side armor plates were four inches thick. The vehicle was crewed by four men. The driver and gunner sat in the front hull, while the loader was at the left rear of the fighting compartment with the commander located at the right rear behind the gunner.

Because of the vehicle's great weight, the T28 rode on a double-tracked suspension system. To aid in transporting this behemoth by road or rail, the outer track suspension system could be removed. This made the T28 only ten feet six inches wide.

The T28 was powered by the same Ford 500hp engine found in the the M26 Pershing tank. Pushing the ninety-five tons of the T28 dropped the vehicle's top speed down to 8mph. Having four fuel tanks carrying a total of 400 gallons of fuel, the gasoline-powered vehicle had a top operational range of 100 miles.

As the war was quickly coming to a close before any test pilots model of the T28 could be finished. Only two vehicles were ordered and delivered to the Army in December 1945. Testing of the vehicles went on until 1947, when the Army finally terminated the entire project.

Tiger-Based Tank Destroyer

Mr. Underhill goes on in his 1949 article to describe the evolution of German tank destroyers and how they led to the development of a Tiger-based version:

Prior to the war the German Army seems to have given little serious consideration to the development of mobile, well-protected antitank pieces. AT for armored divisions was towed—although in 1939 the title *Panzerjäger* (tank hunter, or fighter) began to replace the defensive-sounding "antitank" designation. In 1939 and 1940 some improvised SP TDs saw action. They consisted of standard or captured AT guns mounted on obsolete tank chassis, and lightly protected by armor. Such a one was the job which mounted a Czech 47mm gun high on a Mark I tank chassis.

Soon after the armies flowed into Russia, and Rommel began desert operations, a crying need for tank destroyers was felt. Antitank guns of all sorts were slapped on motor vehicles and on old or captured armor.

In 1942, German industry utilized production facilities of the outmoded Mark II tank to turn out tank destroyers with ordinary antitank guns perched atop the hull with some splinter-proof armor on the front and sides of their open topped fighting compartment. The guns used were the standard *7.5cm Pak 40* and the captured Russian M1936 76mm field gun *[7.62cm Pak 36(r)]*. Production facilities of the Prague BMM tank factory, which had turned out the *Pz.Kwfw. 38 (t)'s* were used for the same purpose, and were furnished with the same guns.

In 1943, new carriages began to appear. The motors of the Mark II and Pz 38(t) tank chassis were moved forward to permit the gun to be mounted low, and the crew to stand on the bottom rear of the hull. Guns were

The heaviest armored vehicle deployed during World War II was the seventy-five ton German *Jagdtiger* (Hunting Tiger). Armed with a 128mm gun, the *Jagdtiger* was a turretless tank destroyer who's gun was too large to fit into a normal Tiger tank. The *Jagdtiger* pictured is currently on display at the British Army Tank Museum in southern England. This particular vehicle is fitted with a Porsche designed suspension system that is missing many of it's road wheels. *British Army Tank Museum*

the *7.5cm Pak 40*. French tank chassis were also used, as was the big Lorraine ammunition supply tractor. In all cases the fighting compartment was open-topped, and the guns provided with little traverse.

For a while there was as much variety in terminology as in types. *Pak (sf.)* (for *Panzerabwehrkanone* and *Selbstfahr*—in other words, SP AT) and *Panzerjäger* plus gun caliber, were widely used. (Improvised chassis were called *Selbstfahrlafette* (SFI)). At first the revised were called *Panzerjäger*, followed by II or 38(t). Complete weapons got the *"suggestiv namen"* Marder (Marten). Complete weapons were also designated by gun title, *(sf.)* and *auf* followed by the name of the chassis.

Finally, *Panzerjäger* was reserved as a name for chassis of the hybrid assault gun-TD's, the improvised chassis all being called *Fahrgestell* (motor carriage). The complete weapons became *Pak(Sf.)*. Thus, *7.5cm Pak 40/2 (Sf.) Marder II*, with detailed title *[7.5cm Pak 40 (L/46) Fahrgestell II]* following, if it was necessary to make clear just what weapon was being dealt with.

In 1943, the new long 88 was mounted on a *Fahrgestell* IV chassis, the resulting TD being called the *Hornet* then *Rhinoceros (Nashorn)*. In 1943 there also showed up for the Kursk offensive an Army attempt to salvage the Porsche Tiger. These had the new 88 mounted in the front of a heavily armored box placed toward the rear of the chassis. At first called the *Ferdinand* after its designer, these were re-named *Elefant*. Some were used in Italy.

The *Elefant* and *Rhino* epitomized German troubles with early TD efforts. To say they were mechanically

unreliable would be an understatement. In one Elephant company, more vehicles fell out during their baptismal approach march than went into action. But at least the Elefant had armor—which the clanking, wheezing tinplate TD's did not.

All the light, open-topped *Pak (Sf)'s* might best be called self-propelled antitank—to differentiate them from real tank destroyers. While their firepower and mobility were fully exploited, their vulnerability did not permit offensive action. When engaging tanks, they did not follow up defensive action with immediate counterattack, as did the better protected assault guns.

Many of these light TD's were used as single support or AT guns in Italy and in the West in 1944-5.

But in 1943 work was going forward on tank destroyers which met assault gun requirements, if they did not satisfy armored force demands for a turreted TD. What the armored people wanted was a tank.

These re-workings of the assault gun design principle had better-sloped armor than the original *Stu.G.'s*. They adhered to the original low silhouette gun with limited traverse, and good frontal armor — with fair armor all over. These new vehicles used the Pz 38(t), Mark IV, Panther, and Royal Tiger tank chassis, and were classed as light, medium, and heavy tank destroyers. The Germans used the title *Panzerjäger* or *Jagdpanzer* for these chassis (as in *Panzerjäger Panther*). Guns were called *Pak*.

Armament followed the system laid down in assault gun development; each class of *Jagdpanzer* mounted the gun of the next heavier class of tank.

The medium hybrid TD was the 46-ton *Jagdpanther*. It mounted the Royal Tiger's 88 *(Pak 43/3 or/4)* on the *Panther (Pz. V)* chassis. The gun had only 26 degrees traverse, but the transmission and suspension enabled the driver handily to swing his tank to pick up targets on which the gunner couldn't otherwise lay.

While not as scarce as hen's teeth, nevertheless *Jagdpanthers* were never plentiful enough to be used in by-the-book tactics — either in assault or TD roles. In Normandy the Germans dug them in (the kind of thing that normally would give the armored force school faculty apoplexy), and used them to connect up sparsely settled German positions with the telling fire of their powerful gun.

The heavy hybrid TD was the *"Jagdtiger"* (*Jäg. Tiger* or *VI* chassis). This monster weighed close to 75 tons. Its frontal armor didn't have the slope of the light and medium TD's, but its thickness was about 10 inches. It mounted a relative of the 128mm *Flak 40*—a *12.8cm Pak 44 (L/55)*. However useful such a weapon might have been in assaults on fortified positions, with a speed of 9 to 12 mph cross-country, it was no asset in mobile warfare—especially considering that it represented the steel weight of about a half-dozen Hetzers [lightweight German TDs armed with a 75mm gun].

Only around 74 were built. On one of the rare occasions when one was used against Anglo-American forces, a US TD got on its flank, penetrated its 80mm side armor, and blew it to pieces.

Otto Carius spent the last few weeks of World War II in command of a company of Hunting Tigers. In the following extract from his 1960 book titled *Tiger im Schlamm* (reprinted with the publisher's permission) he describes his impressions of the vehicle: "When the assault guns were calibrated in Sennelager, we experienced our first failure. Despite its 82 tons, our Hunting Tiger didn't want to act like we wanted it to. Only its armor was satisfactory, its maneuverability left a lot to be desired. In addition, it was an assault gun. There was no traversing turret, just an enclosed armored housing. Any large traversing of the main gun had to done by moving the entire vehicle. Because of that, transmission and steering differentials soon broke down. That such a monstrosity had to be constructed in the final phase of the war made no sense at all."

A US Army technical intelligence report, dated May 10, 1945, describes many interesting features of a captured *Jagdtiger*:

1. General

A *Jagdtiger* (Panzerjäger , Tiger) mounting the 12.8 cm. anti-tank gun has been examined in the First US Army area. The vehicle has been knocked out with a *Panzerfaust*, minor damage having been sustained by the engine.

The chassis and engine are those of the normal *Pz.Kpfw.* Tiger Model B tank. A new type of AA machine

This frontal view of an abandoned *Jagdtiger*, armed with a 128mm gun, is from a US Army technical intelligence dated 10 May 1945. This vehicle was knocked out by a German Army *Panzerfaust* (rocket launcher). The report doesn't state who fired the *Panzerfaust*. However, the *Panzerfaust* was often used by Allied troops when they captured them, since it packed a much bigger punch then the American-made bazooka. The frontal armor on the vehicle's superstructure was almost 10in thick. The object lying flat on the vehicle's front hull plate is a travel lock, which helps to steady the large gun when not in combat.

This US Army photo of an abandoned *Jagdtiger* shows the angled rear-engine deck shared with the Tiger II. Visible are the two mufflers and the vehicle's towing cable. On top of the rear engine deck is an monopod antiaircraft mount for the fitting of an MG42 machine gun. Behind the machine gun mount, in the rear of the armored superstructure, can be seen the twin rear-access doors. These doors could be used as a means of loading the vehicle or as an escape hatch for the crew. Unlike a tank, the *Jagdtiger's* main gun was not traversable except for a few degrees on either side. To aim the main gun the entire tank had to be turned.

gun mount had been welded to the hatch of the engine compartment.

2. Weight and Dimensions:

The chassis and engine are those of the normal Pz.Kpfw. Tiger Model B tank. A new type of AA machine gun mount had been welded to the hatch of the engine compartment.

Weight (from documents)	77.3 US. tons
Chassis No.	305058
Manufacturers code	nhr
Overall length including gun	40 ft.
Overall length excluding gun	25 ft. 11 ins.
Length of top plate over driver	3 ft. 8 ins.
Length of superstructure top	9 ft. 3 ins.
Length of superstructure bottom	10 ft. 4 ins.

Length of engine deck	6ft 7in
Overall width	11ft 9in
Width of superstructure top	5ft 7in
Width of superstructure bottom	7ft 8in
Overall height	9ft 2in
Height of superstructure (front)	3ft 4in
(rear)	3ft 3in
Ground clearance	1ft 8in

3. Superstructure

Plate	Armor Thickness	Angle to Vertical
Front plate	250mm (9.84in)	15°
Side plates	80mm (3.15in)	25°
Rear plate	80mm (3.15in)	6°
Top plate	45mm (1.77in)	0°
Gun mantlet	60-93mm (2.4-3.6in)	——

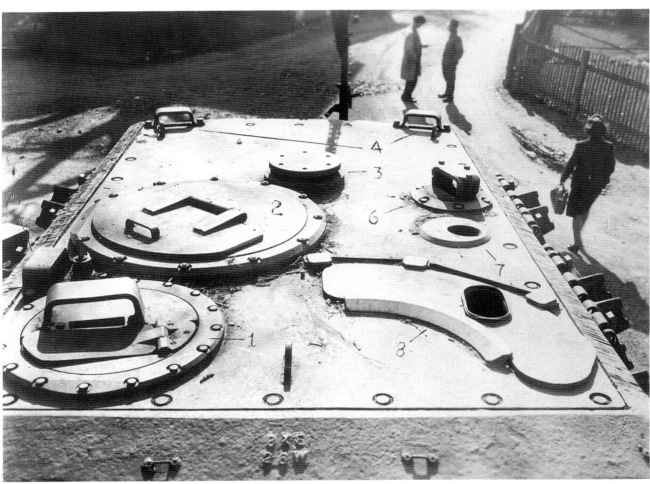

From a World War II US Army technical intelligence report, comes this picture of the upper details found on the superstructure roof of an abandoned *Jagdtiger*. Object (1) is the vehicle commander's hatch which is fitted with a periscope having 360 degree traverse. Object (2) is a rotating semi-circular hatch that could be used by the crew to exit or enter the vehicle. Object (3) is the top of a ventilator. Object (4) are two fixed periscopes located in the rear of the *Jagdtiger's* armored superstructure. Object (5) is an another fixed periscope located alongside an antenna base. Object (6) is a traversable periscope. Object (7) is an opening for a launcher for either smoke or antipersonnel grenades. Object (8) is a sliding plate for a gun sight.

The tank commander, at the right front of the fighting compartment, is provided with a periscope mounted on a circular plate with 360° traverse. The plate also has a hatch permitting the use of an observation periscope. An additional fixed periscope at his right is set at an angle of 90°. A fixed periscope set at an angle of 15° is located at each rear corner and a periscope with a 360° traverse is at the left center. A rotating semicircular hatch is located to the rear of the tank commander's position.

4. Armament

a. Description

The 12.8cm Pak 44 L/55 is mounted centrally in the superstructure. The trunnions are supported on fabricated arms extending upward and forward from the floor of the superstructure. The recoil cylinder and recuperator are mounted above the tube to the left and right respectively. No equilibrator is fitted: neither is the piece fitted with a muzzle brake. A folding bracket attached to the glacis plate supports the tube in the traveling position, and a clamp applied to the breech acts as *a traveling lock.*

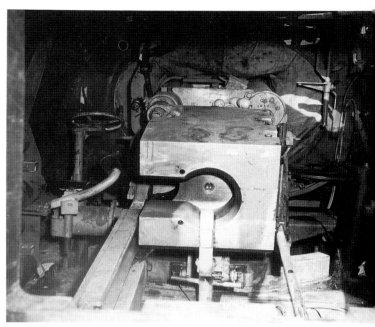

This US Army picture, taken through the rear-loading hatches of an abandoned *Jagdtiger*, shows the interior of the armored superstructure with the massive breach end of the vehicle's 128mm main gun in the center of the photo. Some of the gunner's control can be seen on the left of the picture. Also visible in this picture is a large strap attached to the bottom of the breech, used as an internal travel lock. The main gun rounds for the 128mm were so large and heavy that they had to be broken down into two parts, the projectile and the cartridge. As a result, the *Jagdtiger* had two loaders instead of one like all other German tanks.

The Germans managed to produce only seventy *Jagdtigers* during the closing stages of World War II. Due to it's deadly long-range 128mm gun and thick armor protection, the vehicle was no-doubt a very formidable threat to Allied armor when used in the right defensive situations. Unfortunately, the *Jagdtiger* suffered from the same poor automotive features that plagued the entire Tiger tank series. Being both very large and slow, the *Jagdtiger* would also prove to be both difficult to transport or recover if it broke down. *US Army*

b. Data

Maximum elevation	15° 30'
Maximum depression	6°
Traverse (estimated)	6° 30' R, 6° 30' L.
Breech block	RH horizontal sliding block
Firing Mechanism	Electrical
Traverse mechanism	Segment and pinion
Elevating mechanism	Arc and pinion
Length of tube	21ft 8in
Length of tube plus breech ring	23ft 3/4in
Length of tube projecting from mantlet	12ft 11in
Rifling	Uniform RH twist
Number of grooves	40
Length of rifling	17ft 11in
Width of bands	3.75mm
Diameter of rear chamber	6.93in
Markings on breech of gun	R101Bs.Fl.135bwn bwn TmR 101 Jr.Fl.140 bwn Gerät 13

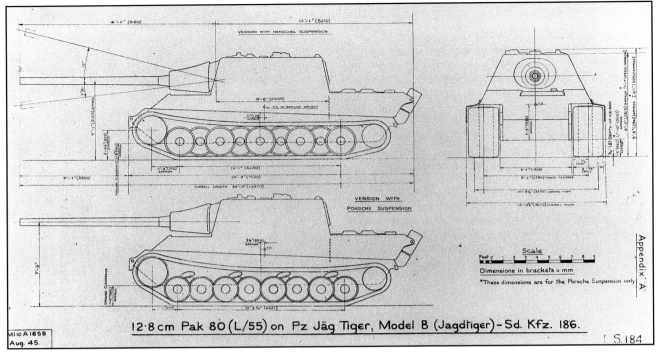

From a British military report—supplied to the US Army after the war was over—comes these comparison drawings of the *Jagdtiger* fitted with both Henschel and Porsche designed suspension systems. Information gathered by Allied technical intelligence teams indicated that the Henschel type was the original version fitted to the *Jagdtiger*. Problems with the Henschel design led to the development of the alternative Porsche design that was to go into full production. The surrender of Germany in May 1945, ended this plan.

5. Subsidiary Armament

The normal hull machine gun ball mount for the MG 34 is provided. In addition, a simple monopod AA mount for the MG 42 had been welded to the engine compartment cover (Photo 9). A rack and pinion arrangement with a ratchet stop permits the extension of the mount from forty-four inches to sixty-eight inches in height. The position of the mount prevents the use of the weapon from inside the tank and consequently no protection is afforded the gunner.

A normal 360° smoke projector is mounted in the top plate to the rear of the gunner (Photo 5).

6. Ammunition Stowage

Racks are provided in the superstructure for stowing thirty-eight cartridge cases and thirty-eight projectiles. On the vehicle examined there were twenty armor piercing and eighteen high explosive projectiles. A diagram of the ammunition stowage is attached as Appendix "A".

7. Communication Equipment

All radio equipment had been removed or destroyed. Visual telegraph communication between the tank commander and driver is provided, the system used being of the marine type with a moveable hand and warning bell.

Tiger Command Vehicles

Standard crew equipment for almost all German tanks was the *Bordsprechanlage B* inter-communication (intercom) set. This system provided a headphone set in conjunction

Pictured on display at the US Army's Ordnance Museum, the massive size and bulk of this German Army *Jagdtiger* is clearly visible in this picture. Based on the lengthened hull of the Tiger II, the vehicle weighed close to seventy-seven tons. The vehicle was about 9ft 3in tall, 25ft 7in long, and 12ft 3in wide. It carried forty rounds for it's 128mm gun. With a crew of six and powered by a Maybach gasoline engine, the *Jagdtiger* had a top speed of 24mph and an operational range of only 68mi. *Michael Green*

with a set of throat mikes worn dog collar fashion for each tank crewman.

For radio communication between vehicles of the same company, the Tiger had an *Fu5* AM radio set operated by the vehicle's radio operator, whose secondary job was to operate the bow machine gun. (Fu stood for wireless/radio in German military terms.) Because of its very limited range of no more then seven miles, a number of Tigers were modified into command vehicles by the addition of second longer range AM radio set. In German military terms, the Tiger I became the Panzer-*Befehlswagen Tiger I* (8.8cm) Ausf. E; SdKfz 267/268, and the Tiger II became the *Panzer-Befehlswagen Tiger II* (8.8cm) Ausf. B; SdKfz 267/268.

That additional radio set could be either an *Fu7* or an *Fu8*. Vehicles so modified also retained their standard *Fu5* AM radio set. Externally, the command version of the Tiger were outwardly similar to the standard production vehicle, the only difference being the mounting of a second large antenna on the outside of the vehicle.

Because the vehicle-mounted radio sets of the era were so large and bulky, the Germans were forced to mount one of the two radio sets in the Tiger's turret. To make enough room in the turret of the Tiger I for this second radio, the coaxial machine gun along with its ammunition, spares, and tools had to be removed. The number of main gun rounds carried in the Tiger I command tank was also cut down to provide additional room for the crew. In the command version of the Tiger II, the rearrangement of certain internal components allowed the vehicle to carry more rounds then the standard production vehicle.

As the command versions of the Tigers were not supposed to engage in combat, the normal crew arrangements were slightly changed. In place of the gunner and loader positions there was now two radio operators. They could if necessary operate the main gun in an emergency.

Selected Bibliography

Fletcher, David. *Tiger! The Tiger Tank. A British View*. London: Her Majesty's Stationery Office, 1986.

Gudgin, Peter. *The Tiger Tanks*. London: Arms and Armour Press, 1991.

Forty, George. *German Tanks Of World War Two In Action*. London: Arms and Armour Press, 1988.

Spielberger J. Walter. *Tiger & King Tiger Tanks And Their Variants*. England: Haynes Publishing Group, 1991.

Perrett, Bryan. *The Tiger Tanks*. London: Osprey Publishing Ltd., 1981.

Tom Jentz, Hilary Doyle, and Peter Sarson. *King Tiger Heavy Tank 1942-1945*. London: Osprey Publishing Ltd., 1993.

Klein, Egon. Kuln, Volkmar. *Tiger The History of a Legendary Weapon 1942-45*. Winnipeg, Canada: J. J. Fedorowicz Publishing, 1989.

Icks, J. Robert. *Famous Tank Battles*. New York: Doubleday & Company, Inc., 1972.

Gillie, Hanson, Mildred. *Forging the Thunderbolt*. Harrisburg, Pennsylvania: The Military Service Publishing Company, 1947.

Baily, M. Charles. *Faint Praise American Tanks and Tank Destroyers during World War II*. Hamden, Connecticut: Archon Books, 1983.

Grandsen, James. Zaloga, J. Steven. *Soviet Tanks and Combat Vehicles of World War Two*. London: Arms and Armour Press, 1984.

Jones, T. Gregory. *Panzerheld, The Story of Michael Wittmann, World War II's Greatest Tank Commander*. Self-Published by author, 1993

INDEX